HUMAN NATURE AND EDUCATION

HUMAN NATURE
AND
EDUCATION

BY

A. S. WOODBURNE

THE MADRAS CHRISTIAN COLLEGE

HUMPHREY MILFORD

OXFORD UNIVERSITY PRESS

LONDON NEW YORK TORONTO BOMBAY

CALCUTTA MADRAS

1926

PRINTED AT
THE WESLEYAN MISSION PRESS
MYSORE CITY

PRINTED IN INDIA

PREFACE

THERE is no science that is of greater importance from the teacher's standpoint than psychology. The person who is engaged in the task of directing unfolding personalities needs above all an understanding of the processes with which he has to deal. As Sir John Adams has put it, the teacher who would teach John Latin needs to know John as much as Latin. Happily for us, the science which studies John has made great progress in recent years. An enormous amount of experimental work has been done, and is being done, which is increasing the precision of our knowledge about the mental processes. That is one reason for offering an additional contribution to the literature in the field. The science is constantly having to adjust itself to the increased knowledge brought by research. The significance of this growing knowledge for education calls for reconsideration rather frequently. The present volume is intended as one in which old problems are reconsidered in the light of the increasingly exact psychological science.

There is another reason for offering this volume to those who are interested in educational psychology. Some years of experience in India have led to the hope that some of the problems may have been viewed from an angle somewhat different from that of books published in the West. The author has had Indian conditions in mind as he has dealt with the subject, and has drawn many of his illustrations from school life in India. To be sure mental processes function in the same ways in India as in Britain or America, so that the strictly psychological portion of the work is as applicable in the West as in the East. It is hoped that the book may be both interesting to western readers and serviceable to teachers in India.

Some of the material embodied in this volume was used in a course of special lectures on 'Modern Development in Educational Psychology' delivered in 1924 under the auspices of the University of Madras. But there are several subjects which are treated in

the published work which were not included in the lectures.   For
the convenience of those who desire to pursue the subject in
greater detail, a short selected bibliography is appended at the
end of each chapter.   There are several more familiar works
which are not repeatedly mentioned and which are invaluable to
the student of the subject.   References to the footnotes will
show that the author is under obligation to many scholars for
suggestion and inspiration.   To the works of James, Angell,
Ward, Woodworth, Stout and McDougall in General Psychology,
and those of Thorndike, Dewey, Drever, Kennedy-Fraser, Adams
and Ballard in Educational Psychology the author is heavily
indebted.

A. S. W.

THE MADRAS CHRISTIAN COLLEGE,
January, 1926.

SYNOPSIS OF CONTENTS

CHAPTER I

THE BIOLOGICAL VIEWPOINT IN EDUCATION

CHAPTER II

INSTINCTIVE TYPES OF BEHAVIOUR

CHAPTER III

THE NATURE OF INTELLIGENCE AND METHODS OF MEASURING IT

CHAPTER IV

THE FEELINGS

CHAPTER V

ATTENTION AND ITS CONTROL

CHAPTER XII

THE WILL

CHAPTER XIII

THE PSYCHOLOGICAL BASIS FOR INSTRUCTION

CHAPTER XIV

THE OLD EXAMINATION *VERSUS* THE NEW

CHAPTER XV

THE ACHIEVEMENT OF PERSONALITY

CHAPTER I

THE BIOLOGICAL VIEWPOINT IN EDUCATION

A HISTORICAL study of psychology discloses such a striking development that we can only speak of its earlier and later stages as constituting a contrast. For many centuries it was a branch of philosophy, owing its tasks and privileges to the benevolent control of metaphysics. To-day it has assumed all the proportions of an empirical science, and even ventures to tell metaphysics what may or may not be said with reference to mental facts. Formerly it was customary to group it with the philosophical disciplines; now it prefers to be counted among the biological sciences. It is one part of the scientific attempt to study life, having for its particular sphere the mental aspects of life. It recognizes first, last and always that life is an integral unity, and that there is no mental life as such, separate and distinguishable from the physical life. Life is the life of a psycho-physical organism which is a unity, and the mental portion of it is something which is never separable from the physical in actual experience. It is solely for theoretical purposes that we essay to make the separation, and as such the separation may often be serviceable. In dealing with the mental life then, psychology does so with a full recognition of the close connection between mental and neural processes.

One of the results of the consideration of the mental life from the biological point of view, is that the centre of interest and study is in reactions, rather than in states of consciousness as hitherto. Now a reaction is simply a response to a stimulus. This relationship between stimuli and responses is full of suggestiveness for the facts of the mental life, and the psychological approach from that angle is proving to be immensely fruitful. One advantage is that it fits in well with the evolutionary point of view. We are able to study psycho-neural reactions from the developmental standpoint, beginning with the simpler reflex actions, and proceeding towards the most highly complex, such as are involved in the higher reasoning processes. Another advantage is that it sets into proper relationship the native and the acquired elements, which have become so inextricably fused in our life experiences. Still again, the biological approach enables us to appreciate the integrative unity of the life of the organism, and to set the mental portion of it in its proper place with reference to the neural.

The essential unity of the psychical and the psychological is demonstrable from evidence of different kinds. There is, first of all, the fact that our consciousness of the environment depends primarily on the functioning of sensory processes. These are the channels through which knowledge is carried to the central nervous system. And second, consciousness ordinarily expresses itself in the form of muscular or glandular movements, which we designate as acts, and acts are observable phenomena for the scientist. In the third place, we observe that pathological conditions of the brain or nerves are accompanied by pathological conditions in some elements of the conscious life. There is an abundance of illustration from the various mental processes to substantiate the integral unity of the life. One of the most fruitful of the recent investigations is into the physiological concomitants of the emotions. It has been pretty well established that if the physiological elements are removed there can be no emotional experience, and now many of these physiological facts have become explicable in terms of chemical processes, such as the changing of the starch of the liver into sugar. What a transformation has taken place in our approach to the mental processes: (i) metaphysics, (ii) mental science, (iii) physiology and (iv) chemistry. It illustrates the way in which psychology has changed companions, and entered the field of empirical science. Thus we study the mental life as one phase of a unified life-process, and action of any sort is in relation to some stimulus. It sometimes happens that one element is affected more than others in our way of reacting to stimuli, but the organism which responds is a unity. The reaction is the reaction of a single unified organism.

Mental processes of all kinds are reactions. The simplest form of reaction we describe as reflexive, and is so simple that it does not usually require any action of the brain at all. Somewhat more complex are instinctive reactions which are organically coordinations of reflexes, but still may be performed with only the lower brain centres. But when we come to the material of consciousness, the higher brain centres are involved, and complexity is increased. Whether we are dealing with sensory or perceptual processes at the one end of the scale, or reasoning and judging processes at the other, these reactions are only possible when called forth by appropriate stimuli. So that the study of psychological science to-day is always with reference to the environmental factors, which function so largely in providing stimuli for action. Very often we find that there is a keen competition of stimuli seeking the attention of the organism, and the task of consciousness becomes that of selecting the one or ones to which it will respond. The learning process is largely that of acquiring a set of reactions which will be the most serviceable to us when presented by various stimuli.

It must be apparent that this change of attitude on the part of psychology is of immense significance for the science of education. For one thing we appreciate the impossibility of training a mind or stuffing it with information apart from a body. We are not trying to educate minds, but children, and the futility of trying to deal with their minds as abstractions must be apparent to the most casual observer. The core of personality is action, so that the goal of education is in the development of persons of right action, and not merely thinking machines. Education thus conceived is a process of constant adjustment, whereby we learn to modify our responses to stimuli until we develop personalities of right reactions. Since the individual is a unity, the process of education must take cognizance of the whole person, and not merely of one section, however important that may be. The modern idea of education discloses that such a conception is becoming increasingly evident, and this has resulted, on the one hand, in a larger recognition of individual interests, and on the other in a development on the vocational side. It is not a mind that is to be educated, nor a body, but a person; and the goal is not the possession of a given body of information, but the development of a person of right thinking, right feeling and right action.

The end of education may be described as producing persons who will react in the best way to the various situations which they will be required to face. Reacting in the best possible way involves the exercise of choice with reference to definite purposes. We cannot react to every possible situation merely by the exercise of our native equipment. We may be able to respond in a satisfactory manner to the more simple demands of the environment by means of instinctive behaviour, but there are a great many complex situations which the experiences of every day present to us, that must be met by responses that have been consciously learned. Now the great need is to achieve the ability to meet these difficult situations and respond to them as satisfactorily as to the more simple. Many of the more important reactions are deliberately selected with reference to conscious ends. It is the function of education to prepare the person to be able to react appropriately, and that involves guidance in the matter of ends and of means to ends. The school and the home (for parents are, whether they know it or not, just as truly educators as teachers) ought to furnish discriminating guidance to the child, both in the formation and execution of purposes. The school is thus a training-ground for the development of persons of worthy purposes and appropriate reactions. There rests upon it the obligation to provide for sufficient freedom, and along with that, wholesome guidance to the child whom we desire to educate into a person of right reactions. Any act of behaviour may be described as a response to a stimulus. There are certain responses which experience teaches us to regard with preference to others. We regard them as successful because they yield a great degree of satisfaction, or we regard them with satisfaction because they have been successful. At any rate, success and satisfaction go together. And, conversely, failure and annoyance are correlatives. Either satisfaction or its opposite is related to a felt need. Thorndike writes as follows concerning the original nature of wants:

'Reason finds the aim of human life the improvement and satisfaction of wants. By reducing those to which the nature of things and men derive satisfaction, or by increasing those which can be fulfilled without injuring the fate of others, man makes his wants better. By changing the environment into a nature more hospitable to the activities he craves, he satisfies them. The sciences and arts arose by the impetus of wants, and continue in their service. They are the ultimate source of all values.'[1]

Whenever a response to a stimulus is accompanied with satisfaction there is a tendency for a bond to be formed between the stimulus and the response. The satisfaction which is the accompaniment of the response becomes the basis for an association between that particular stimulus and its accompanying response. The stimulus and response having occurred together, the tendency is for them to recur together. So that when the same type of situation arises again there is suggested by association the type of response which gave satisfaction on the previous occasion. One can illustrate by scores of examples from everyday experience, such as eating when hungry, drinking when thirsty, resting when fatigued, moving when refreshed, seeking companionship when lonely, etc.

One way to describe the goal of education is that of acquiring a set of bonds between stimuli and satisfactory responses. The well-educated person is one who meets situations which present themselves to him with the most appropriate actions. Obviously the ability to respond appropriately and persistently to the multiplicity of situations which continually arise is the outcome of an educational process. The uneducated person may hit upon the right thing to do occasionally, but to persist in right behaviour is only possible if a set of bonds has been established which ensure that as soon as a particular stimulus is presented, the suitable response will suggest itself to the person.

One of the aims which the advocates of the Project Method

---

[1] E. L. Thorndike, *Educational Psychology*, Briefer Course, p. 50.

emphasize is precisely this one of establishing a system of bonds between stimuli and responses. Such bonds involve a preference that becomes so ingrained in the nervous system that they function with satisfaction. It is true that there are some bonds which have become established in the nervous systems of the species. Among these native bonds there is the response of crying to the stimulus of hunger on the part of the infant. But many of the bonds are acquired in experience. The truth is that a great many reactions are far too complex to be simply native in character. This process, whereby we acquire new bonds or modify existing ones, is called learning. The scientific description of the conditions under which bonds are established or modified is known in psychology as the laws of learning. These laws have been carefully studied and formulated for the educationalist by Prof. E. L. Thorndike as the laws of readiness, exercise, and effect. The law of readiness means (i) that when a bond is ready to act, to act induces satisfaction whereas not to act induces annoyance, and (ii) that when a bond is not ready to act, to act induces annoyance whereas not to act induces satisfaction. The law of effect is that when a modifiable bond acts, it is strengthened or weakened in proportion to the satisfaction or annoyance which results from the reaction. The law of exercise includes the tendencies of use and disuse, use strengthening and disuse weakening the bond between situation and response. In some instances when a situation arises there may be more than one bond suggested to consciousness, and the person has the task of selecting the one which will be considered most worthy. In this type of situation the attitude or mental set of the individual will do much in determining which of the bonds showing readiness to act will be selected. Such attitudes or dispositions are, of course, the results of bonds which owe their existence to the satisfaction which has accompanied certain reactions to characteristic situations. Attitudes are themselves in this sense a type of bonds. They are dispositions to attend or to act in a certain manner, and thus the outcome of an associative process, becoming in their turn the unifying principle of the mental life. Attitudes have been divided into those of habit and accommodation. The attitude of habit is the tendency to conserve the type, and that of accommodation is the tendency to modify the type with reference to the needs of the situation. Both of these attitudes find expression in the bonds. Where the satisfaction accompanying the response to a stimulus is relatively large, the tendency will be in the direction of conservation of the type or habit. After all, the formation of habit is explicable in terms of an attitude of conservation, or the establishment of bonds between response and stimulus, which gradually results in the response following more or less automatically after the stimulus. The second type of attitude is that of modification or accommodation. In these cases the response is changed in some degree, and a new bond is set up as a substitute for the existing one, in the interests of producing more satisfying reactions.

Modifiability is a characteristic of the psycho-physical organism. It is fact which biologists are unanimous in recognizing, though there may be some difference among them as to the manner in which modifications take place. The manner of modification need not greatly concern the psychologist. The point in which he is interested is that modification does take place. It is a neurological fact. Alterations take place in the function of the neurones themselves, and possibly in their structure. It is generally supposed that when a bond is established between a stimulus and response, the neurones assume a characteristic set. But the modification of the bond means some sort of concomitant alteration in the set of the neurones. The bases for all acquired reactions, which at some stage or stages are reactions that have undergone modification, are native reactions. Reflexive and instinctive behaviour is native, but a vast amount of conscious behaviour, both mental and motor, is acquired by modifying the native ways of doing things.

All knowledge is acquired, the complete stock of our ideas, and motor skill also. Knowledge is not to be thought of as consisting in a mere strengthening of native reactions. Neither is motor skill to be so conceived. The modifications which take place are much more profound than that. Indeed many of the native impulses are very plastic, and admit of a considerable degree of free play, though they become stable through exercise.

But when reactions take a particular set of which we are conscious, we may build up a body of knowledge. Mental images of past reactions remain even after the concrete experiences are over, and these form the basis of our stock of ideas which are organized in accordance with experienced needs. Moreover, knowledge itself is continually undergoing modification. As we experience what we call 'new experiences' these new experiences, or the knowledge concerning them, are assimilated or welded into an organized coherent whole with the body of knowledge which we acquired previously. The process of forming concepts is a generalizing process, whereby certain particular bits of knowledge are brought together into classes containing some common bond. Doubtless there are also many items of experience, many units of knowledge, which never admit of classification or abstraction, but remain as isolated bits. But even in these cases the bits of knowledge stand in relationship to other parts of the knowing process. Thus all knowledge is relative to other knowledge, and so is modifiable.

What has been said about the modifiable character of knowledge is applicable also in the case of motor skill. Even here exercise of original tendencies tends towards modification, by giving to it a greater degree of precision than that which it possessed in the beginning. A very familiar illustration may be taken from the behaviour of young chicks. If grains are thrown down before a chick one day old, it instinctively pecks at them with the bill and swallows them. Its aim, however, is inaccurate, and it only succeeds in getting about one grain out of every five at which it pecks. But improvement comes very rapidly through practice, so that on the second day it gets more than half. Within four days it succeeds with over three-quarters, and after about ten days it reaches its maximum of accuracy, that is about 85 per cent. accuracy. Thus we see that exercise of a native reaction tendency induces modification in the nature of accuracy and precision, which results ultimately in the fixation of a definite habit. The same matter may also be illustrated by the increasing ability of the human infant to gain precision in control over the use of its hands. To begin with, the majority of its movements are random. It is only gradually that it is able to co-ordinate its movements in accordance with what it desires to do. We have seen a ball suspended from a string before a young infant lying on its back, and the infant attempting to grasp the ball and manipulate it. At the beginning the attempts are so inaccurate as to be ludicrous. But little by little the child gains motor control, so that it can manipulate objects according to its desires, always, of course, within the limitations set by the structure of the organism. The method of gaining control is the method of trial and error, the method whereby unsatisfactory responses are discovered and eliminated and satisfactory responses established.

This method of trial and error is the typical characteristic of learning. We have already observed that learning belongs to the acquired group of reactions. One of the best illustrations of learning by trial and error is that of the white rat learning to run the maze. At first there is a strong tendency to run back and forth over the runways, and sometimes to get into a *cul-de-sac*, and lying down in the corner, give up the hunt. But the drive of the hunger instinct keeps the animal alive to make further trials, until eventually it learns to avoid every *cul-de-sac*, to avoid retracing its steps, and to go straight to the food box by the shortest possible route. Again it is a case of ' varied reaction with gradual elimination of the unsuccessful responses and fixation of the successful one '.[1] In other cases, as, for example, the cat and the puzzle box experiment, substitute responses are made for the original and most impulsive one. The substitute response is only induced where there is a distinct tendency to achieve a certain goal and the original response has failed to attain the purpose. Then the dammed-up tendency seeks for another outlet, in the manner of another trial response in the direction of the goal. When success is eventually achieved, the tendency towards the substitute response is strengthened and becomes firmly attached to the situation.

Voluntary action is characterized by modifiability much more than is instinctive. In voluntary behaviour there is consciousness of the end in view as well as of the means being taken to achieve

[1] R. S. Woodworth, *Psychology: A Study of Mental Life*, p. 309.

the end. Here we may observe the method of trial and error under conscious direction. The situation presents a problem which the individual attempts to solve by means of a specific response. If the response fails to bring him satisfaction, he makes another attempt to find a solution, and continues the process until satisfaction is attained. In all of this consciousness is operating, as has been indicated, both as regards the means and the end. In the process of selecting between alternatives, and of adapting means to an end, consciousness is operating in the sense of modifying reactions. Many psychologists are of the opinion that a completely involuntary act is rather exceptional, and that in almost all human behaviour, as well as in much of animal behaviour, there is a tendency of striving towards an end. The word 'voluntary' may indeed be used as a synonym for 'purposive'. Actions may be classified into impulsive and voluntary, the latter being a development out of the former. The attainment of a desirable result in the voluntary sense is the outcome of the process of trial and error until the satisfactory and successful response is attained and deliberately established as a method of behaviour. The time may come when the desired response becomes habitual and is made largely automatically. But during the process of attainment and organization, attention is required for the execution, and attention is the heart of voluntary behaviour. Moreover, attention goes hand in hand with interest, and one of the factors in a stimulus which determines attention is change. A steady noise ceases after a while to be noticed, but a change from noise to quiet at once arrests attention. We grow accustomed to the noise on a railway train so that after a while we fall asleep. But we frequently waken when the train stops at stations, because of the change from noise to quiet and from motion to immobility. So that change or modifiability is a distinct advantage in estimating the power of any stimulus to attract attention.

The importance of this factor of modifiability can scarcely be over-estimated for the educationalist. The educational process is the modification of our reactions in the light of past experience. Education is a process of acquirement based, to be sure, on the native equipment and on native reactions, but modifying them in the interests of the end in view. The entire mental life is conceived in terms of process, and hence education must be conceived as a process, and that means modification. If one could imagine an individual as unmodifiable, he would be picturing to himself a mechanism and not a person. A machine is lacking in the capacity of profiting by experience, and consequently cannot be educated. But a person possesses the capability of adaptation to environment and is able to profit by experience, and consequently is educable. Moreover, the degree of educability depends upon the degree of adaptability. The great difference between the feeble-minded person and the intelligent person is to be seen precisely in this matter of the degree of educability, which rests on the capability of profiting by experience. The intelligent person continues to develop mentally through childhood and adolescence, reaching maturity of capacity perhaps about the age of sixteen. But the feeble-minded person's mental development is arrested, so that when the maximum ability is obtained, his intelligence is comparable to that of a child. Putting the same thought in other language, we may say that the intelligent person is more educable than the feeble-minded, that educability is a characteristic of intelligence.

The educative process rests upon the assumption that mental development is a fact of experience. It is a fact that such development takes place independently of the educative process. There are different ways of describing the way in which development takes place. Frequently the description is made in terms of levels or stages of development. The earlier is described as reflexive or instinctive and the later as conscious ; or the lower level is described as sensory, the next as perceptual, and the higher as conceptual ; or still again the lower level is described as sensori-motor and the higher as ideo-motor. Whatever be the basis of our description, it must be remembered that the analysis is made for practical purposes to enable us to understand the facts of development, and that there is no sharp line of division between the different levels. This is of the utmost importance for the educator. Education is a recognition of the possibilities of development within any living organism, and is also intended to direct and encourage the process of natural development. Education is related to the facts of mental development in two ways. One is that it recognizes the natural processes and organizes its own methods so as to fit into the facts of natural development. The other is that it functions as a supplement to the native capacities, stimulating them to a healthier and stronger development than might otherwise be possible. Without the stimulus of education the development of human beings would stop at a much more primitive level. All that is necessary to realize this fact is to compare the cultural levels of two groups, of which one has enjoyed and the other has been deprived of educational advantage. A very patent example, observable in South India, is the difference between a Brahman and an Audi-Dravida community. We all know the difference in the cultural atmosphere as one enters the two communities. In the Brahman community there is an ease and polish of manner which is the outcome of generations of educational advantage ; whereas in the Audi-Dravida community there is a crudity and primitivity that characterize those less favoured educationally. The psychologist knows that this difference is due to the presence or absence of the advantages of education much more than to any inherent difference in the capacities of the two social groups. Many are familiar with the experiment made by the Rev. D. S. Herrick, M.A., of Bangalore. By means of the Goddard form-board, Mr. Herrick tested the performance of 710 children, of various ages from four to fourteen, 355 of whom were Brahmans and 355 Panchamas. The task was simply to fit the blocks of wood into the corresponding holes in the form-board as speedily as possible. The time of the fastest performance in each child was regarded as the index of the child's psycho-motor ability. The time allowed was five minutes, and any performance that took a longer time was not recorded. The matter of interest for us is that the average performance of the Panchama took only two and a half seconds longer than that of the Brahman, a difference certainly not very significant in a test for which five minutes was allowed. The test seems to indicate that the difference between the cultural levels of the two communities is due not to capacity, but to education.

An example of a similar character came before my notice

while in the United States of America.   An American missionary,
who was working in a tribe of primitive peoples in the heart of
Africa, took a bright looking little boy with him to America to
educate him.   That boy, who came from a tribe of people in the
pre-cultural stage of society, went straight through the American
schools without difficulty, took the B.A. degree, and went on,
completing his Ph.D. at one of the universities.   The study
of anthropology does not indicate any great disparity between
the intelligence of different peoples of the genus *homo sapiens*.
The greater differences that exist are obviously not of
capacity, but of attainment.   Even the peoples of the lower levels
of culture—the Toda, the Badaga, the Panchama—possess
capacity for development as well as those who have been more
favoured.   This fact serves to deepen our responsibility to those
classes which we call 'backward' according to our official
terminology.   We know that backwardness is not something
inherent in the character of the people, but has to do only with
their lack of opportunity.   The backward classes are probably
as educable as the more privileged, and the community owes it
to them to provide them with the necessary opportunities that
will enable them to develop up to their maximum capacity, or
at least to provide opportunities equal to those of other
members of the community.

The educationalist needs to be a keen observer of the manner
in which mental development takes place.   Prof. James Drever,
in his *Introduction to the Psychology of Education*, has summarized the principles of mental development[1] on the basis of the
work of James, McDougall, and Shand.   He finds seven laws, and
we cannot do better than follow Drever's summary of the matter.
The first law is the law of 'development by stimulation': 'The
more frequently a natural tendency is evoked, other circumstances remaining unchanged, the more readily can it be
evoked, and the more powerfully does it operate.'   Various
qualities of character, both undesirable and desirable, may be
developed by repeating the types of stimuli which call them out.
The second law is the law of 'selection by experienced results'.

[1] pp. 64-74.

'Those actions tend to be discontinued which lead to unsatisfactory or disagreeable results; while, on the other hand, successful reactions, or those which involve agreeable results, are established.' It is an observation of common experience that we tend to persist in the actions which we find pleasurable and satisfying, and to avoid a repetition of those which have the opposite results. The third law is what James called 'inhibition by habit'. Drever adopts James' phraseology here: 'When objects of a certain class elicit from an animal a certain sort of reaction, it often happens that the animal becomes partial to the first specimen of the class on which it has reacted, and will not afterward react on any other specimen.' Reactions which at first are on the purely perceptual level may arouse such affective concomitants that in process of time sentiments grow up in regard to stimuli of a specific type. Drever's fourth law is also adopted from James. It is the law of 'transiency or transitoriness'. 'Many instincts ripen at a certain age and then fade away.' Certain of the child's interests and impulses come to focus at definite periods. Consequently James adds: 'In all pedagogy the great thing is to strike the iron while hot, and to seize the wave of the pupil's interest in each successive subject before its ebb has come, so that knowledge may be got and a habit of skill acquired— a headway of interest in short, secured, on which afterwards the individual may float. There is a happy moment for fixing skill in drawing, for making boys collectors in natural history, and presently dissectors and botanists, then for initiating them into the harmonies of mechanics and the wonders of physical and chemical law.' Drever's fifth law is called the law of 'transference of impulse', and is adopted from McDougall: 'Under certain more or less definite conditions, and as a result of experience and circumstances, an instinctive impulse may come to be evoked in connection with objects or situations different from, and sometimes entirely unconnected with, those which originally evoke it.' This matter of transference in education will be discussed later, when we are considering the learning process. The sixth law is called the law of 'fusion of feeling or emotion', and is expressed as follows: 'Primary emotions, simultaneously evoked, fuse so as to produce an emotional experience, different from the emotions involved, and *suo genere*, but generally analyzable into its elementary components.' This principle furnishes a basis for explanation of the more complex emotional experiences as developments from the more elementary types. The seventh law Drever calls the law of 'complication of behaviour': 'Where different impulses are evoked by the same situation simultaneously, and different emotions fuse in the resulting emotional experience, the behavour will tend to be always a complication for the behaviours corresponding to the respective impulses and simple emotions involved, with a varying emphasis according to circumstances.'

The educationalist must ever be an idealist if he is to be a successful leader of child life. He must keep persistently before him the ideal end of education—persons who have been so developed that they behave in the best possible way under all circumstances. The truly educated person is the person of finest character.

> ' We live in deeds, not years ; in thoughts, not breaths ;
> In feelings, not in figures on a dial.
> We should count time by heart-throbs.
> He most lives who thinks the most,
> Acts the noblest, feels the best.'

At the same time, the educationalist must be a thorough pragmatist, keeping in vital touch with real situations and real persons, studying needs in the concrete, and striving to meet them with specific appeals and devices. There is no such thing as human nature in general which the educator must study. There is no environment in the abstract in which personality must unfold. The educational process must proceed in a social environment, but it must be a separate process in each individual who is a candidate for development.

It is the function of the school to provide a specialized social environment. As Dewey says: 'The development within the young of the attitudes and dispositions necessary to the continuous and progressive life of a society cannot take place by direct conveyance of beliefs, emotions and knowledge. . . . The deeper and more intimate educative formation of disposition comes, with conscious intent, as the young gradually partake of the activities of

the various groups to which they may belong.'[1]   The school
provides a special environment, which helps to prepare the young
for the social life of which they are eventually to partake.   It
does this by offering a simplified environment, selecting the more
elementary features to which the young may be capable of
responding, and thus providing a developing environment for the
developing personality.   Furthermore, the school has an idealistic
mission to perform.   It has an obligation to provide the young
with the best, so that they will grow up with high ideals of what
the social life ought to be, and with a determination to play their
part in helping society to realize that ideal.   But society must
make provision for personality, so that it may unfold without
undue limitations in moral character and strength.   And the
school, as a model society, must make sufficient provision for the
freedom of its members, that they may grow into ideal citizens.

[1] John Dewey, *Democracy and Education*, pp. 26, 27.

LITERATURE

E. L. Thorndike.   *Educational Psychology*, 3 vols.; also Briefer Course,
    published by Teachers' College, Columbia University, 1914.
John Dewey.   *Democracy and Education*.   Macmillan, 1915.
W. C. Bagley.   *The Educative Process*.   Macmillan, 1905.
James Drever.   *An Introduction to the Psychology of Education*.   Edward
    Arnold, 1923.
D. Kennedy-Fraser.   *The Psychology of Education*.   Methuen, 1923.
R. S. Woodworth.   *Psychology : A Study of Mental Life*.   Methuen, 1922.
A. G. Tansley.   *The New Psychology and Its Relation to Life*.   George
    Allen & Unwin, 1920.
H. Crichton Miller.   *The New Psychology and the Teacher*.   Jarrolds, 1921.
Wm. Brown (Editor).   *Psychology and the Sciences*.   A. & C. Black, 1924.

CHAPTER II

INSTINCTIVE TYPES OF BEHAVIOUR

REFLEX BEHAVIOUR—NEUROLOGICAL BASIS OF INSTINCTS—CHARACTER-
ISTICS OF INSTINCTIVE BEHAVIOUR—INSTINCT AND EMOTION—DEFINITION
OF INSTINCT—TYPES OF INSTINCTIVE BEHAVIOUR.

THE character, personality and skill of any individual are the
outcome of the native capacities plus the development which they
attain. The individual is social and his native tendencies develop
in the environment in which his lot is cast. Human personality
in the large is the product of the individual's native tendencies,
the learning process, and the environmental influences in which
he lives and develops. The main task of the educator is to try
to provide an environment in which the native tendencies of the
child will have a maximum opportunity of developing along
wholesome lines. Obviously, if he is to be a minister to the
unfolding personality, he must have a thorough acquaintance
with human nature, on the side both of original tendencies and
of the capacities for development.

We can never understand the meaning of our task nor the
method of its accomplishment until we first appreciate the fact
that the child is a product of native equipment plus attainment.
There are some who think of human nature as an old Adam
that is unalterable except by miraculous intervention. But that
is to attribute, as Prof. Dewey says,[1] ' to native activities the
permanence and inertia that in truth belongs only to acquired
customs. To Aristotle slavery was rooted in aboriginal human
nature. Native distinctions of quality exist; such that some
persons are by nature gifted with power to plan, command, and
supervise, and others possess merely capacity to obey and
execute. Hence slavery is natural and inevitable.' In the same

[1] Dewey, *Human Nature and Conduct*, pp. 109, 110.

2

way, Dewey says that 'the worldly wise Aristotles of to-day assert that the institutions of war and the present wage system are so grounded in immutable nature that effort to change them is foolish'. The criticism of this doctrine is, as that writer goes on to show, that its adherents have confused native capacity with the attainments of group custom, whereas the truth is that 'native human nature supplies the raw materials, but custom furnishes the machinery and the designs'.

One of the most fruitful sources for the study of original human nature is the study of the behaviour of lower animals. Here we see reactions of less complexity and less consciousness, which therefore lend themselves more readily to observation. At the same time, if we hold to the evolutionary hypothesis, we must believe that these more elementary reactions of animal behaviour stand in very close relation to the more elementary human reactions. Moreover, it is possible to experiment with them in ways that would not be possible with human subjects. The biological point of view has been of immense value to the psychologist in this matter. It has helped very much to a clearer understanding of the differentiating characteristics of different types of behaviour. Biologically we study behaviour in terms of reactions which are responses to stimuli, and we find that such reactions vary in the matter of complexity from the simple spinal cord reflex to the most complex types of reasoning. Although there is no sharp line of distinction between the different types of behaviour, they are generally distinguishable into the reflexive, the instinctive, and the conscious. The reflexive and instinctive are native types of behaviour, whereas the conscious is acquired. So that an examination of these forms of conduct is what gives us our knowledge of the original nature of man.

The first observation which we ought to make on the basis of biology is that reflexes and instincts are types of behaviour, and not organic forms. It is not always easy to say when an action is reflexive or instinctive, so much do these types of behaviour merge the one into the other. The same remark applies to certain actions which are on the border line between the instinctive and the conscious. This leads to the conclusion that there are no such things as a reflex, an instinct, or consciousness. These terms would be much better used only in the descriptive sense as adjectives qualifying the words 'act' or 'behaviour', and should not be used as substantives. The inevitable temptation in using the words in the substantive sense is to conceive of each of them as a form of act belonging to the organism. It is, of course, the organism that behaves reflexively or instinctively or consciously, as the case may be, and the centre of focus is the behaving organism. So then we find behaviour increasing in complexity as we ascend the scale from the reflexive to the conscious. The unavoidable conclusion is that in the evolution of human behaviour the instinctive has developed out of the reflexive, and the conscious out of the instinctive.

A reflex act is the simplest possible reaction, being a prompt motor response to a sensory stimulus. Some of the more familiar types are the 'pupillary reflex', in which the pupil of the eye is contracted as a protection against a bright light shining into the eye, the 'flexion reflex', or jerking of the leg in response to a painful stimulus to the foot, the 'patellar reflex', or knee-jerk incited by striking the patellar tendon immediately below the knee when the leg is bent, the flow of tears when a particle of dust gets in the eye, the discharge of saliva in the mouth in response to a tasting substance, swallowing, breathing, hiccoughing, movements of the stomach and intestines, circulation of the blood, and so on. If we study the characteristic features of these various reactions which we class as reflexive, we shall note that they are (i) congenital, (ii) permanent, (iii) automatic, (iv) deep-seated in the organism, (v) essential to the organism's welfare, and (vi) close co-ordinations between stimuli and responses. The simplest mechanism of the reflex is the arc, which consists of a sensory or afferent nerve, a nerve centre, and a motor or efferent nerve. The connection of the nerves in the system is analogous to a telephone system, in which the nerve current, which is chemical and electric, resembles the electricity of the telephone, the nerve centre the switchboard, the sensory nerve, the person making the call, and the motor nerve the person answering the call. The simplest of all reflex acts is the spinal cord reflex, in which case the nerve centre is the spinal cord, the stimulated nerve current passing from the sensory neurones to the motor neurones without having to pass through the brain centres.

Experiments in regard to the neurological bases of reflexive and instinctive acts have led many biologists to conclude that the lines of demarcation between the two are very vague, and that the distinctions must be regarded as simply a matter of relative complexity. The fact that instincts are native tendencies to relatively definite types of behaviour puts them in the same genus with tropisms and reflexes. Thus Jacques Loeb, the mechanistic biologist, identifies the three. As long ago as Herbert Spencer[1] the suggestion was made that instincts are compound reflex reactions, and this position has been adopted latterly by Maurice Parmalee,[2] C. Lloyd Morgan,[3] and L. T. Hobhouse.[4] The later biologists are finding explanations for the distinctions on the basis of neural associations, and this matter applies also to the differences between instinctive and conscious behaviour. In the ordinary reflex, unless it be one of the reflexes connected with the eye, which is itself a protrusion from the brain, the nerve current passes from the afferent nerve through the spinal cord and out by the efferent nerve without involving the brain centres at all. In contrast with that, intelligent or voluntary behaviour, which involves more delicate adjustments, necessitates the passing of the nerve current over pathways which involve the cerebral centres. The property of consciousness has been located in the cerebral cortex, and hence behaviour which involves experience and which is conative is the outcome, on its neural side, of the functional activity of the cerebral cortex. Between these two types of behaviour—the reflex and the conscious—comes the instinctive, which, while more conscious than the reflexive, is less so than the conscious. Such writers as C. J. Herrick, C. Lloyd Morgan and C. J. Sherrington have put forward the hypothesis that the co-ordinations involved in instinctive behaviour are localizable in the sub-cortical brain centres, in the case of the higher vertebrates. This hypothesis is based on the results of

[1] Herbert Spencer, *Principles of Psychology*, vol. i. p. 427.
[2] Maurice Parmalee, *The Science of Human Behavior*, p. 203.
[3] C. Lloyd Morgan, *Instinct and Experience*, chap. iii.
[4] L. T. Hobhouse, *Mind in Evolution*, p. 53.

experiments on decerebrate animals, i.e. animals from which the cerebral hemisphere and cortex have been removed, but have the sub-cortical region and spinal cord intact. In so far as the investigations have proceeded, they seem to justify the conclusion that such animals are capable of behaviour which, in the biological usage of the term, may be designated as instinctive. To apply this hypothesis to human behaviour is, to be sure, analogical reasoning, and it is obviously the type of behaviour that cannot be verified in the case of the human animal. Herrick records[1] the case of an infant who lived to the age of three, and who was so inert that absolutely everything had to be done for it. It showed no signs of hunger, though it swallowed food when placed in the mouth. After the infant died an autopsy was performed, and it was ascertained that everything was normal save for the absence of the cerebral hemispheres and cortex. And the child was incapable of any of the types of behaviour which are called instinctive. Dr. Sherrington[2] has shown that hemicephalic children, in the absence of the cerebral hemispheres and mid-brain, respond similarly to normal children in the presence of unpleasant stimuli. Nevertheless, a good many experiments have been performed with decerebrate animals of various kinds which verify the hypothesis, and it may well be that the congenital defect in the case of the infant of whom Herrick tells, was so great as to impede the proper functioning of any of the nerve processes.

One of the great problems is as to the relation between consciousness and instinct. There are a good many psychologists who believe that there is an element of consciousness in instinctive behaviour, and even an occasional biologist has followed that theory. G. J. Romanes,[3] for example, differentiated between reflexive and instinctive behaviour on the ground that consciousness was operative in the latter but absent from the former. McDougall[4] is another writer who, from the psychological angle, has reached a similar conclusion. He has defined instinct as 'an

[1] C. J. Herrick, *Introduction to Neurology*, p. 312.
[2] C. S. Sherrington, *The Integrative Action of the Nervous System*, p. 254.   [3] G. J. Romanes, *Animal Intelligence*, pp. 3, 17.
[4] W. McDougall, *Social Psychology*, p. 29.

inherited or psycho-physical disposition which determines its possessor to perceive, and to pay attention to, objects of a certain class, to experience an emotional excitement of a particular quality upon perceiving such an object, and to act in regard to it in a particular manner, or, at least, to experience an impulse to such action'.   Parmalee has offered very incisive criticisms of McDougall's definition, as follows: (i) McDougall treats instinct as psycho-physical, his definition involving cognitive, affective and conative factors, whereas biological investigation has shown that instinctive behaviour is frequently devoid of any psychical element. (ii) The expressions 'to perceive' and 'to pay attention to' imply the presence of consciousness, which is not necessarily present. (iii) The experience of 'emotional excitement', which McDougall posits is not the concomitant of all instincts.[1]   President Angell is another psychologist who holds that 'instincts, in the higher animals at all events, appear always to involve consciousness.[2] Presumably the criticisms which Parmalee levelled at McDougall's positions are equally applicable to Angell.   It would seem that confusion has arisen in regard to the functioning of instincts because we are sometimes conscious of being hungry, or thirsty, or lonely, or curious, or of seeking to preserve ourselves from danger.   But it is a very doubtful procedure to conclude on such evidence that consciousness is operative in instinctive behaviour.   It is much more likely that Lloyd Morgan is right when he describes the functioning of consciousness in such instances as that of 'a mere spectator'.   It will be worth our while to quote from his statement of the matter.   'Intelligent guidance is the function of the cerebral cortex, with its distinguishing property of consciousness; the co-ordination involved in instinctive behaviour, and in the distribution of physiological forces to the viscera and vascular systems, is the primary function of the lower brain centres; in instinctive behaviour as such, consciousness correlated with processes in the cerebral cortex is, so to speak, a mere spectator of organic and biological occurrences at present beyond its control, but, as spectator, it receives information of connexion between the lower and higher parts of the brain.'[3]

[1] Parmalee, *The Science of Human Behavior*, pp. 218-21.
[2] J. R. Angell, *Psychology*, p. 339.
[3] Lloyd Morgan, *Instinct and Experience*, pp. 7, 8.

Instinctive behaviour differs from reflex in being more complex. Not all compound reflexes are instincts, however. Coughing and swallowing are examples of complex reflexes, which do not come under the designation of instincts. From the standpoint of complexity there could be made out a gradation of behaviour from the simplest form like the knee jerk or the papillary reflex to the mating or nesting instinct. There is no sharp line, as we have said, to demark one from the other, so that we may speak of the instinct as a complex of reflexes that have been neurally integrated into a unitary type of behaviour. They probably originated as situations arose which were too difficult to be met by the simple reflex reaction. In a parallel way, we may think of consciousness having arisen to meet situations that were too acute for satisfactory responses by means of instinctive reactions. For example, so long as it would be possible to respond to the need for food by partaking of the supply provided by nature, the hunger stimulus could be responded to by the food instinct without the intervention of consciousness. But if there were two or more kinds of food provided by nature, and it was necessary to weigh the one against the other and make a choice, consciousness would be required to select between the alternatives. Or, if the supply of food proved to be inadequate to meet the needs of the individual or the group, and some other device had to be sought to meet the hunger need, that would constitute a crisis incapable of solution instinctively, but requiring the functioning of consciousness. Thus either a luxurious nature or a niggardly nature would present a situation to which man could not respond instinctively, but for which conscious deliberation and action would be required. The cortical centres are the centres which come into play when a reasoning process is required, so that they would be called into function when the lower brain centres were found inadequate to cope with the situation.

It is necessary to note the characteristics of instinctive behaviour which have been disclosed by the aid of biological investigation. And in this connection let us observe that a good deal of the difficulty in reaching a tenable definition of instinct on the part of psychologists is due to their failure to remember that they must really depend on the biologists for scientifically justifiable conclusions. The necessity for this will be all the clearer when it is remembered that many instinctive reactions are wholly physical. The trouble with such writers as McDougall comes from the introduction of too much psychical matter. And the advantage of such psychologists as Lloyd Morgan grows out of their beginning to speak where the biologists stop.

1. In the first place, instinctive behaviour is plainly native as distinguished from acquired modes of behaviour which involve intelligence. It is an inherited mode of reaction, though the theory that instincts are inherited ancestral habits has gone by the board. No biologist would accept that any longer, for it is no longer believed that acquired behaviour traits can be transmitted by heredity. Learned reactions, skill and knowledge cannot be transmitted. Such abilities as typewriting, motor car driving and gymnastics, no matter how well we may be able to perform them, are not passed on to our children. But instinctive behaviour, such as shrinking from danger, striking at an enemy, mating, procreating, resting and mothering, is congenital. It is part of our original equipment when we come into the world. That does not mean that all instincts appear at birth, but some of them appear later. Hans Driesch is of the opinion that when they do appear they are 'perfect the very first time'[1] that they function. Lloyd Morgan is wisely more moderate in his statement that they are 'serviceable on the occasion of their first appearance'.[2]

2. In the second place, instinctive behaviour is characteristically performed by all the members of a group of species. It tends towards the well-being of the species and of the individuals composing the group. Some of the best known instincts, such as the migrations of birds, hibernating of frogs, feeding, mating, flight and fighting are quite essential for the survival of the species or of the individual members composing the group. There are some types of instinctive reactions the survival value of which is very dubious, such as the crowing of cocks at dawn, but it may be that these reactions, as some hold,

---

[1] Hans Driesch, *The Science and Philosophy of the Organism*, vol. iii. p. 110.   [2] Lloyd Morgan, *Instinct and Experience*, p. 22.

were originally serviceable, though the serviceable character does not now appear. Though one must be ready to acknowledge exceptions when they occur, we may accept it as the rule that instinctive reactions are useful to the species or individual.

3. At the same time, instinctive reactions are capable of modification and adaptability under the guidance of experience, even as the structures themselves are possessed of these characteristics of modifiability and adaptability. Angell has described instincts as 'structurally pre-formed pathways in the nervous system', standing 'functionally for effective inherited co-ordinations made in response to environmental demands'.[1] Sometimes these reactions are strengthened or stimulated, while others of them are obstructed or inhibited, where reinforcement or inhibition are necessary in the interests of the welfare of the organism or of the species.

4. The fourth point on which psychologists are agreed is that instinctive reactions are relatively complex. As Lloyd Morgan says: 'Such behaviour is a more or less complex organic or biological response to a more or less complex group of stimuli of external and internal origin, and it is, as such, wholly dependent on how the organism, and especially the nervous system and brain centres, have been built through heredity under the racial preparation which we call biological evolution.'[2] Insects afford very good examples of highly organized instinctive reactions. 'Their behaviour is extremely regular and predictable, their progress towards the end-result of an instinct remarkably straightforward and sure. They make few mistakes and do not have to potter around.'[3] Bergson tells of a certain wasp which is the traditional enemy of a particular beetle. There is but one vulnerable spot on the otherwise hard back of the beetle, and the wasp unfailingly alights on the beetle and pierces its sting into the beetle through the vulnerable spot. The nesting and incubating behaviour of birds furnishes us with further examples of very complex and well-organised instincts. In all of these instances the preparatory reactions are very closely linked to the principal reaction-tendency, so that when the principal tendency is

[1] Angell, *Psychology*, p. 339.
[2] Lloyd Morgan, *Instinct and Experience*, p. 5.
[3] Woodworth, *Psychology*, p. 111.

once stimulated to activity, the preparatory reactions follow closely and surely afterwards. Exactly the required preparatory reactions are associated with the principal reaction, so that the entire series of acts follows in order with precision.

Before offering a definition of instinctive behaviour, it will be helpful to quote Prof. Lloyd Morgan's suggestions in regard to a scientific approach to the problem. He says:

'I suggest that, for the biologist and the psychologist a criterion—not the only criterion, but a criterion of instinctive behaviour—is that it is serviceable on the first occasion. But the biologist for the purposes of his interpretation of animal life will ask: Serviceable to what end? First of all, serviceable as affording the congenital foundations for an improved super-structure of behaviour. That is one way in which instinctive behaviour is serviceable, the way which is of special interest to the psychologist. From the more distinctly biological point of view, instinctive behaviour is broadly and generally serviceable for survival for avoiding danger, by shrinking, quiescence or flight; serviceable for warding off the attacks of enemies; serviceable for obtaining food, capturing prey, and so forth; serviceable for winning and securing a mate, for protecting and rearing offspring; in social animals, serviceable for co-operating with others, and so behaving that not only the individual but the social group shall survive. But it will be said, these are the very ends for the attainment of which intelligence is serviceable. Unquestionably it is so. It is just because the many and varied modes of instinctive behaviour are serviceable for the attainment of the same ends for which intelligence is serviceable, that their consideration is essential to the right history of experience. Instinctive behaviour, which has its roots in organic evolution, affords the rude outline sketch of that far less imperfect and far more fully serviceable behaviour, the finishing touches of which are supplied by practice under the guidance of intelligence. The net result (what is for popular speech the perfect instinct) is a joint product of instinct and intelligence, in which the co-operating factors are inseparable, but none the less genetically distinguishable.'[1]

[1] Lloyd Morgan, *Instinct and Experience*, pp. 25, 26.

There is another characteristic of instinctive behaviour which, while it does not find a place among the biological factors, is yet psychologically important, and particularly important for the teacher. McDougall has the merit of developing the intimate relationship which subsists between instinctive reactions and emotional experiences. He has made a very useful analysis of the primitive instinctive tendencies which lie at the root of the affective and conative activities of consciousness. There are instinctive reactions which occur so quickly in response to their stimuli that they are almost entirely reflexive, and in such cases emotional qualities are almost entirely absent. But there are many other instances where the instinctive reaction and its emotional correlate are almost simultaneous. But even if the emotional quality always succeeds the action, as is suggested by the theory of James and Lange, the emotional accompaniment follows very soon, and is characteristic. Experiments on the emotional reactions are indicating that they have their neurosis which corresponds to the neurosis of the instinctive experience. There is a considerable body of evidence to lead to the possible conclusion that such neuroses are identical. Emotional experiences are reduced by many scholars to purely physiological reactions,[1] such as changes in breathing, in circulation, in the churning of the stomach and in the kneading of the intestines, change of the starch of the liver into sugar, and changes in the secretions of the endocrine glands—in particular the thyroid and adrenal glands. The chief concern for the present discussion is that there are intimate associations between certain types of instinctive reactions and certain emotional experiences. McDougall's list[2] of 'simple instincts' includes fourteen, the names being taken from the characteristic conation in each case. The following is the list with the corresponding emotional experience placed after it :

1. Flight, *fear.*
2. Pugnacity, *anger.*
3. Repulsion, *disgust.*
4. Parental instinct, *tenderness.*

[1] *Vide* W. B. Cannon, *Bodily Changes in Pain, Hunger, Fear, and Rage.*
[2] McDougall, *Outline of Psychology,* p. 324.

5. Appeal, *distress*.
6. Reproduction, or the sex instinct, *lust*.
7. Curiosity, *wonder*.
8. Submission, or self-abasement, *subjection* (*negative self-feeling*).
9. Self-assertion, *elation* (*positive self-feeling*).
10. Gregariousness, or the herd instinct, *loneliness*.
11. Food-getting, *appetite*.
12. Acquisition, *feeling of ownership*.
13. Construction, *feeling of creativeness*.
14. Laughter, *amusement*.

On this basis McDougall proceeds to account for the 'complex emotions', which he says are compounded of two or more simple emotions, and the 'sentiments' which, after Shand, he describes as mental dispositions formed by the association of affective experiences with concrete objects.

The psycho-analysts are also very much interested in the question of instincts. They introduce the matter in connection with their discussion of complexes. To quote from Tansley: 'The term *complex* was introduced into psychology, in a definite technical sense, by Neisser and Jung, in order to present a clear picture of the manner in which affectively toned groups of presentations, which have been repressed from consciousness (i.e. have become secondarily unconscious), because they are out of harmony with the rest of the mind, suddenly make their presence felt in consciousness and give rise to the symptoms of hysteria or insanity.'[1]   These complexes, according to the psycho-analysts, are caused by instincts which come into conflict with one another. For example, if the instincts of self-assertion and self-abasement, with their concomitant effects, come into conflict with one another, the outcome will be the 'ego-complex'. Pugnacity is contrasted with flight, and curiosity with repulsion. Pugnacity and curiosity are expressions of the instinct of self-assertion, whereas repulsion and flight belong to self-abasement. These various complexes, of which one example is given, constantly interplay upon and modify

---

[1] A. G. Tansley, *The New Psychology*, p. 59.

one another. The normal development of consciousness and personality depends upon their harmony and poise. The educational significance of this theory is obvious. Opportunities for development should be presented so that the life processes will unfold with that harmony and poise which makes for a normal, healthy character. The observant teacher will easily detect tendencies toward over-emphasis in one direction at the expense of some other direction.

We are now in a position to sum up the characteristics of instinctive behaviour in the form of definition. Prof. James Drever says: 'As a factor determining the behaviour of living organisms, Instinct, physiologically regarded, is a congenital predisposition of the nervous system, consisting in a definite, but within limits modifiable, arrangement and co-ordination of nervous connections, so that a particular stimulus, with or without the presence of certain co-operating stimuli, will call forth a particular action or series of actions; this predisposition, biologically regarded, is apparently due to the operation of natural selection, and determines a mode of behaviour which secures a biologically useful end, without foresight of that end or experience in attaining it.'[1]   Drever has a different psychological definition, however, to his biological definition 'proposing to call the conscious impulse "Instinct" when and so far as it is not itself determined by experience, while itself determining experience, in conjunction with the nature of objects or situations determining experience as sensation. . . .   Instinct is the "life impulse" becoming conscious as determinate conscious impulse. But this, in itself, is only one side of the psychological fact, and an abstraction. The other side—also an abstraction—is sensation. The psychological fact itself is experience in its lowest terms.'[2]   The crux of the problem is as to whether it is legitimate to have a psychological definition distinct from the biological. If once that procedure is granted, there is no good reason why the metaphysician should not also offer a definition, which, as a matter of fact, has been done, as e.g. by Von Hartmann, who says: 'Instinct is purposive action without consciousness of

---

[1] Drever, *Instinct in Man*, p. 81.   [2] Ibid., p. 80.

the purpose';[1] and again, 'Instinct is conscious willing of the means to an unconsciously willed end.'[2]   But it would seem as though this *laissez-faire* policy in the matter of defining instinct is directly responsible for the well-known, lamentable fact that scarcely any two writers use the term in precisely the same sense. I have made a collection of about forty definitions of 'instinct', and their dissimilarities are much more striking than their likenesses.   For that very good reason it would seem to be the part of wisdom for the psychologist to accept the biological meaning of the term, concerning the main factors of which there is pretty general agreement.   Otherwise it would seem that there is no hope of ending the confusion.

I have elsewhere defined instinct from the biological point of view as 'a congenital co-ordination of reflexes, neurally integrated and effecting an organic response characteristic of and serviceable to the species, and in some manner capable of subsequent modification.   The character of the response depends on the character of the stimulus, and the presence or absence of any obstruction to its normal expression.'[3]   If we confine our use of the word 'instinctive' to those reactions which fall within the biological description, and which have their neurological connections in the sub-cortical regions of the brain, we shall have a much more definite concept.   We may say that it is the biologist's task to define, and the psychologist's task further to interpret, instinctive behaviour with reference to its relation to the mental life.

The lists of instinctive tendencies will be found to vary widely in different books on the subject, largely because the authors start out from different views of what constitutes an instinct. Some sociological writers[4] are inclined to group them all under two classes as elementary—food and sex—but that usage of the word is more as a synonym for the great life interests.   There is no doubt that these fundamental life needs have been the stimuli which have often called forth instinctive responses.   But to

[1] E. Von Hartmann, *Philosophy of the Unconscious*.   Translation by Wm. C. Coupland, vol. i. p. 79.   [2] Ibid., vol. i. p. 88.

[3] A. S. Woodburne, *The Relation Between Religion and Science*, p. 52.

[4] e.g. W. I. Thomas, in *Sex and Society*, pp. 97-99, 118-19.

identify them is scarcely a tenable position. The diametric-
ally opposite tendency appears in such writers as Wm.
James and E. L. Thorndike, whose lists are exceedingly long.
James thought that the human instincts were very much more
numerous than those of lower animals. The list which
Thorndike has made covers three pages,[1] and includes what
we would break up into reflexes, instincts, inborn capacities,
and some even more complex forms of behaviour. Between the
two extremes are lists of various lengths. It is more serviceable
to us from the point of view of psychology to group them into
classes than it is simply to enumerate them separately, as they
appear in biological investigation. From the psychological
viewpoint we may group the instinctive reactions then into five
classes, namely (i) reactions connected with the securing of food,
(ii) reactions connected with mating and procreating, (iii) reactions
associated with self-preservation, (iv) reactions stimulated by
contact with the strange and the unusual, and (v) reactions
connected with gregariousness. Possibly this list of types may
not be exhaustive, but it will nevertheless be found to include all
the more important reactions which we think of as instinctive.

1. Instinctive reactions connected with the securing of food
include such reactions as sucking, swallowing, chewing, putting
food into the mouth. The end-result is having food in the
stomach, and the affective concomitant of uneasiness is hunger.
Sucking and swallowing appear practically at birth, and chewing
with the coming of the teeth. Movements of rejecting food
when satiated or when the food is ill-tasting appear very early.
Putting food into the mouth by the hands is evidently instinctive,
but it has to be regulated and fixed by the method of trial and
error. In animals the food-getting instincts include such movements as crouching, stalking, creeping, and pouncing upon prey,
such as are evident in hunting. It need scarcely be pointed out
that thirst and nausea belong to this same general group of
experiences.

2. Instinctive reactions connected with mating and procreating
are sometimes known as the sex instinct. Attraction towards

---

[1] Thorndike, *Educational Psychology*, vol. i. pp. 17-20.

members of the opposite sex is usually experienced first
during the adolescent period, when the sex organs themselves
come to maturity. In the lower animals these instinctive
tendencies appear much earlier than in man, and manifest
themselves in characteristic reactions, such as strutting, spreading
of the feathers in birds, and such attempts at display to attract
attention. In most instances, both human and lower animal,
the aggressive is taken by the male, while the female appears
as shy. As Woodworth has pointed out, ' the " survival value " of
the instinct is absolute ; without it the race would not long survive.
But it has " play value " also, it contributes to the joy of luring
as well as to the struggle for survival.'[1] This instinct has been
made to do duty as an explanation for a very wide range of
human activities. Some sociologists have made it the basis
of the entire social life. It has been credited with being the
foundation of both religion and morality. And the Freudian
psycho-analysts have made it a sort of universal explanation for
all mental facts, both individual and social. Most complexes are
sexual. Practically all the good and the bad of life are alike
traceable to this wonder-working tendency.

In the general grouping here adopted the parental or mothering instinct is also included in this class. In some animals the
care of the young is shared by both parents ; in a few, such as
fish, the male takes care of the young ; in mammals it is always
the work of the mother. We have most of us at some time
experienced the instinctive reaction towards a helpless infant.
The petting of young animals is probably an expression of the
same tendency. In some instances, no doubt, the attraction
between the sexes is a compound of the mating and parental
tendencies. The parental instinct, in the opinion of most
psychologists, is at the foundation of all education. The process
of education is undoubtedly one in which the school and the home
share. The parents recognize that they have a great responsibility
in the development of the immature life. And the establishment
and maintenance of schools is an expression of the recognition by
the adult members of a community of their responsibility towards

[1] Woodworth, *Psychology : A Study of Mental Life*, p. 148.

the child life of the group. In a parallel way this instinctive tendency to protect the helpless, an essentially parental attitude, lies at the root of all philanthropy.

3. Instinctive reactions connected with self-preservation are of two main types—the tendency to avoid dangers with its appropriate defensive reaction of flight, and the tendency to overcome opposition with its concomitant conation of fight. With the former is associated the emotional experience of fear, with the latter, anger. There are some psychologists who include self-preservation under the instinctive reactions associated with the securing of food, regarding food-getting as basal to the life processes, and self-preservation as subsidiary thereto. But if they are to be grouped together at all, it would seem a sounder argument to place food-getting under self-preservation, as one of the processes necessary to that end. There is even some justification for using the term ' self-preservation ' in a wide enough connotation to include all instinctive behaviour. But the commoner usage of the term is to restrict it to the two types of behaviour mentioned—the defensive and offensive reactions in the presence of danger and opposition. It might be spoken of as the way in which the organism expresses the will to live in the presence of circumstances which seem ready to crush it. Woodworth analyzes the self-assertive tendencies into four groups.

' (i) Defensive reactions to things, overcoming obstruction, putting through what has been undertaken—the success motive.

' (ii) Defensive reactions to persons, resisting domination by them—the independence motive.

' (iii) Aggressive reactions to things—the seeking for power.

' (iv) Aggressive reactions to persons—seeking to dominate.'[1]

There is obviously important educational significance in the functioning and development of these tendencies. Take, for example, the fighting tendency. If this be allowed to develop selfishly and cruelly, it may become a social menace. The warring tendency of our so-called civilization is an illustration. But, as William James has shown,[2] it is possible to find a moral

---

[1] Woodworth, *Psychology : A Study of Mental Life*, p. 162.
[2] Wm. James, *The Moral Equivalent of War*.

equivalent for war, which will give the fighting tendency wholesome expression in combating moral evils.   Again, the desire for
domination may be given opportunities to develop in connection
with problematic situations in the school, and in that way be
utilized for the child's best interest.   The teacher needs also to
understand that such undesirable tendencies as sulking, sullenness,
peevishness, stubbornness and defiance are very often due to the
thwarting of the self-assertive tendency. Jealousy, envy, embarras-
ment and shyness also owe their significance to their relation to
this group of instincts.   The educator needs to be a real
psycho-analyst in the sense of being able to relate various moods
and attitudes to the child's instinctive tendencies.   Only by means
of such analyses will he be able to meet the child's needs and
remedy his deficiencies.

4. Instinctive reactions arising out of one's contact with the
strange and the unusual frequently go by the generic name of
curiosity.   There are some who deny that curiosity is instinctive,
but biologists are agreed that there are in man and in many of
the lower animals tendencies to distinctive reactions in the
presence of the strange and the unusual.   The behaviour of
dogs and of monkeys is particularly illustrative.   And the same
disposition is apparent in young children.   There is no doubt
that this tendency is at the basis of much of the acquisition
of knowledge, which is so vital in the educational process.   This
has been brought out by Mr. Shand, who says that to the impulse
of curiosity we surely 'owe most of the disinterested labours of the
higher types of intellect.   It must be regarded as one of the
principal roots of both science and religion.'[1]   It is a root of
science, inasmuch as it germinates in an attitude of insatiable
desire to add to the stock of knowledge by the methods of
investigation and experimentation.   In that way it lies at the
root of many of the most brilliant scientific achievements of
mankind.   On the other hand, it is a root of religion, in that it
moves mankind to pry into the superhuman, to investigate the
unknown, and to seek to establish helpful relationships with it.
The educator will clearly desire to make the greatest possible

[1] A. F. Shand, *The Foundations of Character*, p. 59.

use of this instinctive tendency for the development of the personalities entrusted to his care and guidance.

5. Instinctive reactions connected with gregariousness are otherwise called 'the herd instinct', or 'the socializing tendency'. It is more difficult to analyze this group of reactions than some of the others. Yet most biologists agree that certain co-ordinations of reflexes have taken place in such a way that the resultant neural integration is serviceable in helping the group as well as the individual in the struggle for existence, that is, is serviceable for co-operation. Prof. Brooks has shown convincingly that the adaptations developed in the various species are many of them to be considered as ' for the good of the species and not for the individual ' as such. He claims that ' the law is universal, but since the welfare of the species is usually identified with that of the constituent individuals it is not obvious unless the good of the species demands the sacrifice of the individuals '. He further argues that the general law of nature which refers the properties of all living things to a social, utilitarian basis, affords an explana- tion for such varied gregarious activities as the migrations of salmon and the altruistic moral sense of man.[1] Those who argue for the instinctive character of gregariousness refer to such pheno- mena as the swarming of bees, the migrations of birds, colonies of ants, packs of wolves, herds of deer, flocks of sheep, droves of cattle, shoals of fishes, and the like. There is an important school of biologists to-day who hold that ' mutual aid ' or co-operation is much more characteristic of the struggle for existence in the animal kingdom than is the principle of ' natural selection '. The socializing tendencies are surely very prominent also in the human race. Group life is much more characteristic than soli- tary life, both in primitivity and in the age of sophistication.

It is not necessary to go into greater details from the point of view of educational psychology. It will suffice to refer to the great importance of these tendencies from our point of view. The family and the school are both social institutions. So also are the state and the religious community. These all give opportunities for the education of the person in consonance with

[1] W. G. Brooks, *The Foundations of Zoology*, pp. 117-19.

his fundamentally social nature. Education itself from this point of view is a co-operative enterprise, in which teacher and taught struggle together and help one another to develop their personalities. It is of inestimable value to the teacher if he is able to instil in his pupils the sense of co-operating in a common task. And it will develop the social tendency of the child in a way that will be incalculably worth while in his mature life.

LITERATURE

C. Lloyd Morgan. *Instinct and Experience.* Methuen, 1912.

W. H. R. Rivers. *Instinct and the Unconscious.* Cambridge University Press, 1920.

J. B. Watson. *Behaviour.* Henry Holt, 1914.

R. S. Woodworth. *Dynamic Psychology.* Columbia University Press, 1922.

W. McDougall. *An Outline of Psychology.* Methuen, 1923.

Maurice Parmelee. *The Science of Human Behavior.* Macmillan, 1913.

E. L. Thorndike. *The Original Nature of Man.* Columbia University Press, 1913.

W. Trotter. *Instincts of the Herd in Peace and War.* T. Fisher Unwin, 1916.

James Drever. *Instinct in Man.* Cambridge University Press, 1923.

John Dewey. *Human Nature and Conduct.* George Allen & Unwin, 1922.

C. J. Herrick. *An Introduction to Neurology.* W. B. Saunders, 1918.

A. S. Woodburne. *The Relation Between Religion and Science.* University of Chicago Press, 1920.

C. S. Sherrington. *The Integrative Action of the Nervous System.* Scribner's, 1906.

CHAPTER III

THE NATURE OF INTELLIGENCE AND METHODS OF MEASURING IT

THE place that is accorded to the subject of intelligence in modern educational psychology is one of the features which distinguish it from the older treatment of the subject. One is amazed to look over some of the older books and find how little reference there is to that exceedingly important topic. Probably the reason for its infrequent use in the older writers was that they thought of it as synonymous with the knowing faculty. They believed that in describing that faculty, they were describing intelligence. This conception has some justification from the etymological significance, the word being derived from the Latin *intelligere*, to understand, as is also our other English word, *intellect*, the French *intellect* and *intelligence*, the Italian *intelletto* and *intelligenza*, and the German *intelligenz*. On the other hand, the reason that intelligence has come to occupy such an important place in modern psychology is due to the experimental work in the measurement of it during the last two decades.

We have noted that the words *intellect* and *intelligence* originated from a common root. Though they have the same meaning philologically, the two words have grown apart in usage, the word *intellect* being used for the distinctly conceptual processes, and the word *intelligence* for mental capacity or ability. This distinction is serving a very useful purpose to-day in the realm of Comparative Psychology. Baldwin and Stout have pointed out, in the *Dictionary of Philosophy and*

Psychology, that it is quite customary to speak of 'animal intelligence', but that the phrase 'animal intellect' is not generally used. Lloyd Morgan, who wrote the article on *Intelligence* in the *Encyclopaedia Britannica*, elaborates the same differentiation, saying that 'the term may be conveniently restricted to the capacity of guiding behaviour through perceptual process, reserving the terms intellect and reason for the so-called faculties which involve conceptual process'. Proceeding, he says, 'It is probably best, for strictly psychological purposes, to define somewhat strictly perceptual and conceptual (or ideational) process, and to leave to intelligence the comparative freedom of a word to be used in general literature, and therein defined by its context.'[1] The writer then proceeds to show that experiments with animals have proved that they are quite lacking in the abilities of analyzing and abstracting, even in the more elementary phases, and without analysis and abstraction conceptual processes are impossible. On the other hand, animals are quite capable of perceptual processes. By means of associative representation, animals are able to learn. A good deal of experimentation has been done on the learning ability of animals, and so far as perceptual learning is concerned, they sometimes compare very favourably with human beings. But in the matter of conceptual learning, which demands the ability to generalize, they show a great disadvantage.

The story of the beginnings of the measurement of intelligence is now quite familiar. It is not necessary in this connection to tarry over the antecedents to it in cranioscopy, phrenology, psychiatry and physical anthropology. The name with which we rightly associate the real beginnings is Alfred Binet. The Board of Education in Paris was anxious to learn the causes of retardation, and turned to Binet to conduct an investigation in the matter. Binet realized that the chief difficulty was not environmental but congenital, not bad teaching but feeble-mindedness, but he needed an instrument whereby he might be able to detect the feeble-minded so that they might be separated from the normal for special treatment. The instrument which

---

[1] *Encyclopaedia Britannica*, 11th edition, vol. xiv. p. 681.

he devised was the scale of intelligence tests. His first scale was issued in 1905, a second and revised scale in 1908, a third and still further revision in 1911, and at the time of his death he was at work on a fourth scale.

The principle which Binet adopted, and which other scholars have found to be sound, was that no one test could be used as an adequate measurement of intelligence, because intelligence is much too complex to be so measured. It is obvious to even the least scientific observation that intelligence does not always express itself in one way. Arthur is a good mathematician, but poor in language; James is very good in language, but mathematics is a constant struggle for him. Yet on the average the two boys are fairly equal. It is difficult to say that either is more intelligent than the other. The only fair way to measure intelligence is therefore some such way as Binet adopted. It is necessary to provide a sufficient number of tests so that different sorts of ability may have a chance of expressing themselves. Either a purely mathematical test or an entirely linguistic test would fail. It is to be questioned as to whether any of the scales so far devised are yet broad enough to measure intelligence. For intelligence may possibly be rather motor than mental, and the majority of the tests so far devised are measures of mental abilities only. In that sense the still more recently devised vocational test is really a test of intelligence in its motor expressions.

The Binet scales and the scales which followed the revisions of the Binet scales—the Point Scale, and the Performance Scales—were graduated so as to test the intelligence of children at various ages from three years to maturity. It was necessary to ascertain what tests would be appropriate for subjects at the various stages of maturity, before it would be possible to have a scale. Binet began by testing a very large number of children, and he endeavoured thereby to ascertain at what particular ages children would be able to pass the various tests. If seventy-five per cent of the children of a particular chronological age were able to pass a particular test, and yet only a much smaller percentage could succeed in a more difficult test, he then fixed the test as suitable for that age. He thus made the measurement of intelligence on an age basis. The average child is the child who is just able to pass the tests for his own age. Working on that basis, he would say that the child who passes the tests of his own chronological age has a mental age corresponding to it. Indeed, his mental age is determined by the place in the scale of the tests which he is able to pass. This plan has an obvious advantage over the old examination system in vogue, in that it not only offers a basis for determining who were dull and who bright in a school, but also the degree in terms of mental age of that dullness or brightness. A further development of a measuring basis was put forward by the German psychologist, W. Stern. He proposed that, although the determination of the mental age of a child served a very useful purpose, what we really want to know is what relationship subsists between the mental age and chronological age. He therefore invented the term, 'Intelligence Quotient' (conveniently abbreviated as 'I.Q.'), to express that relationship, and the method of ascertaining it is to divide the mental age by the chronological age. Thus if the two ages correspond, as in the case of the average child, his I.Q. is 100, which really means one hundred per cent. If he be of superior intelligence, say at nine years able to pass the twelve-year tests, his I.Q. is $\frac{12}{9}$ x 100 = 133; if he be sub-normal, and at nine only able to do the six year tests, his I.Q. is $\frac{6}{9}$ x 100 = 67. Nobody would say that this is an absolute method of measurement, but there is one claim that may be made for it with real justice, namely that it affords a basis of comparison. It may well be that further tests would make us revise the I.Q's of different subjects who have been tested, but it is unlikely that there would be any marked difference in the relative positions of the subjects. Further testing would be altogether unlikely to change classifications from superior to inferior, or *vice versa*.

The most important element in Binet's contribution was the substitution of a scale of tests for the older fashioned all-or-none performance. Binet really built larger than he knew. His own purpose was, as we have seen, the device of an instrument whereby he could detect the feeble-minded. But it has been found to serve an even wider function in educational psychology, for the age-scale has been an aid to the grading of children in school. It is necessary to be on our guard, however, against the temptation of using the age-scale or intelligence quotient as the sole basis for educational organization. A school cannot be organized without any reference to the attainments of the children, no matter how detailed be our knowledge of intelligence. The attainment tests are thus supplementary to the intelligent tests.

There has been a great expansion of this measuring activity since it was begun by Binet. A host of workers in the field have been at work, devising tests, testing the tests, revising them, building up standards, and so forth. Among the best known workers mention may be made of Simon, Terman, Goddard, Kuhlmann, Schwegel, Ballard, Burt, Whipple, Thorndike, Pintner, Paterson, Yerkes, Otis, McCall, Haggerty and Hollingworth. But mention of these names must not be interpreted as indifference to the invaluable work of many others whose names do not appear. By far the most significant advances that have been made are, first the devising of performance tests, and second the institution of group tests.

In regard to the performance test, the *raison d'être* will be fairly obvious. Tests of the Binet type obviously suffer from the defect that they depend on language stimuli and language responses. The defect was very soon realized in the United States when psychologists began to investigate the intelligence of foreign-born immigrants. The difficulty is two-fold: (i) those who do not understand the language in which the test is given cannot respond intelligently, and (ii) one cannot be certain that a translation is an equally difficult test to the original. Further, there is the difficulty in the case of the deaf or dumb. To remedy this language difficulty the performance test was devised. The aim which the performance test has is that of presenting problems the solutions of which depend entirely on manipulations which require the functioning of capacities or abilities, but which may be responded to at a given signal, and quite as effectively in the absence as with the use of language commands. The performance tests have been and are of inestimable value to those who are trying to estimate the intelligence of illiterate peoples, and it frequently happens that people whose intelligence it is desirable to measure are not literate.

Those who have been experimenting with the intelligence test in India are impressed with the possibilities of the performance test, since there are so many people who, though they may be literate in their own vernacular, are not literate in the language of the test. The census reports indicate that there are approximately four hundred languages and dialects spoken in this country. It is enough to show the impossibility of devising a language test that can be standardized for the whole of India. One of the great values of the measure is that it can be so standardized as to enable psychologists to make comparisons not only between people in different parts of India, but between people of this country and others in other countries. Even supposing it were possible to have a language test translated into all known languages, it would be an impossible task to determine whether the test represented the same degree of difficulty, and consequently presented a problem demanding the same degree of intelligence for its solution everywhere. But a performance test is not subject to this difficulty. Take such a test as placing geometrically formed blocks into the appropriate recesses in a form-board, or that of tracing a pencil through a maze. These are tests which do not require any language test, nor do they require any previous experience with the types of response for which they call. So they do not require either translation or modification. They are used in precisely the same way, no matter with whom they are used. Consequently they seem to be much more the type of test which is needed for building up universal standards. And particularly in India, where we want to test people belonging to such a variety of language areas, and many of whom are illiterate, the possibilities of the performance test seem to be much greater.

The exigencies of the Great War are responsible for the introduction of the group testing of intelligence. Soon after America entered the War as a belligerent, a meeting of the American Psychological Association was held and the psychologists of the country were mobilized for service. It was speedily seen that it would be impossible to do any satisfactory work with the immense numbers of men who were assembling at the training camps if they had no instrument other than the individual test.

If all the men were to be tested, each man requiring from forty minutes to an hour, a tremendous amount of time would be wasted, unless there was a small army of psychologists to test the larger army of soldiers. It was to remedy this defect that the group test was introduced. Even before the War some preliminary work had been done on the innovation of the group test, that of Otis being the principal test devised. But a committee was appointed, with Prof. (afterwards Major) R. M. Yerkes as chairman, and as a result of its labours two sets of group tests were devised, which were named the Alpha and Beta. The Alpha scale was composed of language tests, whereas the Beta was a scale of performance tests, provided for those men who were illiterate in the English language, and arranged so far as possible, test for test, corresponding to the tests of the Alpha scale, only performance was substituted for language. There were several points which were kept in mind in devising these group tests, the more important being: (i) to have a test that would enable a large group to be examined rapidly; (ii) to be able to measure a wide range of intelligence; (iii) to be able to score objectively and rapidly; (iv) to make the tests 'foolproof', i.e. with no possibility of error in scoring; (v) to provide against possibilities of cheating; (vi) to reduce schooling advantages to a vanishing point; (vii) to reduce written responses to a minimum; and (viii) to enable the examiners to get an accurate and valid measure of intelligence in as short a time as possible. The men who devised the tests were all experts, and consequently they were able to work out scales which possessed a large measure of validity and reliability. To be sure, there would be some instances where the results were unsatisfactory. In such cases the group test can be supplemented by the individual test. The group test has been very largely used in schools since its introduction in the American army. It enables the psychologist to go quickly through a school and get a rapid and general, while fairly accurate, classification of children. It will sometimes be found that there are cases which demand more detailed investigation, and then the individual test is used to secure the desired result.

What are some of the results which have been achieved by the intelligence test? One of them is to enable us to classify people on the basis of intelligence. There were one and three-quarter million men tested in the American army, and the results were classified according to intelligence, and also according to vocations. These results correspond fairly closely with the results obtained throughout in the public schools. Of course, results that have been obtained from college students, indicate, as is to be expected, a higher degree of intelligence on the average than in an unselected group. The following table shows the distribution of intelligence as obtained from the tests:

Those with I.Q. below 70			..	..	..	1 per cent.
,,	,,	I.Q. from 70 to 79	..	..	5	,,
,,	,,	I.Q. ,, 80 ,, 89	..	..	14	,,
,,	,,	I.Q. ,, 90 ,, 99	..	..	30	,,
,,	,,	I.Q. ,, 100 ,, 109	..	..	30	,,
,,	,,	I.Q. ,, 110 ,, 119	..	..	14	,,
,,	,,	I.Q. ,, 120 ,, 129	..	..	5	,,
,,	,,	I.Q. of 130 or over	..	..	1	,,
					100	,,

This new method of classifying intelligence has quite displaced the older and rougher method of classification. Formerly children (or, for the matter of that, adults) were called 'bright', 'dull', 'average', 'idiot', 'imbecile', 'genius', etc., with nothing more than subjective notions of what these words meant. Even the definitions of such words as 'feeble-minded', 'imbeciles,' and 'idiots', in the Mental Deficiency Act of 1923, in England, were quite vague, and admitted of a wide divergence in interpretation, so that the same person might conceivably be put into all three classes by different people. For convenience these terms are still used to some extent, but a much more definite meaning is given to them, whereas a great deal of the time the terms are not used at all, but a person is described by his intelligence quotient. Roughly speaking, idiots are those whose I.Q. is between zero and 20; imbeciles those between 20 and 40; morons those between 40 and 70; all of those three classes together make up the 'feeble-minded'; from 70 to 85 or 90 are the slightly sub-normal, or border-liners; from 85 or 90 to 110 or 115 are the average; from 110 or 115 to 130 come the superiors; and those who are over 130 correspond to the older word 'genius'. Thus from the point of view of the I.Q. about 60 per cent. of people are of average intelligence, one per cent. are idiots, and one per cent. are geniuses. It has already been indicated that the I.Q. is of great value for purposes of comparison. Thus to say that a person's I.Q. is 85 means that his capacity for learning is 85 per cent. of the average person's. Moreover, experiments indicate that the I.Q. of a person remains fairly constant, and that no matter how often he be tested, the same relationship with average intelligence will hold good. For example, if a child be tested at six years chronological age, and passes all the tests for nine years, his I.Q. will be $\frac{9}{6}$ x 100 = 150. It will be found that at eight the child will pass the twelve-year tests, and at ten the fifteen-year tests, thus maintaining the constancy of the I.Q.

One of the points on which there is a difference of opinion among psychologists is as to whether there is any such thing as a general intelligence, or whether that which we call intelligence is made up of a number of specific abilities. First class authorities may be quoted on either side of the question. Those who argue for a unitary general intelligence do so on the ground that there is a common central factor or central tendency, which cannot be defined with precision, but which functions in a greater or lesser degree in all types of psychical activity. They also argue that intelligence is something that shows itself in all sorts of ways when it is present, but its absence is marked by all around failure. Ballard, who is an adherent of the doctrine, puts it trenchantly: 'Generally speaking, a wise man is wise in all things, a fool is a fool all round.'[1] The opponents of the theory might say that wisdom and intelligence are not synonyms, neither are foolishness and feeble-mindedness. Spearman, in his work on *The Nature of 'Intelligence' and the Principles of Cognition*, supports the general intelligence theory on the ground that consciousness is a fundamental unity. He claims that to say that intelligence is composed of a number of specific abilities is a reversion to the old faculty psychology. Intelligence

[1] P. B. Ballard, *Mental Tests*, p. 27.

is rather to be considered a general ability or capacity that characterizes all of the mental processes. This argument is further supported by the fact that it may be proved mathematically that there is a positive correlation among all forms of native ability. Spearman ascertained that there was correlation, for example, between adding numbers and correlating words. His results led him to conclude that a person who is good in one subject is usually good in another. The person who is able in one direction only is the exception. Native abilities hang together, as it were. Mathematical ability and linguistic ability, even excluding any factors which may appear to be common to the two, still exhibit a relationship, unaccountable save on the ground of a general factor of intelligence, common to all the multifarious operations of consciousness. Spearman thinks of it as a sort of general store-house of intellectual power from which the person is able to draw to meet the particular demands of any given situation.

The adherents of the opposite view include such men as Prof. Thorndike in America, and Professors Brown and Thomson in Great Britain. And the strange thing is that these scholars have reached their conclusions from precisely the same kind of data as have led Spearman, Hart, Ballard and others to the opposite conclusion, i.e. from the mathematical data of correlation. Thorndike's investigation was concerned with specific mental abilities, such as the addition of numbers, the discrimination of lengths, the memorization of words, and the sorting of cards, and his findings were that there was very poor correlation indicated between the various abilities. He thinks that a person who is a good linguist may be a complete failure in mathematics ; one who is brilliant in science may be stupid in poetry. He further made comparative tests of the inmates of institutions for dependent children with ordinary public school children, using two types of tests, one requiring language and the other mechanical ingenuity. He found much wider divergence between the results of the two groups in the language than in the performance tests, and concluded that the abilities are specific, with no special relationship between the two. Brown and Thomson[1] attacked the

---

[1] Brown and Thomson, *Essentials of Mental Measurement*, pp. 176-90.

arguments of Spearman and Hart from the standpoint of superficial mathematics, claiming that they had over-simplified the whole matter. Spearman and Hart had attempted to establish the presence of a hierarchical order among the co-efficients of correlation, to account for which it is necessary to posit a general factor of intelligence. They believed that in the absence of such a general factor the average correlation among the several abilities would be either zero or negative. Brown and Thomson proceeded to show that such a hierarchical order among the co-efficients of correlation could be secured by a random overlap of group factors, and illustrated their contention with a pack of cards from which a card was drawn, a great many times, shuffling taking place before each draw. They were able to establish a hierarchical order for the drawing of a card from the pack, and for the throwing of dice, two procedures for which surely Spearman and Hart would not claim a general factor. This led Brown and Thomson to agree with Thorndike in the doctrine of specific abilities. They offered what they called 'a sampling theory of ability', preferring to think 'of a number of factors at play in the carrying out of a mental test, these factors being a sample of all those which the individual has at his command'. The sampling theory insists that the theory of general ability is incapable of proof, though it does not go so far as to deny its possibility.

It is not easy to reach a hard and fast conclusion on the basis of the evidence available. It will be seen that there are some parts of the evidence that support the theory of a general factor of intelligence, and others which support the doctrine of specific abilities. The correlation between various sorts of abilities, while in some cases it is quite low, is at least positive. So that we may conclude with Woodworth, that 'there is no evidence of any antagonism between different sorts of ability, but there is plenty of evidence that different special abilities may have little or nothing in common.'[1] Though there is not enough evidence to pronounce with finality on the matter, the conclusion which we must reach on the available data is that there is no

---

[1] Woodworth, *Psychology : A Study of Mental Life*, p. 284.

such thing as a general intelligence in the form of a mental power that can be directed at will to different sorts of tasks. It is unsafe to conclude that exceptional ability in one direction will carry with it outstanding ability in another, or even that the development of one will be paralleled by development of another.

The next problem is the analysis of intelligence to ascertain what are the factors that may be considered, as Thomson suggests, as samples of what the individual has at his command. The value of the tests is that succeeding in them demands intelligent behaviour, so that an analysis of the psychological abilities which the tests call into function ought to disclose something in regard to the character of intelligence. This has a three-fold importance for the psychology of education: (i) the necessity of understanding what are the principal significant abilities in each group, and the relation of them to the various processes involved in education taken as a whole; (ii) the necessity of recognizing special abilities as well as general in the individual, and of providing educational facilities to develop these abilities; and (iii) the necessity of knowing something about the order and method of development of the various abilities in the individual, so as to plan the curriculum and school organization accordingly. As a matter of common knowledge, interest can only keep pace with the educational process, if that process takes cognizance of the facts concerning the unfolding of the capacities, so that an educational system that is to succeed in gaining and holding the interested attention of the child must be one that is built on sound psychological knowledge of human personality in the making.

In the analysis of intelligence, the first point to be remembered is its complexity. Intelligence, as a substantive, is really an abstraction used as a convenient way of accounting for a certain kind of conduct. That with which we actually have to deal is intelligent behaviour, and intelligent behaviour is otherwise describable as appropriately responding to stimuli. The experiences of life are multiform. We are daily confronted with all sorts of stimuli, a great many different kinds of things that have to be done. The intelligent person is the one who does the greater number of them correctly. Of course, that does not mean that there is any uniform type of correct response for every stimulus. The possibilities of variation are as great as human personality plus the environment, social and physical, in which persons live and act. Precisely the same physical stimulus may be quite a different stimulus to different people from the psychological viewpoint. Take, for example, a rainbow. The stimulus of the visual process from the rainbow may call forth a great many different types of response: in the child the emotion of wonder, in the saint inspiration to devotion, in the artist the æsthetic attitude, in the physicist a desire to study the refraction of light, in the sailor a sign of meteorological significance. Yet no one can say that any one of these responses is any more or less intelligent than the others. Each of them may meet with success in its own field of stimulus and response, and to the extent that it brings satisfaction and success we may say that it was intelligent.

Experimental psychology is another source beside that of mental testing, disclosing important facts in regard to the complex character of the mental processes. The psychologist in the laboratory studies various forms of sense-perception, visual, auditory, tactual, and so forth. He investigates reaction-time, phenomena of association, emotion, and so on. Some of the results obtained are contributing to our knowledge of intelligence, in helping us to build up standards of human behaviour and in offering explanations of abnormal behaviour. Take, for example, such a finding as that expressed in Weber's law. Briefly stated it is the conclusion that ' equal relative differences are equally perceptible '.[1] For example, if it transpires that a given percentage of errors—say 25 per cent.—are made in the perception of differences between two weights of 100 and 104 ounces, according to Weber's hypothesis we might expect to find the same percentage of errors, i.e. 25 per cent., if we were to compare 400 ounces with 416, or 100 pounds with 104 pounds. Now the comparison of weight is one of the tests used as a test of five-year intelligence. We know from the law of Weber what the normal type of response ought to be.

---

[1] Woodworth, *Psychology : A Study of Mental Life*, pp. 449-50.

4

But we find that an imbecile, instead of performing the test in accordance with instructions, as he seems to be going to do when he begins, very often ends by playing with the weights instead of trying to compare them. And if we found that our subject actually tried to compare them, and in a given number of instances showed a great variation in the percentage of errors, we might take that as diagnostic of something abnormal, and seek by other tests to check our findings.

All branches of psychological science—experimental, theoretical, animal, social, and educational—are very closely interacting. The more that the educationalist knows about theoretical and experimental psychology, the less liable is he to reach hasty or unwarranted conclusions about a child's intelligence. He may find by means of tests that a child is abnormal, but may also find the abnormality to be symptomatic of an unhealthy environment rather than of a congenital defect. The remedy may not be to put the child in a school for the feeble-minded, but rather to apply practical sociology in cleaning up the neighbourhood from which the child comes. Clean streets, comfortable houses, good drainage, sanitary school buildings, good drinking water, sufficient nourishing food, and the inculcation of self-respect will do much in a country like India to eliminate that invidious classification which we sometimes make—'the depressed classes'. The mental processes of the child-life which is committed to the hands of our school-teachers are too intricate, too complex, too big with future possibilities for us to be indifferent in this matter. The day is fast approaching when we shall consider the teacher who is ignorant of the mental processes as much a danger as the physician who is ignorant of physiology and anatomy.

The second observation that must be made is that intelligent behaviour is purposive. We have been using such words as 'capable', 'able', and 'intelligent'. We need only remind ourselves that there are no concrete or absolute things corresponding to our abstractions, capacity, ability and intelligence. They are all relative terms, and the question that we have to ask is: 'Able for what?' or 'Intelligent in what?' The difference between a person and a machine is that the person acts for the sake of some end in view, whereas the mechanism only goes when it is started from without. As James said: 'The pursuance of future ends and the choice of means for their attainment are the mark and criterion of the presence of mentality in a phenomenon.' With reference to the universe he adds: 'If we find ourselves, in contemplating it, unable to banish the impression that it is the realm of final purposes, that it exists for the sake of something, we place intelligence at the heart of it and have a religion.'[1]

Purposiveness simply means the consciousness of ends and the adoption of means for their attainment. Binet considered this to be the principal characteristic of intelligence. In his analysis of intelligence he had three factors: (i) the consciousness of an end to be obtained, (ii) the trial of possible means for attaining the end, and (iii) auto-criticism of the trials made. In devising his tests he made it a point to judge their worth by this three-fold criterion. Take such a test as that of drawing a geometrical figure from memory. The mental image of the completed figure is the end of which the child is conscious, his own attempts at drawing are his trial or means to the end, and the corrections or modifications made indicate his auto-criticism.

Adaptability is obviously the ability to adapt means to ends, and is therefore another word for purposiveness when it is performed consciously. We have observed that modifiability is a characteristic of the native tendencies of the psycho-physical organism. The very organism itself is characterized by plasticity, without which the faintest effort at adaptation of means to ends would be fruitless. The intelligent man is one who sets about adapting means in his environment to his own ends. The observant teacher will pay particular attention to the degree in which the child exhibits this capacity. A generous capacity for it is indicative of superiority, and a lack of it of inferiority in intelligent behaviour.

Purposiveness includes the ability to comprehend meanings. Some of the intelligence tests are devised for the express purpose of measuring that ability. Take, for example, the completion

---

[1] Wm. James, *Principles of Psychology*, vol. i. p. 8.

test, which was first devised by the German psychologist, Ebbinghaus. One form of the test is to give the subject a number of sentences or a paragraph from which significant words are here and there omitted, the subject being asked to complete the sentences or paragraph by filling in the words which are required to make them meaningful. Besides the ability to comprehend meanings, such a test has the value of giving an opportunity for expression to the creative capacity for combination, which is a factor of intelligence. Creatively combining words into sentences that are meaningful involves a responsiveness to relationships. The intelligent person we have already described as one who makes successful and satisfying responses to stimuli. Sometimes the stimulus comes in the form of a new and problematic situation. How will the person behave himself under these circumstances? Will he adjust himself readily and successfully? The ability to do that depends on the consciousness of the purpose to be fullfilled, the means to be used, and the relationship between the person and the situation, all of them factors of intelligent behaviour.

A third factor in intelligent behaviour is conscious conation. The intelligent person knows what he is doing. Reflexive behaviour is involuntary, and habit becomes automatic. That does not mean that an action performed out of habit is devoid of intelligence. But the element of intelligence is in the conscious formation of the habit rather than its involuntary perpetuity. The importance of this factor for the teacher is largely associated with the subject of attention. Attention is necessary for conscious control, and is a *sine qua non* for success in school work. Moreover, attention is the heart of voluntary activity. It signifies the conscious direction of the mental processes on a given focus, an activity impossible to the idiot or imbecile. One of the first evidences of feeble-mindedness is the inability to keep the mind on a problem long enough to attain a solution. It is usually symptomatic of a deeper defect, a defect in regard to voluntary behaviour of any kind. That is the reason that persons so deficient require to be placed under the care and control of the State or of other persons, who will do for them what they are unable to do for themselves—namely, make intelligent responses to the situations with which they are confronted.

A fourth factor in intelligent behaviour is the explorative tendency. This is very closely allied to the factor of persistency, which manifests itself in the tendency to preserve and assert one's mastery over circumstances. Curiosity is very intimately related to self-assertiveness. In the discussion of instinctive behaviour a brief description of this tendency was given. Here we may observe that it is significant of intelligence. If a subject who is faced with a problem, such as those presented in tests, gives up after one or two desultory attempts, it is indicative of a defective capacity. The form-board tests are particularly good in detecting the presence or absence of this ability. The intelligent will continue to experiment, either mentally or in a motor way, until successful; the feeble-minded will readily give up if the first or second trial results in failure. The best results of scientific research have been achieved by those who have persisted in the faith that ultimately they would succeed. 'If at first you don't succeed, try, try again' is a motto for the intelligent only.

Intelligent behaviour includes a fifth element—retentiveness. By retentiveness we mean the ability to carry around with us learned responses until the stimuli arrive that arouse them again. That which we really retain is the machinery for the completion of the reaction. Retentiveness is not a process or activity, but a machinery of neural associations, so that when the appropriate stimulus is aroused, it arouses from rest the learned response. This ability is without doubt fundamental in intelligent behaviour. Tests of association processes, both free and controlled, measure ability to retain, inasmuch as what one retains is retained by means of associative connections in the psycho-neural system. Persons who are of high intelligence are invariably rich in associations, whereas one of the evidences of feeble-mindedness is poverty of associations. These correlations are without doubt due to the higher degree of retentiveness that characterizes the more intelligent. The digit-repeating test, syllable-repeating test, and analysis test are examples of tests which call into function the ability to retain, and the results of these tests have been standardized, so as to show the progressive degree of ability in that direction as personality unfolds.

We scarcely need to be reminded that intelligent behaviour is characteristic of native reaction tendencies rather than of acquirements.   Ballard has stated the matter with his characteristic penetration in describing it as 'ability as distinct from knowledge, capacity as distinct from content, power as distinct from product'.[1]   In attempting to measure intelligence, we are trying to ascertain what consciousness is capable of doing rather than what it has accomplished.   To be sure, it would be absurd to dream of measuring a contentless capacity.   Unless there is some knowledge acquired, it is useless to apply any kinds of mental measures.   We cannot measure intelligence and leave knowledge out of account, and that is one of the gravest difficulties in the whole task.   At the same time, the intelligence test has done more to acquaint us with the characteristics of intelligence than any other method so far devised.

[1] Ballard, *Mental Tests*, p. 23.

LITERATURE

L. M. Terman.   *The Measurement of Intelligence*.   Harrap, 1920.

Yoakum and Yerkes.   *Mental Tests in the American Army*.   Sidgwick & Jackson, 1920.

G. M. Whipple.   *Manual of Mental and Physical Tests*.   2 vols.   Warwick & York, 1914-15.

Cyril Burt.   *Mental and Scholastic Tests*.   London County Council.   P. S. King, 1921.

P. B. Ballard.   *Mental Tests*.   Hodder & Stoughton, 1920.

P. B. Ballard.   *Group Tests of Intelligence*.   Hodder & Stoughton, 1922.

Brown and Thomson.   *Mental Measurement*.   Cambridge University Press, 1921.

E. L. Thorndike.   *Mental and Social Measurements*.   Columbia University Publication, 1919.

C. Spearman.   *The Nature of 'Intelligence' and the Principles of Cognition*.   Macmillan, 1923.

L. L. Thurstone.   *The Nature of Intelligence*.   Kegan Paul, 1924.

A. S. Woodburne.   *Psychological Tests of Mental Abilities*.   University of Madras, 1924.

CHAPTER IV

THE FEELINGS

There are three elements of the mental life which are irreducible. These are the cognitive, the affective, and the conative. To characterize them as irreducible must not be taken to mean that they exist or function independently of one another. The meaning is simply that in our analysis of mental facts and phenomena we cannot reduce any one of these elements to either of the others. The unity which they display, as well as their irreducible character, is traceable to the very beginnings of mental life. There is no period, however brief or simple, when we may say that any one of the three elements is primordial. The hypothesis has sometimes been proposed that feeling is primordial to either cognition or conation. As a theory it rests on a fundamental misconception of the character of the mental life, one which wholly neglects the fact of ultimate unity. Prof. Ward, in his critical reference to the theory, says that 'So far as we can judge, we find feeling everywhere; but, as we work downwards from higher to lower forms of life, the possible variety and the definiteness of sense-impressions both steadily diminish. Moreover, we can directly observe in our own organic sensations, which seem to come nearest to the whole content of primitive or infantile experience, an almost entire absence of any assignable *quale*. Finally, in our sense experience generally, we find the element of feeling at a maximum in the lower senses and the cognitive element at a maximum in the higher. . . . If, then, feeling predominates more and more as we approach the beginning of conscious life, may we not conclude that it is its only essential constituent?' Dr. Ward hastens to answer his own query: 'On the contrary, such a conclusion would be rash in the extreme',[1] and we suspect that most psychologists agree with him.

The mistaken notion that is largely responsible for the theory of the primordial character of feeling is at bottom that feeling is something which can exist by itself, a sort of 'thing-in itself'. No doubt it is an echo of the old faculty method of interpretation. But we have come to understand the concept as qualitative rather than substantive. It is not a particular type of experience, but the background or undercurrent of all experience. It refers to the colour or tone of experience. Scarcely any psychological term is more difficult of precise definition. There is no such thing as a feeling, and yet there is no experience which is not felt, or has not an affective accompaniment. Various experiences are qualitatively judged by us in accordance with the effect they have on us, and these qualitative effects (or affects) are what we designate as feelings. If the feeling experiences were things in themselves, we would expect to locate them in some particular part of the organism, but they have no sense organs, neither are they localizable in any way, either within or without the organism. The feelings are subjectively experienced by us as persons, and are distinguishable characteristics of total mental conditions, telling us the 'how' of our psychical states. They seem to belong to the totality of shifting tensions, which are taking place all over the organism at once.

Since we regard feeling as one of the primordial mental elements, as well as cognition and conation, the question arises as to the relationship between these elements in actual experience. Here again Prof. Ward's account is particularly clear. He says: 'Broadly speaking, in any state of mind that we can directly observe, what we find is (i) that we are aware of a certain change in our sensations, thoughts or circumstances, (ii) that we are pleased or pained with the change, and (iii) that we act accordingly.'[2] Cognition, or the knowing process, tells us the 'what' of

---

[1] *Encyclopaedia Britannica*, 11th edition, article *Psychology*, vol. xxii. p. 551.   [2] Ibid., p. 551.

our experiences, in contrast with affection, which, as we have said, tells us the 'how'. Cognition has reference to some facts which are external to the process of knowing, whereas affection is an internal affair belonging to the organism. The former has to do with the processes of knowing, whereas the latter gives us a qualitative way of experiencing. On the other hand, it is this qualitative effect of our experiences which we call feeling that forms our incentive to action. We tend to make responses and to continue activities which bring us pleasure, and to inhibit responses and movements which have painful affective tones. A stimulus that proves to have an agreeable accompaniment calls forth an appropriate responsive movement, expressing the desire to continue or to intensify the stimulus, whereas one that proves to be disagreeably coloured leads to retreat or rejection or an effort to substitute some other stimulus. Thus we see the inter-relationship of affection and conation in our unified experiences. The two together constitute our manner of expressing interest. Our word 'interest' is really a Latin impersonal verb which means 'it is of importance', or 'it makes a difference', and that experience of importance or difference may be on the side either of feeling or of action or, quite likely, of both.

If the experiences of feeling are difficult of description, the word is still more difficult to define. And the difficulty is increased by the fact that it is used with a variety of connotations. (i) Popular usuage includes the identification of the word with opinion as based on emotion. A chairman sometimes asks: 'What is the feeling of the house?' (ii) Again it is used for susceptibilty, sensibility or impressionableness, especially in the plural, as in the expression: 'His feelings were hurt.' (iii) There are occasions when the word feeling is used as a synonym for the æsthetic sense, i.e. the appreciation of beauty in some particular object. (iv) Another usage is as an expression of suggestibility or earnestness, as in the expression: 'His address was delivered with fine feeling.' (v) Sometimes the word is indicative of a vague understanding or perception, as 'We all had a feeling that he was describing the situation accurately.' Yet none of these meanings is strictly psychological. However, our difficulty is the more increased because even within the science itself the word is employed in different senses. (vi) It is used, e.g. to mean an emotional experience, which, as we know, has a large affective element. Anger, fear, rage, sympathy and grief are felt experiences, for all emotions are intensely affective. It is not at all surprising that this character of the emotion has resulted in a considerable amount of confusion with regard to the two terms. (vii) The word 'feeling' is still again used in the tactual sense. We speak of feeling various objects, and describe their feelings as rough, smooth, hard, soft, etc. This is quite a legitimate use of the word, and it is difficult to substitute any word which would describe the tactual experience as appropriately. (viii) Another usage of the word is as descriptive of the organic sensations, such as feeling cold, hot, hungry, thirsty, nervous, nauseated, etc., and none will deny that distinctive affective qualities are present in these experiences. (ix) Finally, there is the narrower and more technical use of the term, the experience of pleasurableness or agreeableness, and painfulness or disagreeableness, as affective qualities which accompany different types of experience.

By feeling proper, then, we mean the quality or tone of pleasure or pain which accompanies and colours various experiences. And the extension of the word to further experiences, such as organic and tactual sensations and to emotions, is in a secondary sense, because such experiences have, in addition to the cognitive and conative factors, definite affective qualities. Hunger, thirst, nausea, roughness, fear, anger, grief, etc., are all of them coloured with an element of disagreeableness; whereas satiety, smoothness, joy, wonder, etc., are accompanied by a quality of pleasurableness. Indeed, it is a fiction to speak of any pure sensation or device in the sense that a cognitive experience could be absolutely neutral. To speak of a neutral feeling is a contradiction in language, for an experience which could be neutral could not be felt. Psychologists differ as to whether or not there are such experiences, some claiming that, since the affective is an integral element of the mental life, it is always present, and that any experience which does not arouse a feeling of disagreeableness with an effort to resist or put an end to it, ought to be classed as agreeable. If it were otherwise than agreeable there would be a protest from the organism, and the affective tone of pain is the organism's method of protesting. Those who take the position that some experiences are affectively neutral, base their argument on the routine character of various experiences, in consequence of which they command a minimum of conscious attention, and therefore need not be affective at all. We may be walking on one side of the road, and a bullock-cart passes us on the opposite side, concerning which we have no interest either one way or the other, and therefore we are affectively neutral in regard to it. In reply it may be said that if the bullock-cart has no interest for us, we do not attend to it, and attention is the core of a conscious reaction. In short, if we do not react affectively in ever so small a degree, it is very doubtful whether we react cognitively either. To repeat, it is a contradiction in terms to speak of a neutral feeling. What is not felt is not experienced.

It is of fundamental importance that those who are engaged in trying to stimulate and direct the educative process in children should appreciate the qualitative character of all experience. Sometimes parents and teachers work on the principle that a certain amount of disagreeable work is essential for children, to give them an element of character otherwise unattainable. The truth is that a child requires to face difficult problems and surmount them if he is to develop normally. But that does not argue that the task need be disagreeable. Disagreeableness of tone is an indication that all is not well with the organism, that some adjustment is necessary for its smooth running. It ought to serve as a symptom and a warning that something needs to be done to set things right. On the other hand, agreeableness is an indication that the organism finds the experience satisfying and conducive to its welfare. The intelligent educator will be a keen observer of the indications of the child's affective processes, and will assign tasks and guide activities in accordance with his observations. That does not mean that if a child is found reacting with pleasure to a certain task, he must be kept at it indefinitely. If a child or a class is enjoying a history lesson or an arithmetic lesson, it does not argue that they must be kept at that lesson for the remainder of the day. The factor of change is of fundamental importance because the organism itself demands it, and the most pleasant task may turn into an appalling bore, if persisted in even after fatigue sets in. If you congratulate your cook on serving up your favourite curry, it does not mean that thereafter you want only that particular curry. 'Variety is the spice of life.' In our school work we must guard against fatigue and monotony, for if the child's work becomes disagreeable, interest lags, attention shifts, progress is curtailed, and personality fails to develop normally. And the key whereby the teacher understands in which direction things are moving with the child is the expressive movement that affords an index to the feeling.

What is it, then, we may inquire, which arouses reactions in the affective phase of consciousness? What sort of stimuli arouse feeling reactions? In some cases they are due to the presentation of objects to sense. Presentations may be through vision, hearing, smell, taste or tactual sensibility. The reason that certain objects when presented arouse pleasant feeling, and others unpleasant feeling, is partly subjective in that it depends on the condition, or the welfare, of the organism at the time of the presentation. To some extent the effect is traceable to a racial or generic element, depending on the structure and manner of functioning of the class of organisms to which the individual belongs. Another contributing factor is the environmental. Not only are our ways of doing many things determined by the fact that we belong to groups which act in such ways in the presence of given situations, but our affective reactions are likewise socially determined. There came to my notice the other day a Hindu gentleman, who, while his wife was lying on her death-bed, and five days before her demise, married her younger sister. The idea of such a procedure is to me, with the group sanctions and feelings in which I share, revolting and disgusting. Yet that gentleman claimed that, according to the group sanctions and feelings in which he participated, there was nothing to arouse a disagreeable affect. The social environment is very largely responsible for the types of affective reactions which are aroused within the individual. Recognizing, then, that there are explicable grounds for the stimulation of the affective reactions, we have to observe that these reactions are frequently aroused in the presence of certain objects. Doubtless one reason why an object can so function is that certain associations have been formed between a group of objects and our affects in the past, by which the presentation of the object to sense suggests the disagreeable character of past experience, and thereby arouses a similar affective reaction. In other cases it may be due to a fundamental incompatibility between the object and the sensing organism, as, for instance, the taste of an object that is intensely bitter is disagreeable to practically all human beings.

The sense-perception of objects arouses affective qualities with reference to the duration, the intensity and the extensity of the sensory processes so aroused. The case of duration is fairly obvious. There are a great many stimuli which up to a certain point arouse pleasant affects, but when continued to the point of fatigue or exhaustion lose their agreeableness. There is a tendency for all sensory experiences, when repeated or continued sufficiently long, to lose the intensity of their original affective accompaniments. We grow accustomed both to the pleasant and the unpleasant, until presently they tend to lose some of their power to command attention. Affection also stands in definite relationship to the intensity of sensory processes. Loud sounds, bright lights, strong tastes and pungent odours have decidedly different affective values from subdued sounds, suffused lights, luscious tastes and mild odours. Sensations of great intensity are usually unpleasant. At the same time there is relativity about the affects. If one is suffering from headache, a light, sound or odour that might otherwise produce a pleasant effect, will produce the opposite, because of a subjective sense of intensity due to the malady. In regard to extensity somewhat similar reactions are produced, extensity beyond a certain point tending to give rise to unpleasantness. The matters of intensity and extensity are illustrated particularly clearly in responses of an æsthetic character.

Objects are not the only source of affective reactions. They may also be aroused by ideational processes. Here the basis is undoubtedly associations which have been formed in the past. If an experience when it occurs is accompanied by a definite affective colouring, either pleasant or unpleasant, the tendency is for

images of that experience to involve a recurrence of the same
affective colours. It is this associative tendency which explains
the pleasures and displeasures of desires, motives, memories,
imaginings and processes of reasoning. At the same time it
does not account for all the affective elements, for there is an
added fact that, whatever stimulates and aids us in the ideational
process at any time stimulates pleasure, whereas anything that
impedes the process is experienced as unpleasant. Take the
case of desire. Feeling qualities are greatly influenced by desires,
which vary at different times and in different people. In a battle
the victory of one army gives pleasure to that army and pain to
the enemy. In a game it is the same ; victory and pleasure for
one team entails defeat and pain for their opponents. In either
case the desire is what determines the affective quality. Take
again the case of motives. Motives are impulses to action which
may come into conflict with one another and produce complexes.
Whatever furthers the accomplishment of a motive is pleasurable ;
that which frustrates is painful. Our motives are the outcome
of past experiences, and consequently they are already tinged with
decided affective colours, colours which become more saturated
as the motives are brought into contact with other life phenomena
and activities.

In memory, imagination and reasoning there is a constant
flow of images, and these images are the mental products of
past experiences. These past experiences have been either
satisfying or otherwise. When we recall a past experience there
is a tendency for us to remember whether or not it produced
satisfaction. That does not mean, however, that when recalled
the image calls up the same feeling colour as when originally
experienced. The remembrance of a pleasurable experience may
produce such a contrast with the present as to arouse a painful
quality. The pleasurableness or painfulness will be with reference
to the present, and the way in which the memory or imagination
relates itself to the present experience. It must be said in
passing that we are not able to re-instate with any effectiveness
the affective colouring of a recalled experience. The memory is
much more cognitive than affective. In imagination there is much
more of the creative element, and the affective element grows out

of the satisfaction or otherwise with which the images are combined. Reasoning is imagination in the technical sense, in which the images are manipulated and controlled with reference to a problematic situation. The resultant affective tone is with definite reference to the success or failure experienced in the endeavour to master the situation or solve the problem. That which furthers our mental exploration is pleasurable; that which thwarts it, disagreeable.

A third stimulus of affective qualities is energy. In all psycho-neural activity there is an expenditure of effort, and the effort which it is necessary to expend for the accomplishment of a task or purpose bears a relationship to the capacity of the organism. If the available energy is equal to or in excess of the amount required to complete the activity, the experience will be pleasurably coloured; if the energy be defective with reference to the activity, unpleasantness will result. There is no surer way of making school-work a bore to a child than to keep assigning tasks beyond the limit of his physical or mental energy. To be sure there is the other side to it—we do not want to make the work so easy that it calls forth little or no effort. There is a decidedly agreeable experience in facing a difficult job and realizing that one has the energy to accomplish it. It is the glory of the strong man over the weak. It was that which gave to the great hero of the *Ramayana* the pleasure of conquering what was impossible for others. The intelligence measure gives the teacher the indication of the capacity of his child, and he ought to use that knowledge in the assignment of tasks so as to make the child's work interesting and agreeable, because it challenges him to put forth his best.

There are some who are not inclined to accept the simple bi-polarity of affective qualities, and who urge that we require a more detailed analysis of feeling experiences. Both Wundt and Royce propose to add a second group of feelings—excitement and calm; and the former a third group—strain and relaxation. No doubt it would be possible to differentiate more analytically the different experiences with reference to their affective qualities, as is done, for example, in the case of the emotions which are markedly affective. Even so, such a detailed treatment in no way tells against the wider classification. It is possible, indeed, to classify emotional experiences into those whose affective element is pleasurable and those which are unpleasant. In regard to the proposals of Wundt and Royce the criticism of Angell is most trenchant, that after we subtract the elements in strain, relaxation, calm and excitement which are clearly kinæsthetic and organic, there is surely no residue that does not admit of classification into the pleasurable and the painful. Stout says that it is difficult to reduce all the emotional experiences, such as anger, fear, love and hate simply to pleasure and pain, and so he is inclined to think that there are feeling-attitudes besides pleasure and pain. But surely there is no need of attempting a reduction. A classification of the affective phases of emotional experiences into these two groups need not be interpreted as in any sense a reduction. To be sure there is admissable an indefinite amount of gradedness. The concepts of pleasure and pain are comparable to the white and black qualities at either extreme of the grey line in the colour pyramid. Over 700 distinct shades of grey have been isolated, and analogously we have any number of lighter and darker shades in the affective qualities, and we have many experiences involving elements of both, which at times so nearly balance one another as to create a sense of neutrality.

It is not easy to give a satisfactory neural account of the feelings, because they are not localizable in any definite part of the nervous system. When we feel, we feel all over, and not in any one particular spot. That there are neural accompaniments of the feeling experiences is perfectly clear from the facts of the various expressive movements which can be observed. A stimulus that proves to evoke an agreeable response calls forth appropriate responsive movements which express the desire to continue or intensify the stimulus. These characteristic movements include such items as laughter, advance, appropriation, motion towards, a heightened tone in the voluntary muscles, dilation of the peripheral blood-vessels, decrease in the rate of the heart-beat, increase in the depth of breathing, turning of the body, effort to continue the existing state, or endeavour to intensify the stimulus. A stimulus which evokes a disagreeable response expresses itself in the movements of the opposite type, such as frowning, crying, retreat, rejection, motion away from, endeavour to substitute another stimulus, contraction of peripheral blood-vessels, increase in the rate of the heart-beat, decrease in the depth of breathing, effort to shut out the stimulus or to discontinue the existing order. We tend to make responses and to continue activities which bring us pleasure, and to inhibit responses and movements that have a painful affective colouring. But, since there are no sense organs with connecting nerves which function particularly for feelings, and the possibilities of expression are so varied, the problem of neural explanation has admitted of a variety of attempts.

1. One of the least attractive of the efforts to explain has been with reference to the æsthetic. Sir Charles Walston,[1] believing that the feeling of harmony is the basis of all human conceptions, uses it to account for the feeling of agreeableness. The perception of harmony or symmetry is the basis for the feeling of pleasure, while discord and asymmetry in any form produce an experience of disagreeableness. Not only is the æsthetic instinct the foundation of agreeableness and disagreeableness, it accounts for the ability to form associative bonds and to remember. Herbert Spencer had long ago attempted a somewhat similar theory in proposing that pleasure is induced through a sense of harmony between the organism and its environment, and pain through the lack of such harmony. No psychologist would presume to doubt that symmetry and harmony are elements which play active parts in the stimulating of the affective qualities of experience, but it must be admitted that experience is too complex to try to reduce it to a unitary cause.

2. One theory which undoubtedly explains some of the facts is that of Marshall.[2] His interpretation is in terms of stored-up nervous energy with relation to activities undertaken. If the energy available is equal to or in excess of the amount needed for an activity, the result will be agreeable, whereas a deficiency of energy is unpleasant. There is, without doubt, a pleasurable accompaniment to the experience of being able to do what ought

[1] Chas. Walston, *Harmonism and Conscious Evolution*, pp. 12 ff.
[2] H. R. Marshall, *Pain, Pleasure, and Æsthetics*, p. 204 f.

to be done, and a corresponding sense of pain in being faced with a situation for which the available energy is not sufficient. Moreover, it is a fact, as has already been pointed out, of peda-gogical significance. Agreeableness is the counterpart of effective modes of reaction, and disagreeableness of inability to cope with a situation. Yet that is not the whole story. It sometimes happens that a task that is too easy, that makes too small demands on the stored-up energy, fails to elicit a pleasurable response, and that we sometimes get pleasure from trying to do certain things even when we fall short of success.

3. Münsterberg attempted an explanation by referring pleasantness and its opposite to certain movements of the exten-sor and flexor muscles, which resulted in conditions of innervation in the motor cortex, and in expansion and contraction of the organism. But, as Angell points out by way of criticism, this view 'has despite its suggestiveness, only a very general and indefinite basis'.

4. Another view, which was fathered by Stumph in Germany and supported by Woolley in America, is that affection is definable as an organic sensation. The theory proposes that every stimulus which arouses responses of either the overt or delayed types, stimulates concurrently and reflexively a group of affective impulses from certain tissues which the authors do not specify. Watson[1] in reviewing the theory assumes that the reference is to the tissue of the reproductive organs and related erogenous zones. The erogenous zones are much more widely distributed through-out the organism than is popularly supposed, and are capable of initiating impulses, some of them of the expansive and seeking type and others of the relaxing and inhibitory type. This is really one form of the old theory that regards affection as an attribute of sensation. It was this position that led Wundt and his school to try to work into affection all the breadth of detail which they had previously introduced into cognition. But, despite the fact that both are characterized by quality, intensity and duration, as Titchener has clearly shown, 'the lack of the attribute of clearness is sufficient in itself to differentiate affection

---

[1] J. B. Watson, *Behaviour*, p. 22.

from sensation; a process that cannot be made the object of attention is radically different, and must play a radically different part in consciousness from a process which is held and enhanced by attention.'[1] Incidentally it may be remarked that this is one of the criticisms of ethical hedonism, for pleasure cannot be a moral end itself, precisely because it cannot be made an object of attention.

At the same time it cannot be denied that there is an organic element in feeling. Reference need only be made to the various expressive movements already mentioned in verification of that. Alterations in circulation and respiration indicate that fact. One can even verify it for himself by trying to breathe more rapidly or more slowly, and observing the affective effects of the alterations. The mistake comes in trying to identify either of the affective qualities with any one definite organic sensation or group of sensations. It is another case where over-simplicity condemns the theory.

5. The theory which finds most general acceptance to-day is that the bi-polarity of affective experiences corresponds to two antithetical modes of mental activity. Pleasurable affects are associated with experiences which contribute to the welfare of the organism; pain with those which are harmful. In that way we may speak of the feelings as signs or indices of the condition of the organism with reference to its activities and in relation to its environment. Pleasurableness is the sign of a situation that is of value, harmonious, and needs to be persisted in; painfulness is the index to a situation which is harmful, discordant, and needs to be altered or readjusted. Thus by indicating the needs of the organism, they point the way to appropriate responses, pleasure inciting appropriation or advance, and pain inciting retreat or rejection. Agreeableness arises in association with (a) healthy bodily conditions, (b) the stimulation of nerves within the limits of their ability to respond to a situation with maximum vigour, (c) an unimpeded and effective flow of the conscious processes, and (d) satisfactory relations subsisting between the organism and its environment. Disagreeableness is incited in association

---

[1] E. B. Titchener, *A Text-book of Psychology*, p. 232.

with (a) pathological conditions of the organism, (b) either excessive or insufficient stimulation of the nerves, (c) the repression or inhibition of conscious activity in the direction of activities, and (d) unsatisfactory relations subsisting between the organism and its environment.[1] In short, pleasure is an index to conditions that are serviceable, and pain to conditions that are menacing to the welfare of the organism in any particular time and situation.

The emotional experiences are predominantly feeling experiences. Indeed, the feeling element is so vivid that in popular usage the terms are often used interchangeably. McDougall classifies the emotions[2] into primary and derived, and uses the expressions 'derived emotion' and 'feeling' as practically synonymous. Indeed, the primary emotions also are very much coloured by pleasure and pain. Certainly we must agree with him that the experiences are too complicated for us to succeed in disentangling them at all adequately. At the same time the bi-polarity of feeling affords one basis on which the emotions may be classified, those whose affective tone is pleasurable, and those which are disagreeable, the former including joy, wonder, love, gratitude, reverence, benevolence, etc., and the latter including fear, anger, embarrassment, disgust, grief, etc.

The emotions illustrate the impulsive character of the feelings. In the case of the former there is a close alliance with the instincts, as was pointed out in the chapter dealing with instinctive behaviour. The instinct provides the 'pattern response' whereby the organism expresses itself on the motor side, and that expression is frequently characteristic of an emotional experience. In other words, the impulsive tendencies find characteristic modes of expression. Shand describes emotions as forces which operate in particular ways and in certain definite directions.[3] Stout speaks of them as being of a 'parasitical character',[4] usually being secondary phenomena presupposing the existence of more specific tendencies. This is characteristic of all feeling

---

[1] This doctrine has been ably expounded by President Angell in his *Psychology*, pp. 320, 326 f.

[2] McDougall, *An Outline of Psychology*, chap. xii.

[3] Shand, *The Foundations of Character*, p. 179.

[4] G. F. Stout, *Manual of Psychology*, p. 408.

experiences, since they are effects of something or other. Those other conditions which arouse the emotions may be any number of varied phenomena, including danger situations, food situations, sex disturbances, anticipation, thwarting, herd influences, or other emotions. Some of the conditions are fulfilled in connection with definite objects or ideas, and others are primarily organic. Not only the conditions, but the emotional effects cover a wide range from perceptual consciousness up to the higher conceptual activities, from the lowest form of animal reflex behaviour to the most complex reasoning process among human beings.

It was the combined merit of the American psychologist, William James and the Dane, Lange, to point out the intimate connection between emotional experience on its psychic side and physical concomitants. James said: 'If we fancy some strong emotion, and then try to abstract from our consciousness of it all the feelings of its bodily symptoms, we find we have nothing left behind, no " mind-stuff " out of which the emotion can be constituted.'[1] It is not necesssary to go into the theory in detail or the criticisms levelled at it by such psychologists as Ward and Stout. The main principle involved has received an astonishing vindication from recent experimental work in the field of physiology. The X-ray has disclosed the fact that under emotional stress the churning motion of the stomach and the kneading of the intestines stop. The observations of changes in the rates of circulation and respiration go back to James and Lange themselves. Most illuminating has been the study of the functioning of the endocrine glands. It has been ascertained that during emotional stress or very fatiguing activity the adrenal glands release the adrenin secretion, and that revives the hard worked muscles and glands, and enables us to carry on, in spite of the trying conditions. Some of the actions which take place are purely chemical, such as the changing of the starch of the liver into sugar, and who knows but that bio-chemistry may not ultimately show that all emotional disturbances are chemically explicable ?[2]

---

[1] James, *Principles of Psychology*, vol. ii, p. 451.
[2] cf. W. B. Cannon, *Bodily Changes in Pain, Hunger, Fear, and Rage.*

The theory which Dewey has proposed to explain emotion is
in general agreement with that already referred to in connection
with feeling as associated with the name of Angell. The crux
of the theory is that emotional reactions represent the survival
acts which were originally useful, either physiologically or
socially. We can easily understand that the running away reaction
accompanying fear would in many cases be useful in preservation
from danger. What about weeping under the stress of grief?
This is one of the reactions which might easily be of social
utility. The outcome of these reactions has been the fixing of
definite series of co-ordinations until they became organic and
racial heritages. This account of Dewey's is the best explanation on the basis of the evolutionary hypothesis of behaviour. It relates the emotional disturbances, as we have
already related the affective experiences, to the welfare of the
organism. It thus possesses the great merit of keeping the
welfare of the organism, in the case of human beings the welfare
of personality, at the core of the process, a matter of the utmost
importance in a psychology of education.

LITERATURE

W. McDougall. *An Outline of Psychology*. Methuen, 1924.

A. F. Shand. *The Foundations of Character*. Macmillan, 1914.

James Ward. *Psychological Principles*. Cambridge University Press, 1920.

J. R. Angell. *Psychology*. Constable, 1908.

W. Whately Smith. *The Measurement of Emotion*. Kegan Paul, 1922.

W. B. Cannon. *Bodily Changes in Pain, Hunger, Fear, and Rage*. Appleton, 1915.

E. B. Titchener. *A Textbook of Psychology*. Macmillan, 1909.

G. F. Stout. *A Manual of Psychology*. University Tutorial Press, 1913.

CHAPTER V

ATTENTION AND ITS CONTROL

THE COMPETITION OF STIMULI—ATTENTION A PROCESS OF SELECTION—THE
FACTORS OF ADVANTAGE: CHANGE, INTENSITY, DEFINITENESS, REPE-
TITION, QUALITY, EXTENSITY, AND INTEREST—SOCIAL DETERMINATIONS
OF INTERESTS—THE SPAN OF ATTENTION.

ATTENTION is the heart of the conscious process. When we
are conscious of an object, it means that we are aware of its presence in the environment. To attend to an object means to be
more keenly aware of it than of anything else, to hold it in the
focus of consciousness. But, central though it is to the conscious
process, it must not be thought to be an end in itself. Attention
is for the sake of something else. It is an attitude of prepared-
ness or readiness for action. Woodworth draws upon two familiar
experiences as clearly illustrative. The one is the military command of 'Attention' preparatory to some other command or
commands about to be given. The other is the athletic call of
'Ready' preparatory to the order to start a race. Both of these
are splendid illustrations of that sensitively conscious and preparatory attitude which we characterize as awareness. Sometimes
school teachers resort to the same military method of commanding attention when they are about to impart some instruction, i.e.
to induce an attitude of readiness to receive what is to be given
or to do what is to be commanded. Without pausing to criticize
the method so employed, it may be noted that the attitude sought
is essentially the same as that for which the army officer and the
starter in the races seek when they give their commands.

Living in an environment that is, in both its social and physical
aspects, exceedingly complex, there are an enormous number of
stimuli which are constantly competing for our attention. This
competition is sometimes referred to as objects external to us sending messages along the afferent nerves. If all of these messages

came with equally insistent voices, it would be hopelessly confusing to know what response ought to be made. But happily there are various factors of advantage which characterize certain stimuli, giving them a power to attract attention and secure responses greater than the power possessed by others. These factors of advantage are constantly undergoing change and modification in experience, which is the key to the mobility of attention. And those stimuli which have the advantage constitute the field of attention. The entire field of consciousness is sometimes compared to an iceberg, by far the major portion of which is submerged like the subliminal consciousness, while the portion above the water is analogous to the field of attention.

The phenomenon of the competition of stimuli is familiar to us in many experiences. There is not only a competition between the visual, auditory, tactual and other forms of sensory stimulation, but also within each of these separate fields there is keen competition as to what shall command attention. An example may be cited of a dog which is being called at the same time by two members of the same family where it is a pet. The dog shows its confusion by turning its head, wagging its tail, and wriggling its body, as it hesitates which call to heed. A child taken into a shop or bazaar, where there is a variety of attractive toys, shows the same confusion, looking first at one toy and then at another, shouting to its companions to look at first one thing and then something else, all the time its eyes dancing with excitement, but quite unable to select any one object as the focus of attention to the exclusion of the others. The same phenomenon of competition may be illustrated by an animal or a child in the presence of a variety of good things to eat. The difficulty of decision is rendered more difficult if all of them happen to be articles which appeal to the taste. The teacher knows how difficult it is at times to secure attention in the class-room. The difficulty is not always easy to diagnose, as it is not readily possible to detect just what the competing stimulus may be. Perhaps it may be a mischievous boy making 'funny' grimaces for the benefit of the other members of the class, while the teacher, with back turned to the class, is writing on the blackboard.

There is one thing, however, of which the teacher may be

quite sure, and that is, when there is difficulty in securing the attention of the members of the class, it is due to some competitive stimulus or stimuli other than those which he is presenting to them. It is almost true to say that there is no such thing as inattention. That which is ordinarily called inattention is in reality attention to other stimuli.

In all the conscious moments of a sentient being there is attention of some degree to some object, even though that attention be never so fleeting. We know from our memory of dream experiences that in them there is no conscious process, and the images flow past sometimes with astounding rapidity. Even in reverie the same is true, and in reverie attention is at a minimum. The objects of attention stay at the focus for the shortest possible time, and are displaced by others. This is because there is a minimum of voluntary control. And, as we have seen, attention is a form of voluntary control. Sometimes it may happen that a child in school becomes lost in reverie when he ought to be attending to the work of the class. Thus it becomes the duty of the teacher to study the factors of advantage in attention, and apply them to the matter to which it is desired to attract the attention of the children.

Since the environment is constantly presenting us with a number of different stimuli which are in competition for attention, attention itself obviously involves a process of selection. Woodworth has stated the fact of selection in the form of a law: 'Of two or more inconsistent responses to the same situation (or complex of stimuli), only one is made at the same time.'[1] The same author has a splendid discussion of this matter of selection and control in his volume of lectures on *Dynamic Psychology*.[2] We cannot do better than quote him at this point. He says:

'The fundamental thing in selection is undoubtedly the linkages, some provided by nature and others established by previous training, between actions and their exciting stimuli. Actions are *reactions*, being connected by nature or training with certain stimuli; and unless the stimulus occurs the reaction does not

[1] Woodworth, *Psychology: A Study of Mental Life*, p. 256.
[2] Woodworth, *Dynamic Psychology*, Columbia University Press, New York, 1922, pp. 106 ff.

occur, but its mechanisms remain in the resting condition. The mechanism for flight exists in good working order in an animal, but unless the situation confronting the animal contains something that the animal naturally fears or has learned to fear, the flight mechanism is not activated. Thus the selective agency is very largely to be sought in the situation confronting the animal or man. . . . The same stimulus may have become linked with two or more reactions, and the same act with two or more stimuli; and the situation presented is always complex, containing a number of elements that are capable of acting as stimuli to different reactions. Under such conditions, the question of selection is very real and not at all easy to answer in full.' After illustrating the point by the case of the cat in the puzzle-box, trying to find a method of escape, he proceeds, 'evidently there would be no room for selection except for the existence in the individual of two or more mechanisms responsive to the same object or situation.' This is illustrated from Jenning's work on *Behaviour of the Lower Organisms*, with special reference to the lowest form of animal life. The protozoan has two possible forms of avoiding reaction, the one a simple contraction, and the other more positive, amounting to flight. 'Which of these reactions shall actually be aroused by a given stimulus depends not only on the stimulus, but also on the inner condition of the animal, which in turn is largely determined by the stimuli that have just gone before.'

The matter of selection is best explicable, as Woodworth has shown, in terms of stimulus and response. The necessity for selection arises out of the multiple possibilities of reaction. If there were only one possible course of action, in the absence of alternatives there would of course be no selective process called for. The selection of a particular course of action involves the exclusion of alternative responses. It is difficult to illustrate action of any sort where the factor of conscious selection is absent. Comparative psychologists have found examples by performing operations on such animals as dogs. A cut is made across the spinal cord of the animal, thus severing the connection between the nerves of the hinder half of the body and the brain. This converts the hinder part of the animal into a purely reflex mechanism, and the animal responds directly to stimuli to that portion of its body, with an inhibition of other possible reactions, an obvious case of natural selection. This principle is the reciprocal inhibition of antagonistic reactions. But we do not call such a selective process as this by the name 'attention', because consciousness is not operative, and the response to the stimulus is quite automatic.

In mental operations the factor of selection is seen to be operative in an important way. Ideas or images call up by association a great many other ideas or images. In a chain of thinking or reasoning there has to be constant attention to the problem in hand, for reasoning is a kind of problem-solving process. And attention takes the form of selecting, from the images or ideas which compete, the one or ones which are needed or appropriate to the problem in hand. What then is the psychological explanation for the fact that some are much better at problem-solving situations than others? This is, of course, one indication of intelligence, and takes the form of a multitude of associations that compete for attention. It has already been noted that one of the differences between the supernormal and the subnormal is the wealth of associations in the former case, and the poverty of them in the latter. There can be no doubt that this difference materially affects this question of selection and attention. Where there is an abundance of associations from which to select, there is a much greater degree of possibility of securing the appropriate solution to a problem. But where the number of available associations is very limited, the individual has much less chance of finding the one that is needed to solve the problem. When the available associations have been explored, and no appropriate solution is found, the attention to the problem naturally lags. The greater the poverty of the associations, the sooner will they be explored, and the sooner will the attention lag. That is one reason why the capacity for attention is so meagre in the feeble-minded person. He comes very soon to exhaust the store-house of available associations, and consequently his mind goes on to something else. Persistency of intelligent behaviour, persistency in the endeavour to solve problems and a generous capacity for maintaining attention are all correlative mental processes. If any one of them is weak, they are all weak. They stand or fall together.

The reason why selection is necessary lies in the difficulty of making more than one conscious response to a situation at a time. It is possible that automatic responses, such as reflexive or habitual responses, may take place simultaneously with an attentive response, but any two attentive responses appear to be inconsistent with one another, so that the making of one inhibits all others in accordance with the general principle of selection. The subject of doing two things or more at once is one which is closely connected with this matter of attention and selection. It is possible, if the things attended to are somehow related to one another, so that attention may be so directed as to include all of them. For example, four different colours may be seen at the same time, and sometimes a small group of disconnected letters or even a few disconnected words may be read at once. This is possible simply because the different things are homogeneous, and the responses called for are homogeneous and elementary. Under such unusually favourable conditions attention may be directed and responses made to two, three or four stimuli at once. In the main, however, two responses are possible simultaneously only because one of them has become familiar enough to be automatic. For example, some people achieve the feat of reciting a piece of poetry and adding a column of figures simultaneously, but only by first memorizing the poem so that it can be recited automatically. But this is not making two attentive responses simultaneously. The law of selection holds with very little exception—only one attentive response is possible at a given instant of time.

Mention was made of the fact that there are certain factors of advantage in the securing and holding of attention. The more important among these are change, intensity, definiteness, repetition, quality, extensity, habit and interest. We shall consider these one by one, and the ways in which they function in determining the capacity of a stimulus to attract attention.

1. Change is an important factor in securing and maintain-

ing attention. It is a phenomenon of common experience that attention cannot be held on any object very long, unless it can be seen in changing aspects. A continued sound, even though it be loud, will, after a time, become so familiar as not to be noticed. The ticking of a clock in a room where we are sitting reading is a typical example. We become so accustomed to it that sometimes it requires close attention to be able to detect that it is ticking. But if it should undergo some change, such as difference in the speed, pitch or tone of the sound, or even if it should cease ticking, we would suddenly attend to the change. If we sit in a room that is lighted by a coloured light we may become so accustomed to it that we do not notice the colour. But when we change again into white light, our attention is suddenly drawn to the difference in the light stimulus. Familiarity with tactually sensed objects may result quite similarly. The clothing that is worn day after day fails to attract any attention on the tactual side unless some change is made, something that disturbs the habitual way of feeling clothes. If we put on a garment that, because it is too small or for any other reason, is uncomfortable, attention is quickly directed to the tactual experience. Or, if a garment is removed which we ordinarily wear, attention is drawn to the change. For that reason persons who wish to make any important changes in their habits frequently prefer to make them gradually, to avoid the discomfort that comes from the complete and sudden inhibition of habitual modes of action. If the change in a stimulus is made sufficiently gradual, it may even not attract attention at all.

It is exceedingly difficult to ascertain with any degree of precision how long attention can be held on any object. In the case of voluntary attention, that can be measured to some extent for some reactions by determining the span of attention. But of one thing we are certain, viz. that however constant the external stimulus may remain, we can only attend continuously to an object if we can see it in new lights. This fact seems to point to change as a fundamental characteristic of mental life in general. As Angell has put it : ' Thought processes which cease to move, cease to exist. They simply go out. To keep a thought alive we must keep turning it over, keep *doing* something with it.

Mental paralysis is mental death. . . . What we call attending to a topic for a considerable period of time will, therefore, always be found to consist in attending to *changing phases* of the subject, to ideas associated with it.'[1] This fact can be illustrated from the study of any subject in the school curriculum. A child is able to attend to an arithmetical problem he is trying to solve only because he is constantly looking at it from fresh angles and attempting different ways of solving it.

The problem arises: Why are we unable to attend long to a stimulus unless it appears in changing fashion? Why does attention shift? ' It has been suggested that the rapid changes of attention are due primarily to fatigue in the delicate cortical cells which are connected with conscious process.'[2] We must remember that the old psychological maxim holds good in the matter of attention as well as with other processes: ' No psychosis without neurosis.' In all processes of attention, and ' process ' is the right word to use since change is the characteristic feature, there is constantly going on modification and adjustment. And these mental activities of modification and adjustment have always their neural counterparts. It may well be that the explanation which Angell suggests is valid, that fatigue in the cortical cells is the cause of the shifting character of attention. If attention is to be retained for any length of time on any particular focus, the object must be viewed in fresh lights, so that the energies of adjustment may be distributed among the cortical cells and fresh responses may be possible. It frequently happens that painful stimuli protrude themselves into the field of attention to the exclusion of the pleasant, and the reason is that they call for a process of adjustment and continue to do so until the demand is satisfied. That is the reason why the unpleasant so often monopolizes attention, to the exclusion of the pleasant.

2. A second factor of advantage in attention is intensity. Other things being equal, the more intense stimulus gains attention more readily than the less so. A loud noise startles us into attention where we might pay no heed to a milder one. A bright colour or an intense light attracts attention when a more subdued

---

[1] Angell, *Psychology*, pp. 93, 94.   [2] Ibid., pp. 94, 95.

one would not.   An extra dose of salt or of chillies with rice and curry at once occupies the field of attention, where we might eat a whole meal with normal amounts quite automatically.   So a powerful odour attracts attention more readily than a faint one, intense pressure than light pressure, intense heat or cold than moderate heat or cold, etc.   As Woodworth has shown, $size^1$ has the same effect as intensity in the case of visible objects.   A large mountain will be noticed more readily than a small hill, a large temple than a small one.   The newspapers print important news in large type, and advertisers have recourse to large type also. The cobra may not be so dangerous to us in South India as the krite, because it is usually much larger and consequently more noticeable, so that we can more readily avoid it, though it is just as venomous as the krite.   The truth is that we are often deceived in our value judgements by size, simply because the big thing is quicker to attract attention.   The teacher will make judicious use of his knowledge of the functioning of intensity in stimuli. There are some teachers and some parents who quite overdo the use of intense stimuli by trying to emphasize everything which they wish to command or impart.   The result is, of course, that nothing is emphasized, for if all commands are given and all knowledge is imparted with the idea that it is exceedingly important, the outcome is that there is nothing remaining that can be called ordinary.   The result is the opposite of what is desired, for if everything be emphasized, then the children come to think that this is simply the normal manner of the teacher, and the unfortunate teacher has no instrument left at his command when there is really something important which needs emphasis. There are, however, wise uses to which the teacher may put his knowledge of this factor of advantage.   The blackboard may be used to that end.   Resort to unusual and surprising methods very occasionally may serve the same purpose.   The re-enforcement of a stimulus may also be obtained by so manipulating the lesson that an appeal is made to several sensory processes at once.   If a pupil be made to pronounce the word m-a-n-g-o the sound serves as a stimulus.   If it be written on the blackboard and he

---

[1] Woodworth, *Psychology : A Study of Mental Life*, p. 246.

writes it in his book, it is intensified.   If in addition he handles a
real mango, and tastes it, the various experiences all re-enforce
one another, and serve to intensify the stimulation, so that attention
is much more readily secured.

3. A third factor of advantage for a stimulus in securing or
holding attention is definiteness.   It is common knowledge that
matters that are vague and ephemeral soon lose their hold on us.
This is true without any difference as to the sensory nerves that
are stimulated.   A vague indefinite taste is characterized as
insipid, whereas one that is definite attracts attention either as
pleasurable or painful.   An indefinite odour is ill defined and
fails to attract.   A well defined and relatively small object, such
as an aeroplane flying across the sky, is much more noticeable
than the broad expanse of blue sky itself.   A tune catches and
monopolizes the field of attention to sound, whereas rambling
notes do not.   Knowing this to be the case, the teacher should
present the matters in which he desires the students to be instructed in definite form.   That means that the teacher must have a
thorough mastery of the subject, for vagueness is very often
born of insufficient knowledge.   It must be remembered that the
reason why vagueness fails where definiteness of form attracts
attention is that the psycho-neural organism is of such a
character that the processes of sense-perception cannot well be
carried on unless the stimuli are definite in character.   In other
words, definiteness is a native factor of advantage in attention, and
not an acquirement.

4. Repetition is a factor of advantage to which many
teachers resort in trying to secure or hold the attention of their
pupils.   We are familiar with the function of repetition in
individual experience.   The repetition of a call at first unheeded
will eventually attract attention.   A business firm puts the same
advertisement in a newspaper repeatedly for weeks sometimes, in
the belief that by dint of seeing it over and over again some of the
readers may be moved to try the product being advertised.   Sometimes an infant that succeeds in a reaction for the first time is so
pleased that it wants to attract the attention of its parents to the
new accomplishment, and seeks to do so by doing the thing over
and over again.   Teachers make use of the same device in their

class-room work. One common form is to ask a question, and if the desired response is not readily secured, to repeat it, perhaps altering the form of the question just a little. The method is one that sooner or later succeeds in securing correct answers in many cases where the first asking fails. But it has the disadvantage, if used too freely, of developing a habit of inattention. The pupils get to expect the repetition of questions, and consequently wait for the second or third asking before they voluntarily attend. It is well sometimes to offset such a tendency by recourse to a special oral test or quizz for which the pupils are asked to make special preparation. They are warned that no question will be repeated, and that failures will count against them. If this method is used judiciously, it will serve as an intensified stimulus to attention. Furthermore, there is a danger in too much repetition resulting in a monotony which will eventually cease to hold the field of attention, from sheer force of our becoming too accustomed to it. Repetition continued too long robs the stimulus of the element of change, which we saw was necessary to attention.

5. The quality of a stimulus is another factor which determines the capacity of the stimulus to attract attention. This is not to be identified with intensity. A good illustration of the distinction is from the psychology of colour vision, viz. the distinction between brightness and saturation. The bright colour holds our attention because of the intensity of the stimulus, but a well saturated colour is one that is pure, that has less grey mixed with the original chrome. It is an observed fact that a well saturated colour will hold the attention of a person more readily than a less saturated one, even though the latter be more intense. Quality is also an important element in sound. Pitch is the name given to the quality of a sound, and is determined by the vibration rates per second of the sound waves. There are 11,000 tonal qualities distinguishable to the human ear, ranging all the way from 16 to 50,000 vibrations per second. Our experiences of music enable us to realize how fundamental to attention is this factor of tonal quality. Similarly, with tastes and odours, there are certain objects the stimuli of which possess a quality that makes them at once noticeable, even

6

sometimes to the exclusion of rivals which possess greater intensity. To find a psychological explanation for this factor is difficult indeed. But we do know that certain stimuli have that capacity of attracting attention more than others, and we can offer no more satisfactory description of that capacity than to term it their quality.

6. Extensity is a factor of advantage in securing attention, which may not always be easy to differentiate from intensity. But we know that extensity is sometimes an important element. We are much more likely to attend to the weather signs when the whole horizon blackens for an approaching storm, than when there are a few dark clouds in one portion only. The extensiveness of an odour, particularly if it be a mal-odour, will become very noticeable indeed, and lead us to seek to respond appropriately. The same applies to certain objects which we taste. The taste seems to find its way into so many taste buds that we find it very hard to get rid of it, even long after the object has been swallowed or rejected. We mean by extensity that the object presents to us such a broad range of stimuli that it fairly monopolizes the field of attention. The value of this fact for educational ends must be apparent. If a teacher is especially anxious to exclude all other rivals for the attention of the pupils in a class-room, it may sometimes be accomplished by a broadside attack of stimuli to which the pupils will be compelled to yield. It is common knowledge that, other things being equal, the army with the biggest battalions wins the day. So, too, other things being equal, the object that can outnumber the others in competing stimuli, will win the attention.

7. Habit is an important element in the acquiring and maintaining of the attentive attitude. Indeed, we may go further and refer to attention as itself largely a matter of habit. There are some people who have so little habituated themselves to prolonged attention to anything, that they become vascillating in character. On the other hand, resoluteness of character is in some measure due to the formation of habits of attention to the work that is pressing to be done. Obviously, the school has an important mission to perform in helping young people in the plastic, habit-forming period to form the habit of attentiveness.

Many men owe what success they have attained in life to the fact that they were able to concentrate on the business in hand, to give it their 'undivided attention'. Now concentration is nothing more nor less than an attitude of attention which has been developed into a habit. Habits, as we well know, are backward looking. But in the school we are making experience, forming habits, and preparing for the time when the children, having become men, will have past tenses. It will be fortunate for us who teach if they will then be able to look back to the time when they came under our influence, and think of it as a time when they formed the habit of attention. True, there are some things in the world to which we do not want children to attend. But if they have learned to attend, they will be able to attend to the better things and inhibit the worse.

8. No factor of advantage is more a part and parcel of attention than interest. The two processes go together. We are interested in that to which we attend; we attend to that in which we are interested. Interest is a phenomenon which in a conspicuous way illustrates the union of the cognitive, the affective and the conative elements of the mental life. An interest is always directed to an object which is cognitively recognized. It involves a feeling of satisfaction and pleasure with the meeting of a need. And it has a self-expressive active feature. Interests can be traced, to be sure, back to the primitive needs of the organism, the primary interests of life being food and sex. As food is essential to the existence of the individual, so mating and pro-creation are necessary to the preservation of the species. It is to be expected that man, in his desire to obtain control over the environing forces, should seek to organize his life so as to obtain help in matters relative to these two primal life-interests. Some sociologists are of opinion that all of the interests even of civilized man gather about these two fundamental interests. Be that as it may, we know that civilized man's interests are more varied and much more complex than those of his primitive brother. Yet, in the main, the psychological characteristics are much the same throughout.

It will be fairly obvious that there is the most intimate kind of connection between interest and attention. We are by nature disposed to attend to those objects and those ideas which immediately interest us, rather than to those which do not. This leads some psychologists to make a distinction between what they term 'spontaneous attention' and 'voluntary attention'. Angell says: 'By virtue of the spontaneous characteristic of attention certain ideas will from the first be given preference over others. . . . But when we ask the further question, *why* they interest us, we can only point again to the spontaneous and impulsive nature of attention. We get back here finally to the admission that both the hereditary and the personal history of each of us has produced differences in our impulsive and spontaneous modes of acting which we all recognize in one another, and for which we can offer no detailed explanation.'[1] These 'differences in our impulsive and spontaneous modes of acting' are referable to our interests. In that sense attention is always an expression of an organic mode of consciousness, of an interest that we feel and that moves us to act in one way rather than in another. This explanation may not be as detailed as some would wish, but it must be acknowledged that there is intelligibility in the notion that interests are native predispositions which determine largely the direction that attention shall take. The truth is, there is not much difference between the meanings of the two terms 'spontaneous attention' and 'interest'. There are other psychologists who would prefer to keep the term 'interest' for what Angell terms 'spontaneous attention', reserving the word 'attention' for the more conscious, voluntary process.

Interest and attention are in a measure socially determined. There are, in addition to the interests which originate in our native constitution, others which are the outcome of our being members of a social environment. Our attitudes and dispositions are among the determinants of conduct, and they are to a considerable degree socially nourished. By participating in the activities of the group, we come to share in the interests of the group, to make its interests our individual concern, its purposes our individual aims, its feelings our feelings, its methods our methods, its motives our motives. The obvious result is that the group life

---

[1] Angell, *Psychology*, p. 420.

exercises a large function in determining the direction of attention. From the social point of view, interest is very frequently the forerunner of participation. We become interested in what others are doing, and the next thing we know we find ourselves doing the same thing, whether it be reading a popular novel, playing a popular game, eating a particular kind of food, growing a particular variety of jasmine in the garden, wearing a particular style of clothing, singing a popular song, using a popular phrase, or doing anything else that the group to which we belong is doing. If we are not interested, the activities of others have no meaning for us, and we pay very little heed. In the class-room one of the most valuable means of holding the attention of the children, is to get them to realize a sense of participation in common enterprises. There is no surer way of capturing their interests. Sometimes that is possible by inspiring a class to a healthy rivalry with a class of the same grade in another school. The psychology of rewards and punishments serves the same purpose. A reward is an expression of approval and a punishment of disapproval, both of them socially sanctioned. The punishment is designed to prevent attention and interest from being misdirected, and the reward is to encourage interest and attention along desirable lines. Social approval or disapproval are means to the end.

Attention to and interest in the moral and religious life are special cases of social determinations. One of the foremost ends of education is the development of moral character and personality. The school has an important function to perform in directing the attention of children to, and interesting them in, the socially and morally desirable. Moreover, it ought to be so conducted as to furnish in miniature an ideal environment in which the person with moral interests and aspirations has a chance of realizing them.

It is obviously of the first importance that the teacher should study the interests of his pupils. The psychological test of mental abilities will disclose what the special capacities of a child are. It is very much easier to inspire the child's interest in doing the sort of things for which he has special gifts. The natural talents represent the direction in which the individual is able to offer society his most efficient service. Moreover, in pursuing them he can enjoy more happiness and freedom than in any other activities. The earliest evidence of talents is in special predilections or interests, a knowledge of which is of inestimable value to the teacher. There is no use in trying to get a boy to concentrate all his attention on language when his interests and talents are all scientific. Education involves growth, unfolding, and that includes a knowledge of the talents which will most readily unfold to maturity. Our interest in various activities is a dynamic phase of life, charged with meaning, in so far as it is an expression of ourselves. It is only as we find ourselves and feel our experiences to be real expressions of ourselves that life is interesting, and persistent attention is possible.

One of the most important of modern psychological studies, considered educationally, is investigation into the span of attention. By 'the span of attention' is meant precisely what the phrase indicates—the measure of the limits which attention is able to compass. Woodworth describes it as measured 'by discovering how many (such) objects can be clearly seen, or heard, or felt, in a single instant of time'.[1] The span of attention gradually increases with the advance of age towards maturity. The teacher should be a careful student of the size of the pupil's field of attention as it develops. It is not wise to try to force too rapid development of it, and yet he must not neglect the fact that the span is educable. He ought, therefore, to provide for the pupil's needs so that he may make a maximum use of his abilities at each stage of the process.

There are several ways in which attempts may be made to measure the span of attention. One is to place a number of marbles in a box, let the child have one peep, and then see whether he can tell how many marbles there are. The largest number that he can take in at a single glance is the measure of his span. Another experiment is to allow children (or adults, if you like) to see cards on which there are different numbers of dots, and ascertain the number of dots that they can compass in a glance amounting to one-fifth of a second or less. If letters

---

[1] Woodworth, *Psychology: A Study of Mental Life*, p. 262.

which do not make a word are exposed, one can ascertain how many can be read at a glance, or if the letters make familiar words how many of them can be read. Another test is if the number of colours exposed in the form of small coloured squares can be reported correctly after a brief glance. In all of these experiments the young child falls considerably behind the adult in regard to the numbers of objects to which he can attend. The dot-counting experiment is sometimes varied by arranging the dots in regular groups, and in this case the span is twice measured—by the size of the groups and the number of the groups; in both cases children fall below the ability of adults.

The span of attention is sometimes measured by addition of columns of figures of graduated length. It is possible for a person to measure the span of his attention by observing the point where fatigue sets in, as he adds a column of figures. Frequently one will observe that a tendency to uncertainty sets in, and that it sets in at about the same spot in each column. For a certain number of addition units he feels quite sure that he has added correctly, and then he begins to doubt the result. The point where uncertainty sets in marks the fact that he has just exceeded the span of attention. It will be observed that practice in an exercise such as this will gradually increase the span, up to a certain limit, of course.

Another very practical test of the span of attention is the unit of apprehension of verbal material. One of the Binet tests for five-year-old intelligence is the execution of three simple commands; putting a key on a table, shutting the door, and bringing the experimenter a book. A feeble-minded child's span of attention is so small that he would not be able to hold the three commands in mind long enough to execute them in the order named. The practical work of the schoolroom will frequently measure this capacity. A teacher must not be too impatient with children who fail to carry out all the instructions given, until he first ascertains whether the child is really able to attend to the number of commands which he is giving at once. In some cases children are accused of stupidity or of disobedience for not carrying out instructions, where the fault is really with the teacher or parent who gives them instructions which exceed their spans.

In discussing the nature of intelligence, it was observed that there are two theories, one that intelligence is general, another that it is made up of a number of specific abilities. One theory is that the central factor, running through intelligent behaviour, is voluntary attention. The work of such investigations as Brown and Burnt, while it does not settle the problem finally, points to a very intimate relationship between the central factor and voluntary attention. If this hypothesis be confirmed it would tend to validate the position of Thorndike that mental abilities are specific. The capacity of giving an intelligent response to any stimulus, in that case, would depend to a large extent on whether the person can and does attend to the matter voluntarily. Certainly, attention is a primary requisite for an educative process. The attentive exercise of any function will induce more rapid improvement than its exercise when attention is directed elsewhere.

LITERATURE

Th. Ribot. *The Psychology of Attention.* Longmans, Green, 1890.

W. B. Pillsbury. *Attention.* George Allen & Unwin, 1908.

E. B. Titchener. *Textbook of Psychology.* Macmillan, 1909.

James Ward. *Psychological Principles.* Cambridge University Press.

J. R. Angell. *Psychology.* Constable, 1908.

Wm. McDougall. *An Outline of Psychology.* Methuen, 1924.

A. S. Woodburne. *Psychological Tests of Mental Abilities.* University of Madras, 1924.

CHAPTER VI

THE LEARNING PROCESS

FROM the viewpoint of the stimulus-response psychology,
learning may be defined as the gradual selection of the most
appropriate responses to stimuli. We have previously observed
that some reactions are native, and others are acquired. The
former group includes impulsive behaviour, such as reflexive and
instinctive acts; the latter includes those reactions which are
acquired by a process of learning. The former constitute a part
of the original equipment with which we come into the world;
the latter are either modifications of native tendencies or further
acquisitions through experience and training. The native traits
are independent of the acquired, but the acquired are developed
on the basis of the native. Both resemble one another in being
responses to stimuli. They are aroused to activity by the need
of the organism to meet some situation called forth by the
environment, and are modifiable to meet the requirements of the
organism in its relation to the environment. Learning is only
possible on the basis of native reactions, for one can only learn
to react by reacting, and the native reactions provide the possibility for further acquisition. Learned reactions are all in a sense
native reactions which have been modified under the guidance of
experience and training.

One good example of the way in which learning builds on
native equipment is in the production of vocal music. Obviously,
the production of vocal sound is a native reaction made by the
vibration of the vocal cords by means of a blast of air from the
lungs. But variations in the voice in loudness and pitch, such as

characterize the singing of a tune, involve modifications of the native reaction tendencies that have to be learned. Again, the production of vowel and consonant sounds and the combination of these sounds into words and of words into meaningful sentences are learned reactions. Another example of a native reaction tendency is the closing of the hand over an object, which becomes the basis for the learned reaction of holding a ball and throwing it in a chosen direction. The prying tendency, which determines a monkey or dog to investigate everything possible, or the child to turn itself into an interrogation point, is the type of native reaction which, when developed and modified, becomes the basis of the scientist's research and the scholar's contribution to the stock of human knowledge. The truth is that all learning must start from the native reaction tendencies. Learning is indeed a process whereby the organism expands from its original capacity and condition to greater maturity. The learning process is the heart of the educative process.

One of the most fruitful sources of help for the study of the learning process in human beings is the study of animal learning. We have observed that it is customary to speak of 'animal intelligence', but that we do not speak of 'animal intellect', and that may be expressed otherwise by saying that perceptual learning is possible in the animal but not conceptual learning. It would not be far amiss to define intelligence as the ability to learn perceptually, and perhaps we could say that intellect is the ability to learn conceptually. If such a distinction were made, we would have to say that some of the psychological tests of mental abilities are tests rather of intellect than of intelligence. The fact is, we do not make such a differentiation except when we are interested in distinguishing animal from human learning. In this connection it will suffice to point out that by definition learning or the ability to learn is an integral part of intelligent and intellectual reactions.

Animals are able to learn, in varying degrees to be sure. Yet even the unicellular animal possesses a primitive capacity for profiting by experience and making adaptations to its environment. If a protozoan is disturbed by a sudden current in the water in which it lives, it will respond by some sort of avoiding reaction, such as by a contraction. If the stimulus be repeated at short intervals, the response gradually decreases in strength, until it stops completely. The protozoan has learned to adapt itself to the changing environment, but the learning is only perceptual for, if the stimulus be repeated after a longer interval, the reaction will recur. These unicellular animals, despite the absence of a nervous system, and of sensory apparatus, respond to such stimuli as heat, cold, electricity, light, touch, and to certain chemical stimuli, though there are other agents, such as the X-ray, which do not stimulate them.

An experiment has been tried with some of these simple organisms to test their learning ability in respect to food and non-food objects. They will absorb the juice of meat, and even the tissue itself. One experimenter soaked some litmus paper with meat juice and presented it to the animal. At first it attacked the litmus paper greedily and attempted to digest the whole thing, but gradually it learned to extract the juice and reject the paper, or to attack particles of meat in preference to litmus paper soaked with the juice of it.

Woodworth quotes[1] an interesting example of a spider which was observed to adapt itself to the sound of a large tuning fork. At first when the tuning fork was sounded it performed the defensive reaction of dropping from its web. When it had climbed back to the web, the stimulus was repeated, and the response was repeated for about half a dozen times, after which it grew accustomed to the sound and ceased to respond. The next day when the stimulus was repeated it again dropped from its web, but after about fifteen days of such trials it learned to adapt itself to the sound so well that the adaptation was established, and no further responses were elicited. Another illustration from the same author[2] is in the learning of hermit-crabs, one of which was kept in an oblong aquarium lighted at one end and darkened at the other. The crab remained at the light end, but would go to the dark end when food was placed there. After several repetitions of the food stimulus in the dark end, the crab acquired the habit of going there even when there was no food.

[1] Woodworth, *Dynamic Psychology*, p. 85.   [2] Ibid., p. 81.

'Thus the food-seeking reaction had become attached to the darkening as a stimulus.' Then the situation was made more complex for the animal by the introduction of a wire screen with a small hole in it, which was placed between the food and the crab. 'The crab not only learned the way through the screen, but after awhile reacted to the screen as a stimulus, going behind it as soon as it was placed in position, even without the presence of food. The screen, not itself an original arouser of the food-seeking reaction, came by "association", as the phrase runs, to have the power of arousing it.'

These illustrations from the behaviour of some of the more simple forms of animal life suffice to show that the capacity to learn is found even there. As we progress up the scale to the more highly articulated organisms with nervous systems, such as the mammals, we observe that the same capacity is present in even more mature forms. The behaviour of these animals has been made the subject of many experiments by psychologists, neurologists and zoologists. Some of the most valuable experiments in so far as obtaining psychological results are concerned, are those conducted with mazes and puzzle-boxes. The special purpose of the experiments is to ascertain the accuracy and the speed with which animals are able to learn how to make certain reactions without mistakes. Of course, our ultimate aim is to understand human learning. But human learning on account of its perplexity is much more difficult to examine. Animal learning, to repeat, is learning on the perceptual level, and a study of it is the best preparation for the understanding of human learning, which involves more intricate forms of learning.

Thorndike records an experiment with young chicks and a very simple maze. A number of chicks, six to twelve days old, were kept in a yard (YY) adjoining which was a maze or pen (ABCDE). A chick was taken from the yard and placed at about half-way between the blind alley end of the maze and the entrance to the yard (i.e. at A). The stimuli which it experienced were, in brief, 'confining walls and the absence of other chicks, food and familiar surroundings'. Its reactions consisted of much running around, loud chirping, and jumping at the walls. When it jumped at the walls its efforts were thwarted. When it ran inwards (towards B, C or D) it got a continuance of the problem situation. When it ran toward the yard-entrance (E) it escaped and had the

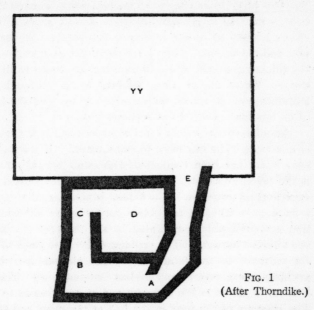

FIG. 1
(After Thorndike.)

satisfaction of the company of the other chicks, of food, and customary surroundings. When repeatedly put into the maze at the same spot (A), it ran less and less frequently towards the blind walls, until ultimately it ran directly towards the yard-entrance and out into it. It had formed an association, or connection, or bond, between the situation due to its removal to the maze (A) and the response of returning to the yard (via E)—in other words it had learned how to escape. The gradual decrease of the useless running, jumping and standing, are the marks of the process of learning. Thorndike's observation was that the chicks averaged three and one half minutes to learn to escape, and, having learned it, the reaction required five or six seconds.[1]

The same author describes another experiment wherein the chicks learned to go through a veritable labyrinth of problematic situations which involved the formation of an extended series of

[1] Thorndike, *Educational Psychology*, Briefer Course, pp. 125-27.

bonds. The chicks first of all learned to escape from a pen by going up an inclined plane. Then a second pen was arranged so that the chick, by walking up an inclined plane, escaped through a hole in the wall to pen number one. After a series of trials the chicks learned to escape from pen number two to pen number one, and thence out. Then gradually other pens were added and the chicken gradually added more and more bonds to its acquirements. Three chicks thus learned to go through a long labyrinth with no errors, the learning representing the formation of no less than twenty-three separate bonds.

Another very common form of experiment is the experiment of observing white rats learn to run a maze. Of course, the maze experiment has been conducted with other animals, but the rat is the favourite subject, because it is easily secured and kept for experimental purposes. The animal is placed at the entrance to a maze, from which it can obtain food only by following a path that is considerably complicated by the presence of blind alleys and alternative paths. The problem is for it to learn to go from the entrance to the food box by the shortest possible path, avoiding delays, returns and useless excursions into blind alleys. The rat is placed at the entrance and at once begins to explore. The presence of the food in the box at the other end stimulates the olfactory nerves, and that is an incentive to continue the process of exploration. Even those who have not watched the rat learning the maze are familiar with the explorative tendencies of the ordinary rat when in search for food. When in the maze it sniffs about, runs hither and thither, tries every passage and several of them many times, until finally it discovers the food box. Occasionally one finds an animal that gets weary with its apparently fruitless efforts, lies down in some blind alley, and goes to sleep. Out of one group of four rats that I experimented with, one was very lazy. It persisted for a long time in giving up. But when one day it discovered that by going on it secured food, it was completely cured of its indifference, and made much faster progress than the other three in the elimination of errors. There are many methods of varying the experiment. Some will replace the rat at the entrance as soon as it has found the food box, and make it run through several times, and it is found that each time it learns to eliminate more errors, until it has learned the reaction perfectly. On the other hand, there is the danger that if the animal is not rewarded with the food when it has found its way through, it may become discouraged and cease trying. So it is usual to have one trial per day for each animal until the maze is learned.

The next question in which the psychologist is interested is the question of how the animal learns. How are bonds formed

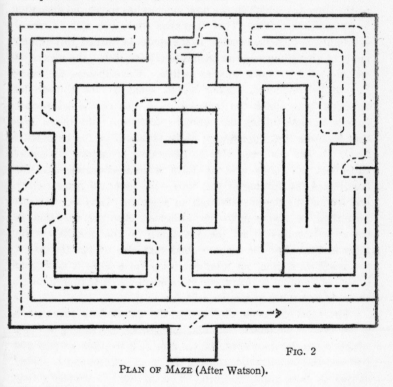

FIG. 2

PLAN OF MAZE (After Watson).

that enable it to eliminate errors? What use does it make of its sensory apparatus? Experiments have been performed with the idea of ascertaining as much as possible in regard to these matters. The experiment is conducted with animals that are blind and deaf, and whose olfactory nerves are rendered insensible. In each of these cases the difference in the animal's capacity to learn is not great. But, when the animal's vibrissæ are cut off, it encounters no end of difficulties, dashing into the sides and ends of the runways, and finding it very hard to thread its ways. It would seem in the case of the white rat that the tactual nerve centres are more affective than any others in the animal's learning process. The kinæsthetic sense is also much used by the animal in its self-guidance. If the maze be shortened, the rat will run headlong into the ends of the runways, which shows how much it has measured distances in kinæsthetic terms. That it makes some use also of visual sensibility is evident, because if the maze be turned through an angle of ninety degrees, the rat has to relearn to run the maze. It will not need so much time as before. Nevertheless, the maze has to be relearned. That would seem to show that the direction from which the light comes is one of the component factors in determining the animal's learning. But more than that, it shows that the learning of the animal is on the perceptual level. It has not been able to generalize in regard to maze-threading, not been able to form a maze-concept, with the result that the turning of the maze—the identical maze that it has learned to thread—through an angle of ninety degrees has perturbed its response to the stimulus. Another variation in the experiment is to set the rat down in the middle of the maze instead of at the entrance, and that also throws the rat off the track for a time, but after exploring for a while it soon gets a feel of familiarity from which point onwards it rushes on to the food box without further mistakes.

The most common subject for the puzzle-box experiment is the cat. The puzzle-box may be opened by raising a latch which keeps the door shut, the cat requiring to place its paw out between the bars in order to raise the latch, whereupon a spring causes the door gently to open. The cat used is usually young and hungry, and outside the cage, just beyond the reach of its paw, is placed food, which serves as a stimulus to the animal to persist in its efforts until it succeeds. The cat is pretty much excited by the combination of stimuli—a closed cage, food just outside and the pangs of hunger. Consequently, it rushes about trying in every conceivable manner to effect an escape from its confinement. In some of its trials it puts its paw on the button and the desired happens—the door opens, and it gets to the food. The experimenter keeps a record of the time, puts the cat back in the cage with more food outside, and repeats the experiment. The same sort of responses are repeated by the animal, except that it probably effects its escape a bit more rapidly. These trials are repeated for a series of successive days until the cat acquires the correct response without any useless movements. Sometimes the animal forms a wrong association, and imagines the existence of a bond that is fictitious, so that it repeats one or more of the useless movements for a long time. But as a rule there is a gradual diminution of useless movements and elimination of errors until an unerring response is secured. The average is from fifteen to twenty trials for that result to be attained.

The maze experiment and the puzzle-box experiment serve as illustrations of the manner in which animals learn. More than that, they illustrate our definition of learning as the gradual selection of the most appropriate responses to stimuli. There is no regularly graded improvement in the way the animal acquires the better reactions. The course of its improvement could not be graphically represented by a curve, but rather by a series of higher and lower peaks. Yet the general trend indicates improvement and indicates that the improvement is gradual. It affords us a good illustration of the working of ' the trial and error method '. The trial and error method confronts a problematic situation with no preconceived idea of how it is to be met. But it consists of a number of successive attempts to discover a solution, with a gradual elimination of the unsatisfactory responses and the fixation of the successful one. It is also an illustration of the substitute response. The animal first responds to the hunger and food stimulus by trying to get at it directly. But it gradually learns that there are other responses which must be made first, must be substituted before the food is obtainable. The repetition of the problematic situation usually results in the animal lessening gradually the time required between stimulus and satisfactory responses, becoming gradually improved until all the useless and unsatisfactory responses are at last eliminated.

7

It will be observed that the learning of the animal is explicable for the most part in terms of bonds which directly connect acts to situations. It is seldom that there is any evidence of anything in the way of ideational response preparing the way for the muscular response. There is no evidence that the animal reasons its way to a solution of its problem, or that it can generalize on the basis of a solution that it has hit upon by trial and error. The behaviour of the animal is impulsive rather than ratiocinative. There is not even much evidence that the animal makes any well defined observations of its own successful reactions. The fact that the rat which is blind does about as well as the one that can see in the maze experiment, whereas the shortening or lengthening of the maze disturbs the animal very much, seems to indicate that the muscular sense functions much more than vision in the animal's learning, and the confusion due to the removal of its vibrissæ shows that tactual sensibility is also an important factor. Tactual and muscular sensibility are fundamental in doing things, and the fact that the animal depends on them so much shows that it learns to do by doing. Interference with the stimulus, either by changing the stimulating object (as in the shortening of the maze) or by mutilation of the sensory end organ (as in the clipping of the rat's vibrissæ), throws the animal quite off, and that seems to indicate that its learning does not involve any use of images or ideas.

The important things in the animal's learning, according to Thorndike, are ' the selection of connections by use and satisfaction and their elimination by disuse and annoyance, multiple reaction, the mind's set as a condition, piecemeal activity of a situation, with prepotency of certain elements in determining the response, response by analogy, and shifting of bonds.'[1] The first factor that he mentions is that which we have already referred to as 'trial and error'. By 'multiple reaction' he means that the animal reacts in several different ways to the same situation which gives it a number of bonds from which it may select the most satisfactory one in the future. The 'mind's set as a condition' means the attitude or adjustment. For example,

---

[1] Thorndike, *Educational Psychology*, Briefer Course, p. 137.

the degree of hunger of the cat will determine to a considerable extent how much it will try to escape from the puzzle-cage. Age, hunger, sleepiness, vitality, and so forth, are all determinants of the attitude. By 'piecemeal activity of a situation' Thorndike means that one or another factors in the situation may be prepotent in determining the response. The 'response by analogy' is a response to a situation the same as the response made to another situation which it resembled. By 'the shifting of bonds' the meaning is that the animal learns to respond in a certain way to a combination of stimuli and that one after another these stimuli may be omitted until the animal responds to one of the least significant elements in the situation. A dog learns to perform a trick, in response to which it secures some food, but gradually the oral signal can be substituted for the food, and the bond between stimulus and response shifts from food-trick to command-trick.

The study of animal learning is of interest to the educational psychologist only as it serves to throw light on the manner of human learning. Human learning is superior to animal learning (i) in that man learns more rapidly, (ii) he acquires a greater variety of reactions as well as more of them, (iii) he is able to make use of ideas in forming bonds, (iv) he is naturally less impulsive and more conscious of his reactions, and (v) he can reason his way to the solution of a problem before he begins to respond in an overt way.

There is a certain amount of human learning, however, which is of the same type as that of the lower animal. There are a good many problems to which we find our solutions by the method of trial and error. We 'muddle our way through' certain situations and 'hit upon' the correct response to a stimulus sometimes just as the animal does, by trying until we succeed. That is particularly true of the way in which the infant learns to exercise control over its own muscles and limbs. Human beings also show a tendency to learn in the same way as animals, when confronted with a puzzle. To be sure, a puzzle-box like that used in experimenting with cats is too simple for human beings beyond the infant stage, but there are many mechanically devised puzzles which present problematic situations of the puzzle variety.

In these cases we see the same sort of muddling as with a completely unfamiliar situation and attempts at a solution until the
correct one is hit upon. Sometimes the puzzle is accidentally
solved, and the subject has to muddle again to discover how he
did it. But he has this advantage over the lower animal, that he
is more likely to notice where he was in the puzzle when he met
with his accidental success, and returning to that point he can
observe more closely until he locates the solution. The human
being has another advantage in being able to study the puzzle
until he can see into the principle involved. Insight is a great
advantage, because it leads to a better plan of attack, even though
the actual concrete solution may be unknown or forgotten. Human
learning also differs from animal learning in sometimes showing
abrupt improvements which seldom if ever characterize the
animal. The subject may work away for a considerable period,
with very little improvement, but a careful study may disclose
the underlying principle of the puzzle, after understanding which
improvement becomes suddenly much more rapid. The human
being learns by analogy to much greater advantage than the
animal. Learning one puzzle and understanding the principle
involved will greatly facilitate his learning of another involving
the same principle.

The trial and error method of learning is the method which
is most useful in problematic situations. In the case of the animal
most of the explorations are of the motor type. But man is at
a decided advantage in being able to explore a situation mentally.
'Reasoning' is the name which we give to mental exploration.
It is a search for relevant facts in which you make use of the
process of manipulating mental images until the one or the group
is found which gives satisfaction in connection with the problem
at hand. The animal does not possess the technique for manipulating images in solving its problems and has to depend on
motor ways of finding solutions. A very good instance of the
use of the trial and error method is in the scientist's attempt to
find a solution to his problems in the laboratory. The example
of the chemist analyzing an unknown compound is one in point.
He tries with his litmus paper and with other chemicals to find
what reactions can be obtained. Then on the basis of prelimi-

nary observations he forms a hypothesis which he puts to the test by the method of trial and error. As mistaken hypotheses are gradually eliminated, he eventually forms one which suits the case, and thus he learns the nature of the compound with which he is experimenting. The hypothesis thus goes hand in hand with the method of trial and error in the higher learning processes of man.

Human learning proceeds through the process of attaching meanings to symbols. One of the performance tests used in

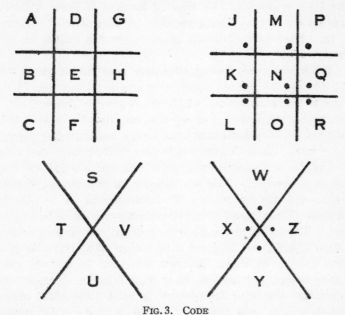

FIG. 3. CODE

measuring intelligence is the test of learning to use a code. One form of the test is one that was actually used as a code of signals during the American revolutionary war. Letters are arranged in certain geometrical designs, and the subjects are required to learn the place occupied by each of the letters. Then the spaces are shown without the letters, and the subject is asked to decipher certain code messages from the signals given. Obviously, this is a test in the use of meanings. Each symbol has its specific meaning attached, and the code becomes meaningless hieroglyphics to those who do not possess the key to the meanings. The same is true of all languages.   Language is simply a convenient method for communicating meanings, having significance only as the symbols are bearers of meanings.   Meanings have to be acquired. The bonds between certain symbols and their meanings have to be learned.   It is in social usage that these meanings are first attached to their symbols, whether they be letters, words, phrases or concepts.   The individual learns them through participating in the life of the group which first formed the bonds.   There is very little evidence of this type of learning in lower animals. Animals are thorough-going realists.   A thing is what it seems to be.   Food is food in the concrete, but the animal has no concept, food.

The human being has an advantage over the animal in the ability to persist without being overcome by distractions.   This is one of the characteristics which we observed to play an important part in attention.   And we observed that the lack of this ability is one of the characteristics of the feeble-minded person. In the test of discriminating weights, the feeble-minded child very soon begins to play with them and forgets that it began with the task of comparison.   This low capacity for attention is, without doubt, one of the reasons why the feeble-minded are so poor in learning.   They cannot attend consistently enough to be able to learn.   The animal also is likely to confront the same difficulty. Rats will sometimes lie down in the corner of a blind alley in a maze and go to sleep.   Animals act more impulsively than human beings, and tend to have their attention distracted to something other than the problem in hand.   The child, whose capacities have only begun to unfold is more easily turned aside than the adult.   The adult is better able to inhibit competing stimuli, and keep consciousness directed to the desired focus.   The more complicated the problem the greater is the necessity of being able to centre the attention on the one thing, and resist all competitive stimuli.

Observation plays an important part in human learning. Learning by observation is another of the advantages which the human being possesses over the animal.   We have made reference to the advantage which the adult human being has in insight.   Puzzle and other problems are solved with much more facility where the person observes and sees into the nature of the problem. While there is much truth in the proverb, 'we learn to do by doing', it does not tell the whole truth for human beings, who possess the additional capacity of learning to do by observing. By observation is not meant visual processes, but mental insight into the principles involved in the nature of the problem and of its solution. When a rat is placed in a maze, and after it has learned it, if the maze be turned by ninety degrees, the rat must learn it over again, but man is not perturbed by such a manipulation, because his power of observation comes to his assistance in the problem. Woodworth records[1] an experiment with a chimpanzee, which is admittedly one of the most intelligent of the lower animals, and which proves that even the most intelligent of the lower animals are lacking in that distinctively human capacity of observation. The experiment was with a puzzle-box such as we have already described. It learned to manipulate the button and open the door after three trials. But a second button completely upset its calculations. It would work with first one button and then the other, but apparently had not the ability to observe the way in which the button secured the door. The chimpanzee even continued to work at the place where the first button had been after the experimenter had removed it, showing that the extent of its observation was that of the locality in which to work. The experiments all indicate that animals acquire most of their learning by doing rather than by observation.

Observation by itself is not enough. It requires to be accompanied by practice. This is but to admit the elements of truth in the proverb, 'we learn to do by doing.' All the insight in the world regarding the principles involved in problems or relationships is of little account unless it is put to use. The native equipment of reaction tendencies is largely of the impulsive type. Control over the impulses, and action as the result of reflection can only come when practice accompanies observation. This is but to admit the potency of the Law of Use. It states that, other things being equal, when a particular

[1] Woodworth, *Psychology : A Study of Mental Life*, pp. 317 ff.

reaction has been used, it will tend to be repeated when the situation is repeated. It is obviously very important that care should be exercised in securing accuracy and satisfaction in the case of the first reaction. This involves great diligence on the part of the teacher who is guiding the child. He must consider the child's capacity in terms of speed, accuracy, development, persistency, etc., in order to direct the child in the acquirement of effective reactions and desirable habits.

Kennedy-Fraser calls attention to a mistake common to many teachers in correcting mistaken forms of reaction by emphasizing the incorrect method. This is to neglect the pedagogical significance of the process of attention. The author cites ' the all too common custom of publicly pillorying the bad spellers by placing before the class a list of the misspelled words, and even leaving it prominently exposed over a lengthy period. . . . The pupils are presumably at the stage of beginning to know these words, and every effort should be made to inculcate the correct spelling on as many different occasions as possible, and to avoid with even greater care any opportunity of stamping in the false impression. The better procedure in this case would be to place a list on the blackboard, or some other prominent position in the class-room, of the *correct* spellings of the misspelt words, and to draw the attention of the children to this correct spelling, without even hinting at the possible mistakes.'[1]

It is an old, old saying that ' practice makes perfect '. Exercise serves to strengthen the bond between a stimulus and its response. This is the reason for drill-work in school. It takes a good teacher so to arrange the time-table that there will be sufficient opportunity for exercise in desirable responses, without thoroughly sickening his pupils with the drill. Such arithmetical operations as are involved in learning the multiplication tables cannot become habitual bonds without plenty of exercise. The problem for the teacher is to make the pupils experience a need for such bonds, and thereafter the drill will not be quite so irksome. If the drill be made irksome, the teacher defeats his own purpose of stamping in the response by repetition and by the

---

[1] D. Kennedy-Fraser, *The Psychology of Education*, pp. 130 ff.

concomitant feeling of satisfaction. The law of exercise and the law of effect work together in close co-ordination.

The results of the learning process are a subject of interesting investigation. One of the results is the acquirement of certain habituated responses, and we shall make that the subject of our next study. Another is the feeling of satisfaction which accompanies a successful response. This affective element is one which cannot be overlooked, for its function is by no means negligible in the learning process. The feelings of satisfaction and dissatisfaction take their origin as 'immediate indices of the significance for the organism of the various stimuli and responses which enter its experience'.[1] They are 'signs in consciousness of the value'[2] of certain reactions with reference to their stimuli. The tendency is for us to repeat those responses to stimuli, when the stimuli reappear, which have on previous occasions been accompanied with emotional satisfaction, and to avoid those which on previous occasions were accompanied by painful consequences. We may revert to Thorndike's way of putting the same matter. He says that in the learning process there is a tendency to 'the selection of connections by use and satisfaction, and their elimination by disuse and annoyance'.[3] The significance of this factor for teaching is so plain that he who runs may read. In the stimulation of the development of learning in children, the teacher who so arranges the stimuli that the things the child ought to learn are accompanied by a feeling of agreeableness, whereas learning of undesirable responses is accompanied by annoyance, there will result a fixation of the desirable and an elimination of the undesirable. The specific ways in which these results are to be accomplished will have to be a matter of constant study on the part of the teacher with reference to the personalities, the problems and the environment. A neglect of the operation of the law of effect may result disastrously for the child's learning, by making the desirable painful and the undesirable agreeable.

One of the problems with which teachers are so often occu-

---

[1] Angell, *Psychology*, p. 320.   [2] Ibid., p. 320.
[3] Thorndike, *Educational Psychology*, Briefer Course, p. 137.

pied is that which concerns the rate of learning. How is a
teacher to know whether a child's learning is proceeding tardily,
normally, or speedily? Is there any exact data available to help
solve the problem? Happily for him, there has been a good deal
of investigation into this problem and the results are being made
available in books and journals. For example, psychological
studies have been conducted in the rate of improvement in
mastering telegraphy and typewriting. Bryan and Harter made
a study of the learning of telegraphy, and have plotted their
results in the forms of curves. The students were given weekly
tests to ascertain their speed in sending messages as well as
receiving them. The number of letters per minute, sent or
received, was regarded as the unit of measurement. The observations were that in the first few weeks there was rapid improvement, and after that a gradual falling off with another spurt later
on which again fell off until all progress ceased. In the 'curve
of learning' this period of scarcely any improvement which
follows the initial success is known as 'the plateau of learning'.
Teachers will have many occasions to observe the plateau in the
learning of children, and many will be able to observe the same
phenomenon in their own experiences. Students of typewriting
very frequently pass through a period of great discouragement.
They attain a speed of thirty or forty words per minute within
the first two months, and then for weeks, no matter how much
they practice, very little improvement is indicated. They become
quite disheartened, and some even give it up as a bad job. But
those who persist wake up some day to find that they are
considerably improved, and can write sixty or seventy words per
minute. The plateau of learning represents a period of practice
in which bonds are being formed to which the student eventually
becomes so habituated that he is able to execute his reactions
with a considerable increase in speed. The phenomenon of the
plateau ought to be familiar to every teacher, so that he will not
be discouraged with the inevitable periods of practice which are
necessary for the fixing of bonds in the learning process, but will
persist in his efforts to make his pupils persist in their practice.

Some of the subjects in an ordinary school curriculum do not
lend themselves as readily to accurate measurement as telegraphy

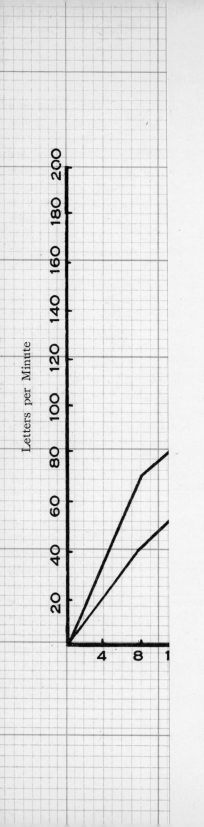

and typewriting, where the number of words or letters per minute in the subjects' performance can be measured with accuracy at any stage in the learning process. Nevertheless, any teacher who so desires can devise experiments of his own for the observation and measurement of the learning process in the pupils under his direction.

One of the pedagogical problems which enters into the discussion of the psychology of learning is the problem of the transfer of training, or formal discipline. In the older educational systems there were included subjects which were regarded as possessing especially formal value, giving a training in certain processes and abilities which was regarded as transferable to other subjects. The basal principles of this view, have been summarized by Drever as follows: '(1) Exercise and effort develop mental power, in so far as they are exercise and effort, and independently of the mode of the exercise, or the direction of the effort. (2) It is possible to develop separately the child's " power of observation ", memory, etc., in a perfectly general way, by the exercise of these " powers " in any material. (3) The exercise of the mind in any subject develops the mind as a whole, although subjects may differ in their value for all-round development.' [1] The first statement is not quite the same as the Law of Exercise, but it contains this much truth that real work is essential to the educative processes. The question that needs to be experimentally verified is whether work in one sphere will develop power for work in another. The second statement is condemned by the fallacy of treating mental abilities as piecemeal and separable in the fashion of the old faculty psychology. The third statement is right, in so far as it treats the mind as a unity in its development, but it is questionable whether there is any general factor of intelligence [2] that profits by work in any direction whatever.

The older idea in education was that such a transfer of the educational benefits of training was possible. For example, if a student proved to be good in mastering Tamil, and afterwards good in mastering Hindustani, it was concluded that the proficiency

---

[1] Drever, *An Introduction to the Psychology of Education*, pp. 165-66.

[2] See above, pp. 45 ff.

gained in studying Tamil had been a decisive factor in enabling him to get Hindustani. But the question probably should be approached from quite a different point of view. The real reason is more likely to be an innate capacity for mastering languages which stood him in good stead in both cases. Other familiar examples are the old notions that the study of mathematics is going to develop some hypothetical general power of reasoning, and that nature study is designed to develop a hypothetical general power of observation. The questions involved are mainly two: (i) whether there are ' general powers ' of reasoning, observation, or anything else; (ii) whether improvement in one mental function has any appreciable influence on the efficiency of other functions. The first of these questions has significance only for those who adopt the doctrine of a general intelligence or mental ability—a general factor underlying particular capacities. For those who follow the lead of Thorndike and hold that abilities are specific, the problem falls to the ground.

As to the second question, it can only be answered satisfactorily on the basis of experiment and observation. A fairly considerable amount of experimental work in the field has been done in recent years. The method frequently followed is by observation of improvement in ' control groups '. A few initial tests are made after which the group is divided into two smaller groups of equal size, and whose abilities are approximately equal according to the indications from the first test: one group, called the ' control group ', is subjected to special training, whereas the other is subjected as much as possible to identical conditions minus the special training. After the period of training the groups are again tested and the relative differences in their performances noted. Some of the experiments tried are as to whether (i) memory for poetry facilitates memory for sounds; (ii) memory for colours facilitates memory for sounds; (iii) memory for nonsense syllables facilitates memory for poetry; (iv) practice with the right hand facilitates skill in the use of the left hand; (v) practice with one eye in controlled perception influences the other eye to improve.

There are a number of cases wherein a certain degree of improvement is noted. But even then the investigators have hesitated to say that it was due to a transfer of training. Bagley was one of the first to suggest that it might be due to the influence of some other factor, hitherto unconsidered, such as the fixation of an ideal which influenced the performance of the student in any subject. Thorndike finds that improvement is evident in so far as the two functions under consideration have as factors identical elements.[1] He puts the matter as follows : ' The bonds whose strengthening and weakening constitute the changes in condition of mental functions in a man are not each utterly independent of the rest, but are related to form the obvious dynamic unity which the intellect, character, taste and skill of any one man displays. What happens to any one bond makes differences to other bonds in the same man that it does not make to those bonds in a different man. The amount of difference made ranges from cases where a change in one bond causes or constitutes an almost equal change in another, to cases where the change in one produces approximately zero changes in the other. The nature of the difference made ranges from cases where the whole effect of the strengthening or weakening of one bond acts to produce a corresponding effect on another, to cases where the whole effect of its strengthening is to weaken, and of its weakening to strengthen the other.'[2]

The same author goes on to show that if there be any transfer of tendencies, it is as evident on the negative as on the positive side. Learning involves the ' dropping out ' or ' driving out ' of bonds which, for some reason or other, are considered to be undesirable. In other words, learning includes inhibition. A transfer of the tendency to inhibit or neglect is as much within the sphere of possibility as the transfer of a tendency towards positive action. But whether the transfer be of a positive or a negative tendency it depends on the degree of identical elements in the two functions. The change, whether positive or negative, in the second function is quantitatively on account of the change in the factors common to the two functions. An example in point is that ability to multiply is facilitated by improvement in

---

[1] Thorndike, *Educational Psychology*, Briefer Course, p. 268.
[2] Ibid. p. 259.

adding, due to the fact that adding is one of the factors in multiplying.

The most significant result of the experimental work has been to give us much more well defined knowledge in regard to the matter of transfer of training. General abstract conclusions have been superseded by scientific inductions on the basis of experiment and accurate observation. The former tendency to emphasize the subject was in part due to the influence of the older faculty psychology which organized the curriculum as it did the mind on the basis of water-tight compartments. The present emphasis is on function and unity, and one inevitable result is that training is regarded as a matter of the person rather than the subject. The Project Method which is based on the purposive act is one of the modern methods which aims at a close correlation of all the activities and processes around a central task. Training and its transfer is not simply a matter of association of ideas, but is tied up with the entire conational tendency of the individual.

LITERATURE

E. B. Thorndike. *The Psychology of Learning.* Columbia University Press, 1913.

S. S. Colvin. *The Learning Process.* Macmillan, 1914.

E. Meumann. *The Psychology of Learning.* Appleton, 1913.

D. Starch. *Educational Psychology.* Macmillan, 1922.

J. Dewey. *How We Think.* Heath, 1910.

I. E. Miller. *The Psychology of Thinking.* Macmillan, 1909.

W. B. Pillsbury. *The Psychology of Reasoning.* Appleton,

L. T. Hobhouse. *Mind in Evolution.* Macmillan, 1915.

J. B. Watson. *Behaviour.* Henry Holt, 1914.

J. Drever. *An Introduction to the Psychology of Education.* Arnold, 1923.

CHAPTER VII

HABIT FORMATION

FROM the biological point of view we have defined the learning process as the gradual selection of the most satisfactory
responses to stimuli.   As that process proceeds these satisfactory
responses have a tendency to become more and more firmly
established.   The more advanced the learning process, the more
facility is attained in the performance, and consequently the less
the amount of voluntary attention that is necessary for the
performance.   Thus, habitual reactions are simply one form of
the learning process, and are best understood in their biological
setting as reactions which by virtue of repetition and satisfaction
have attained such a degree of facility as to demand a minimum
of conscious attention.   In that sense habit may be defined as
'that characteristic set of the psycho-physical mechanism which
accounts for the facilitation of certain reactions, and the inhibition of other inconsistent or opposed reactions, under conditions
dependent upon the previous growth and activities of the
mechanism.   In this sense of the word, there are as many habits
as there are possible groupings of the reactions.'[1]

In the biological usage of the word, we may speak of the
habits of plants and other animals as well as of man.   It applies
in this sense not alone to the fixed tendency to respond in a
particular way to a given stimulus, but also to the characteristic
mode of the organism's growth or of the occurrence of its
structures and functions.   Thus the word is applied both to the

---

[1] *Standard Dictionary*, 2nd Edition.

acquired and the congenital.　Instincts are sometimes spoken of
as racial habits, though, as we have seen, they are congenital types
of reaction.　However, as a general rule the word 'habit' is
reserved for the acquired type of reaction in distinction from
reflexive and instinctive reactions, which share with them in the
tendency towards a particular form of response in preference to
others.　There is, in many cases, a further affinity in that the
selection of reactions which shall become habitual rests upon a
basis of instinctive tendencies.　The habit depends upon the
experience of the individual to the extent that the stimulus is
directed into one neural pathway in preference to another, but
that preference grows out of the nature of the person, the instinctive tendencies to act in a particular way.

At other times the habitual reactions are describable as
modifications of instinctive tendencies and forms of behaviour.
There is an instinctive disposition to run away from certain
animals, and that tendency is accompanied by the emotion of
fear.　Experience may lead to either of two forms of modification.　It may result in an intensification, or in a reduction in
intensity.　A child who is naturally afraid of a dog may learn
to assume an attitude of friendliness, and if any of the original
tendencies remain, they are at least suppressed.　Darwin argued
that many types of emotional expression, both in men and in
animals, are reduced forms of instinctive behaviour.　He claimed
that some of the habitual facial expressions of human beings
are reductions of early forms of activity in the mouth and jaw
muscles which originally accompanied actual combat.　Thus,
our habitual types of reactions to certain situations are reduced
forms of grosser instinctive reactions that were originally useful
in the struggle for existence.　According to this view, while
experience alters the forms of reactions, and directs what shall
become finally habitual, the vast majority of the tendencies and
possibilities in the psycho-physical mechanism are present from
birth.

But this is not the whole story of habit-formation.　Some
of them at least cannot be traced to any typical instinctive
reactions.　There are stimuli with which we are sometimes
presented to which we are unable to respond on the basis of

any inherited tendencies. To be sure, the stimulus will ulti-mately issue in a discharge of motor energy in some part of the body, but that discharge is not pre-determined in harmony with any inherited organization. In some cases the stimulus incites an excitation which is widely diffused throughout the organism, and the organs which provide for its final discharge are selected or learned. The process is one of modification and accommodation in which the organism eventually determines the type of response which will be most appropriate or effec-tive, and practises that until it becomes habitual. We may take the example of a child learning to write. At the outset there is no control but a general diffusion of energy, which may find expression in facial contortions and wriggling of the legs and body as well as movements of the arm and hand. It is only gradually that the child learns that movements of the lips and jaws, knees and feet, are quite superfluous, and inhibiting them, directs all his energy to the arm-hand movements. These two certain co-ordinations require to be definitely learned and fixed. There is no original tendency towards the co-ordination of the thumb and fingers with that harmony necessary to good writing, involved in making the various typical strokes of the pen or pencil. It is not always the case that diffuse movements are quite eliminated even in adults, but the tendency is in the direction of a control which at once eliminates the unnecessary, and fixes the desirable movements. But what-ever be the ultimate result as to necesssary and unnecessary movements, those which become fixed determine the writing habits of the individual. Very frequently it is the unnecessary movements which have not been eliminated or the irregular movements which have not been controlled, that mark the person's writing habits off from those of others.

One of the problems which arise is as to how certain bonds between stimulus and response become so firmly established as to make the reactions habitual, sometimes even automatic. One suggestion is in terms of feeling. Successful acts are said to be accompanied by pleasure, and unsuccessful acts by pain, the tendency being to persist in that which is pleasant and to inhibit that which is unpleasant. Another modification of

8

this explanation is that harmfulness incites an organism to inhibit and helpfulness to establish a reaction. It must be admitted that animals respond positively to certain types of stimuli and negatively to others, and that in the long run a species of animal will respond positively to harmless and negatively to harmful stimuli. On the other hand, there is plenty of evidence for misdirected tendencies of both the positive and negative sorts. Young children and young animals frequently respond positively to certain objects, which are at first very attractive, but which soon prove to be harmful. It is astonishing how few children will accept the judgement of their elders that fire burns. They have to burn their own fingers before they learn, and form a negative habit towards it. Equally so, the child frequently has to learn to establish positive tendencies towards objects such as certain kinds of nourishing food, which he at first regards as unpleasant. This may be taken as a biological tendency then, if not as a basis for universal explanation. In the long run we tend to form positive habits towards the pleasant or harmless, and negative towards the unpleasant or harmful.

Another suggestion has been made by some psychologists, that the successful act is invariably fixed, and the unsuccessful one eliminated. Like the previous explanation, this one accounts for some of the facts, but not for all of them. A little observation will make it plain that there are movements that not only are unconnected with successful responses, but actually delay them which sometimes become fixed. This has been observed with certain animals in puzzle-boxes and mazes. And it may be observed in the case of handwriting. Some people form the habit of making movements with the lips as if pronouncing the words which they write, and find it almost impossible to inhibit the tendency even consciously. The superfluous movements have become so thoroughly fixed that they are not easily eliminated even with conscious attention. If the unsuccessful movements were never fixed along with the successful ones, it would mean a great simplification of the learning process. The investigation of most habits discloses the fact that it is only rarely that successful movements alone are fixed.

The behaviouristic school explains the fixation of reactions as due to two factors which are by far the most significant—frequency and recency. These principles state that the more frequently a given response to a stimulus occurs, and the more recently it has occurred, the greater likelihood is there of its recurrence. It may be that unsuccessful movements may occur along with the successful, and unless the successful is repeated relatively more often than the unsuccessful it will not be fixed. But the repetition of a movement or of any response serves eventually to produce fairly permanent modifications in the nervous system, so that frequency has the effect of making the response more permanent. The principle of drill in subjects of the school curriculum is precisely that. Let the child repeat the operations of the multiplication table sufficiently frequently, and they become a part of him. It is also true that responses which have been made more recently are more likely to recur. That is why so many students burn the midnight oil just before an examination. They believe that the recency of stimulation will be more likely to call forth the appropriate responses. And it is true, providing that other factors are of equal force. But sometimes fatigue more than counterbalances the influence of frequency, and the student's midnight cramming actually does more harm than good.

There is not any single principle which accounts for habit-formation of all types, but we may find it beneficial for educational purposes to summarize the various operating principles, as the principles of (i) stimulus, (ii) plasticity, (iii) impetus, (iv) exercise, and (v) persistence.

1. The principle of stimulus has reference to the characteristic preference for associated stimuli and responses to recur. If a mental attitude or a physical state is made to follow or to accompany a given situation, it will tend to go with that situation in the future. This principle of connection-forming furnishes education, according to Thorndike,[1] with two important maxims: (a) 'Put together what should go together and keep apart what should not go together'; (b) 'Reward desirable con-

---

[1] Thorndike, *Educational Psychology*, Briefer Course, p. 142.

nections and make undesirable connections produce discomfort.'
These principles are particularly valuable for the beginnings of
learning processes. The aim of the teacher is to direct the child
so that bonds may be formed as easily and rapidly as possible
between stimuli and appropriate responses, whether in writing,
spelling, arithmetical operations, the use of language, reasoning
processes, building a house or managing a garden. The most
careful attention needs to be given to the earlier stage of the
learning. Suggestions need to be positive and desirable. Some
teachers make the mistake of putting together, in the form of a
prohibition, perhaps, what they want kept apart, and then blame
the children for the result.   I heard of a teacher who, à propos of
nothing, announced to the class a rule that no one should climb
up the drainage pipe at the side of the schoolroom.   The children had never thought of the idea until the teacher suggested it,
but during the first recess period after the rule was announced
several boys tried the experiment. It is not necessary to ask
whose fault it was.

One form of punishment, which has been all too common, is
that of keeping children in after school hours to complete incomplete tasks or correct incorrect work. This practice has the
tendency to establish an unfortunate association in the child's
consciousness between school work and punishment, so that the
child's habitual attitude towards his school work is one of disagreeableness. If it be necessary to administer punishments,
teachers should avoid the mistake of so administering them that
the child will attach the sense of disagreeableness to the school
activities themselves. If that be done, the teacher defeats his
own ends.

2. The principle of plasticity is simply that the younger the
child is the more plastic will be his mind. By plasticity we mean
that quality which makes a structure or an organism weak enough
to yield to influence, but strong enough not to yield all at once.
One of the characteristics of childhood is plasticity. Childhood
is the impressionable or formative period of thought, speech,
and other forms of activity. The ways of acting and thinking
have not as yet become fixed in moulds or unalterable channels.
The whole psycho-physical organism is pliable, the psychical part

of it just as surely as the physical.   Habit means the formation of a fixed way of doing something.   It therefore depends on a certain degree of plasticity, while it also tends to put an end to that plasticity.   It is only possible to form a habitual way of doing something because the organism is plastic enough to be moulded in a particular fashion.   But once the organism has become so moulded, it is much more difficult to achieve a new way of acting which runs counter to the old.   In other words, the formation of the habit has robbed the organism of a considerable degree of its plasticity in relation to a given situation.

The principle of plasticity reminds us anew of the necessity of exercising great care in the direction of children during the formative period.   Other things being equal, it is just as easy for a child to form a good habit as a bad one during the impressionable period.   There is nothing in the nature of the organism itself that makes it display an appreciably greater degree of plasticity towards undesirable ways of doing things than towards desirable ways.   It is true, of course, that our inheritance sometimes results in the extraordinary persistence of some trait which may modify the amount of plasticity to a certain degree.   This may sometimes be a matter of small significance, but at other times something more serious.   If it be colour-blindness it does not matter nearly so much as feeble-mindedness.   But it is generally acknowledged that the environment has much more to do in determining the habitual forms which our reactions take than has heredity.

The relation between heredity and environment has been very well illustrated from the use of language.

' If a being had no vocal organs from which issue articulate sounds, if he had no auditory or other sense-receptors and no connections between the two sets of apparatus, it would be a sheer waste of time to try to teach him to converse.   He is born short in that respect, and education must accept the limitation.   But if he has this native equipment, its possession in no way guarantees that he will ever talk any language or what language he will talk.   The environment in which his activities occur and by which they are carried into execution settles these things.   If he lived in a dumb unsocial environment where men refused to talk to one another and used only that minimum of gestures without which they could not get along, vocal language would be as unachieved by him as if he had no vocal organs. If the sounds which he makes occur in a medium of persons speaking the Chinese language, the activities which make like sounds will be selected and co-ordinated.' [1]

3. The principle of impetus is that the greater the energy and attention directed to the acquisition of a habit, the more quickly will the end in view be realized. This principle offers a powerful argument for close attention to the question of motive. If the motive force be powerful, the habit-forming tendency will be facilitated; if it be weak the habit-forming tendency will likewise be weak. The advantage of being able to make a powerful appeal to the child's own interests will be obvious to any teacher. A study of each individual personality will disclose to the teacher certain fundamental interests, and he will do well to try to relate the work of the child to those interests, at the same time studying methods for broadening the scope of his interests. The reason for making use of rewards and punishments is to create interests and motives which will aid the teacher in securing the attention of the child to whatever he wants him to acquire. There needs to be a much more rational use of rewards and punishments than sometimes exists. Rewards ought to be associated with good impulses. Some parents pay no attention to their children so long as they are quiet and are not getting into mischief. But if they are cranky and inclined to weep, they play with them. So they encourage the children to simulate crankiness or to form habits of crying, so as to get what they want from their parents. So the good impetus is quite neglected while the bad one is rewarded—an indirect invitation to cultivate undesirable habits.

There is very seldom any doubt about there being energy enough in the child to do all the work which the educative process demands of him. If there is not, of course it is a case for medical advice. The problem is seldom that of arousing energy, but much more frequently that of directing it into

---

[1] Dewey, *Democracy and Education*, p. 87 f.

desirable channels. There is something wrong with the conduct of a school if boys who display boundless energy in such games as football and hockey are not stimulated in such a way that they put themselves into their academic work. Students do not find it difficult to put forth effort if the appeal of the study is of such a character as to arouse their interests. They must be made to see the usefulness or purposefulness of what they are doing. It is only in this fashion that any vital interest is possible. The advantage of such a method as the Project Method is precisely that. It links the school performances of children to purposeful acts which appeal to the children's interests, and give direction to their energies. To make such desirable responses habitual is one of the aims of education, an end that can be attained much more readily if the subject so appeals that the student throws his energy into the undertaking.

4. The principle of exercise is that, other things being equal, exercise tends to strengthen the bond between situation and response. Thorndike includes in his 'law of exercise' the two subsidiary laws of use and disuse.[1] Use strengthens the connection between a given situation and response, and disuse weakens it. This is a principle with the operation of which we are quite familiar from everyday experience. We learn to run by running, to play football by playing football, to write by writing, to speak by speaking, and to reason by reasoning. The knowledge of all the theories of the technique of learning is of much less value than actual practice. No habit is acquired by theorizing, unless it be the habit of theorizing. But habits are acquired by actually doing the thing over and over again, until the connection between the situation and its response becomes so deeply ingrained in the organism that the occurrence of the situation is sufficient to ensure the calling forth of the habituated response, often quite automatically.

It is characteristic of habitual responses that conscious attention to the appropriate response is reduced to a minimum. That is of inestimable value to the advancement of the learning process. If conscious attention can be released from a given

---

[1] Thorndike, *Educational Psychology*, Briefer Course, p. 70.

response which has become so familiar as to be automatic, it is then free for other fresh undertakings, and learning may thus be advanced.   At the same time the removal of conscious attention is not an unmitigated advantage.   For there are some things that we get into the habit of doing so that the habit asserts itself sometimes inconveniently.   James[1] tells of a gentleman who went to his room to dress for a dinner to which he had been invited. It was habit for him to retire when he removed his clothes after darkness had fallen.   His attention became directed to something else so that he simply followed the routine of habit, and when he had removed his clothes he went to bed instead of putting on others. What we call 'absent-mindedness' is explained on this basis. The so-called absent-minded person concentrates his attention on certain activities so thoroughly, that he is completely governed by habit in others, and does certain things so automatically that it would appear that the mind is absent from the performance.   It has frequently been possible to identify criminals and others, about whom doubts have arisen, through certain 'mannerisms' which are nothing more than manners of responding to certain stimuli which through long practice have become so habitual as to be automatic.   Nevertheless, the possible dangers of too much automatism in conduct must not prevent us from appreciating the value of saving energy and labour by learning certain useful things so well that their performance becomes second nature. For the strengthening of a bond through exercise at once increases the efficiency of the response, and releases energy for the conquering of new worlds.

5. The fifth principle of habit-formation is that of persistence or continuity, which is that an uninterrupted continuity of performance under similar circumstances tends to the strengthening of the bond between stimulus and response.   'It was by persistence that the mouse ate the cable,' runs the proverb. And the lesson which Robert Bruce learned from the spider was precisely this lesson of persistence.   This is a principle to which he must attend especially who would overcome an undesirable habit.   If one sets out to overcome a habit, he must be eternally

[1] James, *Principles of Psychology*, vol. i, p. 115.

vigilant so as to win all the battles. We need scarcely be
reminded that habits are not ' broken '. A habit means that a
bond between a particular stimulus and response has been fixed
in the nervous system. But the nervous system is not brittle so
that a habit can be broken off. The only possible way to get
rid of an undesirable habit is to form a new one, a new pathway
in the nervous system, a new bond between the old stimulus and
a new kind of response. The only way to be sure of success is to
keep everlastingly at it, suffering no defeats and no exceptions
until at last the victory is achieved.

One of the most powerful aids to persistency in the habit-forming process is the maintenance of the appropriate emotional attitude.
A persistently repeated stimulus, even when accompanied by the
appropriate and desired motor response, may quite fail to produce
the habit desired if the emotional response or desired success is
lacking. It may even produce the contrary result of repulsion.
When we strive or persist in striving towards a certain end, there
is always present with our striving a strength or intensity which
varies with our striving. That is, there is a qualitative element
in experience which varies with the quantitative. The impulse
to action or to habit-formation carries with it the emotional
element of craving or feeling with reference to the goal. The
element of persistency is thus in part an emotional experience,
and the emotional experience is in part an impulse to action.
So that the securing of that persistency necessary to habit-formation depends in a measure on the appropriate emotional attitude,
the positive self-feeling which determines us to persist until we
dominate the situation.

One of the investigations which modern psychologists have
carried on concerns the most effective way of distributing practice
so as to secure the best results in acquiring new habits. There is
general agreement that there must be persistency, but the
problem is as to how that persistency is best expressed. It has
been found that it does not pay to persist with practising any
functions too continuously without rest, for the element of
fatigue will set in and interfere with progress. Take, for example,
the goal of building up good habits in arithmetical processes—
addition, subtraction, division and multiplication. Experiments

have been tried in varying the length of the practice periods and intervals.   For example, practice periods may be ten of 60 minutes, or twenty of 30 minutes, or forty of 15 minutes, or they may be made a series varying in length, either by gradual lengthening or gradual shortening.   Different practice groups of approximately equal average ability may be tried with the various methods and the results observed.   Thorndike gives the results of a number of experiments from which he concludes that 'the experimental results obtained justify in a rough way the avoidance of very long practice periods and of very short intervals.'[1]

The social significance of habits is a matter of considerable importance for the educational psychologist.   There are two sides to this subject which demand some consideration.   In the first place there is one group of habits which may be called 'social habits', inasmuch as they are the characteristic modes of behaviour of all the members of a group.   In the second place there falls to be considered the significance for the social life of the habits of individuals who comprise society.   We need not delay long in considering so-called social habits, as that is a problem of social psychology into which we cannot enter deeply in this connection. Nevertheless, we would not seem to slight so important a matter. The truth is that a much larger percentage of our habitual ways of acting than we ordinarily acknowledge are to be explained by the fact that we belong to certain groups with customary ways of reacting to various situations.   Facts of social structure are among the most important facts in determining tendencies to behaviour.   The kinds of clothing that we wear, food that we eat, houses that we inhabit, language that we use, books that we read, utensils that we employ, gestures that we make, social etiquette that we follow, colours that we admire, sounds that we prefer, odours and tastes that we enjoy, and rites that we perform are among the scores of habits that are for all of us largely determined by the group.   We are members of various groups, ethnic, national, political, family, academic, literary, recreational, caste, religious and so on.   Each one of the groups has gradually built up its own ways of doing things.   We

---

[1] Thorndike, *Educational Psychology*, Briefer Course, p. 206.

individuals who comprise the groups find ourselves in these groups, dropping into the ways of the social environment, often quite unconsciously. The cultivation of accents and mannerisms is very often a much less conscious process that the uncritical observer thinks. Some persons have a much greater degree of susceptibility to social influences than others, and readily adopt the ways of the groups in which they find themselves. This is sometimes explained as due to an instinctive imitativeness, and at other times as the operation of a group consciousness, which for the time being results in a sublimation of the individual consciousness. Another theory is that it is due either to comradeship or submissiveness. According to this last view gregariousness is not the name of an individual instinct, but a sort of generic term for that element of responsiveness, without which group life would be impossible. That responsiveness may take either the form of dominance and acceptance with the concomitant attitudes of assertiveness and submissiveness, or the form of regarding the other of the social environment as an equal, thus creating a tendency to comradeship.[1] Whatever may be the accepted explanation of the facts, it is plain that the social environment exerts a very marked influence on the individual as a determinant of many of his habits of thought and action.

There is the second phase to the influence of the environment on the habit-forming tendency. The individual who forms habits, be they never so particular, acquires them within the social environment. The environment presents to him the stimuli for action and the limits within which his responses are possible. This function of the social environment has been compared to the use of the air in a biological environment. The organic structures are quite individualistic, each organism having its own lungs and heart and sense organs. But the air is necessary for the functioning of these organs, for the maintenance of life. It is the same air, which carries sounds in waves, and beats down great trees when cyclonic, but in this case purifies the blood and sustains the life processes. So the group may have other functions to fulfil, such as dancing, making war, conducting

---

[1] F. C. Bartlett, *Psychology and Primitive Culture*, pp. 36 and 86.

a political meeting, or performing a religious ceremony. Yet it also ministers to the individual in affording an atmosphere in which native impulses may express themselves. There is no doubt that habits do include elements that are distinctly personal or subjective. But these also depend for their opportunity of expression on a social atmosphere, and frequently their most useful and permanent expressions are of a social character. A love for flowers may be the incentive for interesting one's self in the water supply and the matter of irrigation. Fondness for symmetry may find a useful outlet in architecture or town planning. Taste for outdoor employment might drive on to a study of soil chemistry yielding valuable social results. All of these personal tendencies have their particular drives, frequently leading to consequences of first-rate social importance. Indeed, personal traits can never find satisfactory expression within the limits of an entirely individualistic experience, but demand a world with other people in it. This is one of the essentials at the basis of the modern Project Method. The project is the purposive act which affords the individual the social atmosphere in which he can develop. The purposive act is so because it is socially useful, and that fact offers an effectual stimulus for the child to put the necessary energy into the task. Then the new way of acting has to be acquired in the midst of other people in various stages of progress in the same project. The individual takes his place as a member of the group that is doing things. His newly acquired habits are thus socially motivated, socially conditioned, and socially worthful.

The matter is capable of further illustration from the field of morals. It need scarcely be said that morality depends upon society for its existence. Both as to the attitude it assumes and the technique it employs it is social. There is no such thing as a moral vacuum wherein a person can achieve a moral life strictly his own. 'Some activity proceeds from a man, then it sets up reactions in the surroundings. Others approve, disapprove, protest, encourage, share and resist. Even letting a man alone is a definite response. Envy, admiration and imitation are complicities. Neutrality is non-existent. Conduct is always shared; this is the difference between it and a physiological process. It is not an ethical "ought" that conduct *should be* social. It *is* social, whether bad or good."[1]

Habits serve as social functions in making possible a great conservation of energy, both physical and intellectual. If one could imagine a society in which no activities were habituated, he would necessarily picture to himself a society in which progress was exceedingly slow, if indeed there were any at all. The reason for this is that when a reaction gains in proficiency to the extent that it can be completed without conscious attention, then the attentive processes are released for other activities. So long as we have to focus the attention on a particular performance it means that so much energy is being utilized, while the ability to execute a reaction automatically means that the energy, otherwise required when the reaction is consciously performed, is released for other activities. This results in a great facilitation of the learning process. If we never acquired any reactions with sufficient facility to be able to perform them automatically, we would have to direct the mental and motor processes in a conscious way to every segment of behaviour. The significance of this for education is far-reaching, for progress in learning, such as in memorizing, in the attainment of motor skill or in a reasoning process is possible, because certain responses are learned well enough to become habits, and so can be performed while consciousness is directed to new undertakings. This is quite as true of collective activities as of individual. Certain ways of meeting situations become habits. Social habits are folk ways. Inasmuch as they are performed unconsciously by the various members of a group, the group is left free to expend its collective energy on the facing of new problems. In addition to that there is a division of labour among the constituents of the group, and division of labour is a group habit which plays a very important part in releasing collective energy for a wider range of tasks. If each member of the group had to think about the construction of his own house, the preparation of cloth for the making of his clothes, the production as well as the preparation of his food, and so on throughout all the minutiæ of everything he

---

[1] Dewey, *Human Nature and Conduct*, pp. 16 ff. The entire chapter on ' Habits as Social Functions ' is exceedingly valuable.

uses, it would demand such an expenditure of energy that scientific progress would be seriously obstructed. The division of labour means that certain men are freed for research and other study, and the entire group reaps the advantage.

Habits may also be considered as means to ends. It has been pointed out that in order to appreciate this phase of the habit-forming tendency men have had to take themselves to such undesirable habits as foolish idling, gambling and addiction to alcohol.[1] The net result for some people has been to draw the conclusion that habits are all bad, and the habit-forming tendency an enemy of the race. So-and-so is 'a creature of habit' is thus used as a term of opprobrium. We must remember, however, that there is nothing intrinsically wrong with being a ' creature of habit ', the harm coming only when one becomes a creature of bad habits. It is true that

> ' Small habits well pursued betimes
> May reach the dignity of crimes.'—*Hannah More.*

But it is likewise true that they may reach the dignity of a glorious life and character.

' We may think ', says Dewey, ' of habits as meanings, waiting, like tools in a box, to be used by conscious resolve. But they are something more than that. They are active means, means that project themselves, energetic and dominating ways of acting.' Very frequently the formation of wrong habits is accompanied by a neglect, perhaps deliberate, of the character of habits as means to ends. Whenever we are thoroughly aware of the bond between a means and an end, we are in a position to judge whether or not the end is desirable. If we see that certain tendencies of behaviour are leading in the direction of a habit that will be injurious, the rational thing to do is to inhibit the expression of those tendencies. Conversely, we know that the kind of personality which we desire is only possible by an accumulation of good habits, and, if we are wise, we endeavour to make use of the available means for the accomplishment of the end. Thus the formation of habits has a distinctly conative phase. If the habits are once formed, then we are in a position

---

[1] Dewey, *Human Nature and Conduct*, pp. 24 ff.

to evoke their operation at will, in short to turn them to account for conscious purposes. The significance of this for the teacher is far-reaching. It is not only a matter of helping children build up desirable habits, but also of aiding them in thinking through the consequences of their acts and thoughts in terms of their ultimate effect on the moulding of character. This is a sphere wherein the teaching of history and literature—the teaching of the humanities—may be put to good account in bringing the youth to a clear understanding of the nature of habits as means to ends.

The conservative tendency of habits is of double significance. While it sets free the energies of the individual or group, it has also the tendency of deadening initiative and stifling change. The longer one acts in a particular way, the more difficult does it become to break away from that way of acting. Habits indeed are the inert factor in human nature. It is a constant struggle for the child and for the teacher guiding the child to avoid the temptations of yielding to inertia. But this is a call for the more persistent effort. Even in the realm of physics the doctrine of absolute inertia in any form has been expelled. Man is essentially an active creature. He cannot avoid acting, and there is no need to suppose that in respect of any particular habit he ever attains such inertia that change is impossible. 'While there is life, there is hope' for the building up of new habits and the subduing of old ones. It may require much time and patience to bring about the desired change, but it is characteristic of the organism that it is modifiable, so that attention and persistence may accomplish what seems all but impossible. The other side of the matter is that once a desirable habit has been acquired, the habit tends to conserve for us the acquisition. The problem is to ensure that our acquisitions are worthy of preservation.

LITERATURE

Wm. James. *Principles of Psychology*. Henry Holt, 1890.

J. R. Angell. *Psychology*. Constable, 1908.

C. Lloyd Morgan. *Habit and Instinct*. Arnold, 1896.

J. Dewey. *Human Nature and Conduct*. George Allen & Unwin, 1922.

C. H. Cooley. *Human Nature and the Social Order*. Scribner's, 1902.

E. B. Thorndike. *Educational Psychology*, Briefer Course. Columbia University Press, 1914.

C. H. Judd. *Psychology*. Charles Scribner's Sons, 1907.

W. McDougall. *An Outline of Psychology*. Methuen, 1924.

M. F. Washburn. *The Animal Mind*. Macmillan, 1917.

CHAPTER VIII

THE MEMORY PROCESSES

BIOLOGICAL MEMORY—THE MEMORY IMAGE—ANALYSIS OF THE MEMORY PROCESSES—EXPERIMENTS IN THE PSYCHOLOGY OF MEMORY—ECONOMY IN MEMORIZING—MENTAL INCUBATION—PART AND WHOLE LEARNING—THE PSYCHOLOGY OF FORGETTING.

THE memory processes, like the processes of habit-formation, are special cases of the learning processes, and consequently much that has been said in the last two chapters has reference to the problem of remembering. It may be remarked at the outset that there are differences in the breadth of meaning which different scholars attach to the word, or at least difference in the method of analysis. Some writers[1] use the word as practically equivalent to retentiveness, though they would no doubt admit that the retention was for the purpose of recall. Again others[2] analyze the process into impressions, retention, and recall. Still others[3] distinguish four separate processes, viz. learning, retention, recall and recognition.

Presumably most of us have a general idea of the meanings of remembering and forgetting which serve us for practical purposes, though we may not be able to describe the processes with any degree of definiteness. By remembering we ordinarily mean to keep a thing in mind so that we shall be able to recall it when required, and by forgetting the inability to bear a thing in mind so that it can be recalled when required. But such a popular notion does not explain anything. We are still left with the question of trying to analyze just what the nature of the

[1] e.g. Beatrice Edgell, *Theories of Memory*. Oxford University Press, 1924.

[2] e.g. C. H. Judd, *Psychology*, p. 234, and D. Kennedy-Fraser, *Psychology of Education*, p. 106.

[3] e.g. R. S. Woodworth, *Psychology: A Study of Mental Life*, p 332.

process is whereby we 'keep a thing in mind', so that it can be recalled. It must be admitted that no final solution of that problem has yet been achieved. It is a problem concerning which a considerable amount of theorizing has been done on the basis of introspection. The interest in the problem has been epistemological as well as psychological. But in recent times a good deal of light has been thrown on the problem from two sources, biology and experimental psychology.

Remembering is a biological conception. As far back as 1870 Prof. Ewald Hering read a paper before the Imperial Academy of Science at Vienna on 'Memory as a Universal Function of Organized Matter', in the course of which he once for all established memory as a biological conception. It was his conviction that 'an organized being, therefore, stands before us as a product of the unconscious memory of organised matter, which, ever increasing and ever dividing itself, ever assimilating new matter and returning it in changed shape to the inorganic world, ever receiving some new thing into its memory and transmitting its acquisitions by way of reproduction, grows continually richer and richer the longer it lives. Thus regarded, the development of one of the more highly organized animals represents a continuous series of organized recollections concerning the past development of the great chain of living forms, the last link of which stands before us in the particular animal we may be considering. . . . He who marvels at the skill with which the spider weaves her web should bear in mind that she did not learn her art all on a sudden, but that innumerable generations of spiders acquired it toilsomely and step by step—this being about all, as a general rule, they did acquire. All this is as wonderful as when a grey-haired man remembers the events of his own childhood, but it is not more so.'[1] Butler, in commenting on the passage which he has translated, says: 'Memory was in full operation for so long a time before anything like what we call a nervous system can be detected, that Prof. Hering must not be supposed to be intending to confine memory to a motor-nervous system.'[2]

---

[1] Translated from the German of Hering in *Unconscious Memory*, by S. Butler, pp. 129, 133.   [2] Ibid., p. 115.

What types of biological facts are they that lead to the conclusion that memory is a biological function? One of them is the case where a certain reaction is so acquired that it can be performed without the original stimulus requisite to call it forth. Another is the apparent recognition on the part of lower animals of both qualitative and quantitative variations from the original stimulus. Experiments have been performed by Prof. Lloyd Morgan on chicks which illustrate this matter. Soon after hatching, the chicks were given some caterpillars with characteristic black and gold stripes, and the chicks, finding them distasteful, promptly rejected them. Afterwards, though they freely ate other kinds of caterpillars, they always rejected those with the black and gold stripes, evidently retaining the impression of the original experience which led to future inhibitions.

Yet even among biologists there is no unanimity as to the nature of the process. Dr. Semon thinks that 'without doubt, excitation is at bottom a physico-chemical process and nothing else'. Prof. Jennings thinks of memory as simply the potentiality of a physiological state for change in a given direction. And Butler is of opinion that 'life is that property of matter whereby it can remember—matter which can remember is living'.

One of the most important evidences of the influence of the biological concept on psychology is in behaviourism. Behaviourism is the thorough-going application of the objective method in psychology to the complete exclusion of introspection. The only interest is behaviour in the form of responses to stimuli, all of the old categories, such as consciousness, conation, affection, cognition, sensation, etc., disappearing. This appears to some as a reduction of psychology to physiology. Prof. Watson, who is typical of the school, has defined memory as 'a general term to express the fact that after a period of no practice in certain habits—explicit bodily habits, implicit word habits—the function is not lost, but is retained as a part of the individual's organization, although it may, through disuse, have suffered greater or less impairment'.[1] In another place Prof. Watson says that 'the

---

[1] J. B. Watson, *Psychology from the Standpoint of a Behaviourist*, p. 340.

term "memory" has been ill-advisedly used in the experiments upon the effect of intervals of disuse upon habit functions. The term "retention" has been employed in a static sense in this same connection, referring chiefly to the "persistence of modifications" in the nervous system. Both terms are ill-defined. It seems possible to keep the term retention and make its meaning more definite. In behaviour the term retention covers this phenomenon, viz. that an object to which an animal has learned to respond in a definite way will, for a more or less definite period in which the given response has been prevented (i.e. by not presenting the object) call forth in various degrees of perfection the old (or habitual) response. If the response is as definite at the end of the period of disuse as before, we say that there has been no loss in retention or that retention was perfect.'[1]

The most important contribution of biology to psychology is not to be localized in any specific doctrine or doctrines which it has contributed to that science. It is rather in the field of method. Psychology is a biological science inasmuch as it studies life processes, but it makes use also of the method of introspection. It is a study of the mental life, and biology has infused into it a scientific spirit of investigation, and emphasized the facts of process and change as characteristic of the entire life, mental as well as neural.

Miss Beatrice Edgell has recently made a valuable contribution[2] to the subject of memory. She shows the importance of the memory-image for an understanding of the processes involved. The idea of the mental life inevitably suggests a continuous process. Using the word 'retentiveness' to denote 'the character in virtue of which mental processes are continuous' she regards it as 'involved in the very conception of mental life'. The factor of familiarity which appears in successive repetitions of an act is evidence of retentiveness. This element of persistence involves the functioning of processes of a conative character as well as of cognition and affection. The

---

[1] Watson, *Behaviour: An Introduction to Comparative Psychology*, pp. 241 ff.

[2] Edgell, *Theories of Memory*, Oxford University Press, 1924.

continuity of the cognitive series is only possible because of continuity in the conative series. The process of remembering is explained by the memory-image carrying on the work of the sense-impression. 'The object known is not an event in the life history of the individual, whereas the "given" impression is.' What and whence is the memory-image ? The justification for the concept is our experience of after-images and recurrent sensation. Yet they are different in kind, for the essential conditions for experiencing the memory-image are to be found only within the mental life. 'Memory is cognition of something known before. The particular memory is in continuity with the former knowing. The former knowing was occasioned by sense-impressions ; the image continues the work of the former sense-impressions. Since this continuity is not occasioned by repetition of the sense-impressions, it can only occur as an event because it is "required" by the character of the mental processes themselves. We may say that it stands to those processes in a part-to-whole relation, although we can only trace out the relation in terms of function. . . . If we ask, then, "what brings imagery into being ? " the answer is, "the nature of cognition and conation."' [1] Since we have regarded the image as an event occurring here and now, the pastness cannot be that of this event. 'We have not to claim that the individual is functioning both "here " and "now" and also "then" and "there", in knowing the past. It is the object known which is past, not the knowing.'[2] 'Since the present is always relevant to any experience of the moment, the past which is most strictly akin to the present is not the detached past time of objects known and deeds done, but the personal past of the knowing and the doing.'[3]

Miss Edgell's discussion of the psychological processes in remembering points to two most important matters. One is that remembering is a particular type of imagination, the other that we should think of persons remembering rather than of things remembered. Imagination is a consciousness of objects that are not present to sense, and assumes different forms in accordance with the purpose of the person imagining. It may

---

[1] Edgell, *Theories of Memory*, p. 145.   [2] Ibid., p. 150.   [3] Ibid., p. 153.

be a free flow of images in consciousness without regard to any definite end, what in the narrower sense of the word is called imagination, or sometimes reverie or fantasy. It may be a controlled sequence of images with reference to a problem to be solved, as in scientific imagination which has the element of prediction. It may be a creative combination of images with the object of producing something beautiful, as in æsthetic imagination. Even dream processes are also processes of imagery. Remembering is that form wherein the person endeavours to recall the images in the same sequence that the objects appeared or events occurred in actual experience. In the wider sense of the term, however, all imagery involves an element of remembering in that the images which are brought together, even though they be combined in totally new ways, come to us out of the past. It is impossible for us to create images out of nothing. They are the stuff of experience, perhaps somewhat faded and often appearing with little reference to their original setting, but always coming out of the past.

From the educational point of view the analysis of memory into learning or memorizing, retention, recall and recognition, is probably the most valuable. One of the important desiderata is to be able to recall matters from the past under the stress of particular needs. In order to do that we require to have so learned them that linkages are formed which will fix the matter in mind. That involves the process of memorizing. The second question is as to the manner in which we retain what has been acquired, and this we must observe is a passive state rather than an active process. If a matter is memorized and retained it should be possible to recall it, but there still remains the process of recognizing it as identical with the matter originally cognized.

The process of memorizing has been made the subject of a considerable amount of observation under laboratory conditions. For one thing a number of experiments have been performed in the memorizing of nonsense material. The advantage of observing the process under such conditions is the absence of other complications which might be involved in memorizing sensible material. This may take the form of learning a series of numbers having no other association than that of being members of a series, or learning a series of meaningless syllables, or learning words which together do not make sense. Observations of the process of memorizing in such cases indicate differences in individuals. Some learn by rote, that is by simply repeating the performances until the material is learned. Others will look for ways in which they can form associations which will enable them to attain their end more speedily. Various methods of grouping the material are devised, or the material is linked in some mnemonic system which is designed to convert the nonsensible into the sensible. At other times observations of similarities are utilized, and rythmic groupings are discovered. The entire process is one of exploration and manipulation in accordance with the particular material to be memorized. If the memorizing of nonsense material is difficult, the retention of it is still more so. Studies have been made by Ebbinghaus and others of the forgetting of nonsense material. Obviously, remembering and forgetting are the positive and negative aspects of the same process. Ebbinghaus' experiment was designed to measure the amount of material remembered, by discovering how much time would be required to relearn the same material. He found that if a nonsense series was memorized until it could be barely repeated correctly, and then intervals allowed to elapse, certain percentages of the original memorizing period would be required to relearn, those percentages representing the forgetting, and the differences the remembering. After nineteen minutes, 42 per cent of the original time was taken to relearn the material; after sixty-three minutes, 56 per cent; after eight and three-quarters hours, 64 per cent, and so on. That is, the forgetting was 42, 56 and 64, and the remembering 58, 44 and 36. Others have tried similar experiments, and found that the curve of forgetting was of the same general form, though differing in minor details.

The memorizing of sensible material, such as connected passages of poetry or prose, is along the same general lines as that of nonsense material, except that it has a very great advantage in the matter of being able to discover and form associations of a helpful kind. The presence of meanings calls into play associations from past experiences, which enable the person to achieve the performance in very much less time than is required for nonsense material. Woodworth has very aptly remarked that 'no one in his senses would undertake to memorize an intelligible passage by the pure rote method, for this would be throwing away the best possible aid in memorizing'.[1] Yet we in India are familiar with the pitiable attempts of students trying to memorize passages which they have made no serious effort to understand. The first and indispensable aid to memorizing is to get the sense of a passage, if the material is to be readily fixed in the mind. Recently there came under my observation a college student who was memorizing an American negro's meditations on the game of golf, which he intended to recite at a public gathering. He had no idea either of the meaning of the golf terms, or of the negro dialect, and as a consequence the humour of the piece was all lost on him, although he intended to entertain others. Unconsciously to himself, he had set himself an extraordinarily difficult task because of the lack of meaningful associations linked to the words which he was trying to memorize. The fact is that usually, even where the task is to memorize nonsense material, the subject first of all looks for means of making it meaningful without which the task would be appallingly difficult.

Thorndike's experiments go to show that disuse is the fundamental cause of forgetting what has been learned. The curve of forgetting is so different in different people with different kinds of material that he finds it exceedingly difficult to form any general conclusion. 'About the only facts that they display with any unanimity and brilliancy are the apparent complexity and variability of deterioration by disuse and our lack of knowledge about it.' But even this degree of information about the process is of value, for it enables us to guard against an educational practice which assumes that all learning deteriorates in the same way as learning of the informational type does. It also helps us to guard against the assumption that there is

---

[1] Woodworth, *Psychology: A Study of Mental Life*, p. 337.

'some magical curve of forgetting which every function at every stage will somewhat closely follow'.[1]   In terms of neurological connections the same author suggests that disuse may be conceived as not entirely negative, but a positive 'combination of forces which attack the bonds upon which a function's efficiency depends, making breaches, as it were, in the walls which exercise has built, or conquering certain outposts and redoubts which exercise had won'.   This is a corrective to the popular view that forgetting is merely a negation of remembering.   It means that when learned material is not used there is a constant tendency for other materials which are being learned and being used to make attacks on the bonds which are not being exercised, so that they are gradually weakened.   In a parallel analogy relearning may be interpreted as 'the repair of these breaches, the recapture of the redoubts, the restoration of what was lost during the interval of disuse'.[2]

Another matter which has been the subject of study under experimental conditions concerns the possibility of economizing in memorizing.   We all know from practical experiences that memorizing as a form of mental work is capable of control to a considerable extent.   We know that sometimes memorizing becomes an almost insufferable burden, whereas at other times it is quite an agreeable undertaking.   We would like to know whether the burdensome character of certain tasks can be alleviated. We would like to be sure when we are faced with a particular bit of memorizing that we are accomplishing it as economically and efficiently as possible.   And if there are any such things as 'short-cuts' we want to know about them.

The 'recitation' is one of the aids to economy, and by that we simply mean reciting to ourselves.   Having read the material through once or twice, the subject will find that there is value in attempting to recite it, using the printed or written matter to prompt himself when he lapses.   Professor A. I. Gates has made a specialized study[3] of the relation between recitation and reading in memorizing.   He examined the relationship, with

---

[1] Thorndike, *Educational Psychology*, Briefer Course, p. 251 f.
[2] Ibid., p. 256.
[3] A. I. Gates, *Recitation as a Factor of Memorizing*, 1917.

reference both to nonsense material and to sensible material, in the former case using sixteen nonsense syllables, and in the latter case using five short biographical sketches totalling about 170 words. In each case the time devoted to study was nine minutes, and this time was divided between reading and recitation, according to the proportions indicated in the column at the left. The subjects tested were eighth-grade children, although similar results were obtained in the case of adults. The following is Gates' table of results :

THE VALUE OF RECITATION IN MEMORIZING

MATERIAL STUDIED	SIXTEEN NONSENSE SYLLABLES		FIVE SHORT BIOGRAPHIES TOTALLING ABOUT 170 WORDS	
	Per cent immediately	Remembered after 4 hours	Per cent immediately	Remembered after 4 hours
All time devoted to reading	35	15	35	16
One-fifth time devoted to recitation ..	50	26	37	19
Two-fifths time devoted to recitation ..	54	28	41	25
Three-fifths time devoted to recitation	57	37	42	26
Four-fifths time devoted to recitation	74	48	42	26

If we attempt to read the meaning of the results of Gates' experiments, we shall note certain facts. (*a*) One is that there is a greater disparity in the results between the different proportioning of time to reading and recitation in the case of memorizing nonsense material than in that of sensible material. (*b*) A second is that in every case some help is gained by recitation ; it always shortens the time to some extent. (*c*) Another is that there is a progressive increase in the advantage as fifths are added to the recitation period, except in the case of three-fifths and four-fifths for sensible material, where the results yielded are the same. (*d*) Further, the relative advantage was greater for the tests four hours after than for those immediately after study. The advantage of the recitation is partly that it centres the attention and holds the interest because it is a more active process. Since one soon begins to try out his acquisitions, he is stimulated to observe aids to the process and to do his utmost to achieve the desired end. It is a practical application of the old adage that 'we learn to do by doing.'

A second problem confronts us in examining the question of economy in memorizing, viz. as to whether it is more advantageous to persist steadily with a task or to distribute the task over time intervals. This is an extremely important matter for education, for a teacher may be able to accomplish much more with a class in a given period of time, if he can direct the members as to the most economical distribution of their time and energy. Given a memory lesson which has to be prepared for a coming examination, will it be better to 'plug away' at it, or to spend shorter periods of time interspaced with other work? Woodworth makes reference[1] to the work of Pieron and Jost in this field. Pieron experimented with a certain subject using parallel lists of twenty numbers, and trying the results of unspaced and spaced repetition. With practically unspaced repetitions, i.e. allowing only thirty-second intervals, the subject required eleven repetitions to master the test. But when five-minute intervals were given the same subject was able to master a parallel list with six repetitions. With intervals of ten minutes, five repetitions were found to be sufficient. Pieron went on increasing the length of the intervals, and from ten-minute up to two-day intervals were found to be the most economical. Intervals either less than ten minutes or more than two days resulted in increasing repetitions becoming necessary, and no intervals at all was one of the least economical methods of all.

Jost's experiment was conducted with lists of nonsense syllables. He tried the experiment with two subjects, M. B. and M. M., and arranged the distribution in different amounts, to determine which was the most economical for memorizing. In each case a total of twenty-four readings was allowed, but these were distributed variously through eight, six and two readings per day,

---

[1] Woodworth, *Psychology : A Study of Mental Life*, p. 342.

in immediate succession. One day, after the final reading of each list, the subjects were tested in respect to their memory of it. The following table shows the results:

EFFECT OF DISTRIBUTION OF REPETITIONS ON ECONOMY
IN MEMORIZING

DISTRIBUTION OF THE TWENTY-FOUR READINGS	TOTAL SCORE OF M.B.	TOTAL SCORE OF M.M.
Eight readings per day for 3 days ..	18	7
Six ,, ,, ,, ,, 4 ,, ..	39	31
Two ,, ,, ,, ,,12 ,, ..	53	55

The significance of the experiment is that the best score was obtained from the widest distribution. Children may be shown by the teacher that it is more economical in a piece of memorizing to read the passage once or twice daily for successive days than to attempt to do it all at once. The precise spacing required cannot be anticipated, as that has reference to the particular passage to be memorized, its length and other characteristics. What is still more important for education is that memorizing by distributed repetitions results in greater permanence. Every teacher knows that the student who waits until examinations are near and then crams, at best obtains a superficial advantage, and forgets the greater part of what has been learned soon after the examination. Of course this should not be interpreted as a plea for study of an intermittent sporadic character. It rather argues that a student should vary his subject of study, and not stick too long at the same matter.

The evidence points to the necessity for some time elapsing before an idea becomes an integral part of one's system of ideas. This process is most difficult of description, and is sometimes referred to as 'mental incubation'. While this process of incubation is taking place, the new idea does not become assimilated with the old or with other new ideas to the extent that is possible when the process of incubation is complete. There is one group of facts which serve to illustrate this process, viz. amnesia or loss of memory, which is often the result of a severe shock, such as an accident. Fraser refers to the case of an electrician who has received a severe shock from which he has barely escaped being killed. On recovering consciousness he finds that he can remember everything in the ordinary way up to a few days, say a week, before the accident, but concerning the period of the last few days his memory appears to be a blank. He tries to recall incidents that happened within that time, and only very gradually do they return to him, the return being from the beginning rather than from the end of the period. It is not often that he is ever able to recall events immediately preceding the shock. 'The explanation offered for this is that the ideas or experiences immediately preceding the accident had not enough time to become sufficiently set or fixed in the mental system of the man to be able to withstand the severe shock of the electric current.'[1] A similar case came under my observation in the Government Mental Hospital, Madras, where there are many opportunities to study defects in memory. In this instance the defect was due to a disease, the result of which was absolute inability to retain, recall or recognize any new idea, even for two minutes, while the patient was able to go into unusual details in regard to events which happened years previously.

Pauses are valuable for the process of incubation. During the intervals a process of fixing or assimilation takes place. This was what led James to emphasize the improvement that appears to take place when we are actually resting from practice of a performance. In cold climates it is not possible to enter the lakes or rivers to swim, yet he maintained that 'we learn to swim in winter'. It is sometimes maintained that the elements entering into either a mental or a motor process have different rates of forgetting, and that some of the unessential movements which we have contracted have a rapider rate of forgetting than the essential ones, so that in the interval they drop off.

We may put the matter in another way by saying that mental incubation is a phase of apperceptive synthesis. In apperception 'two mental systems become conjoined in the mind, and thereafter form a single larger system'.[2] We who teach may often observe

---

[1] D. Kennedy-Fraser, *The Psychology of Education*, p. 112.

[2] McDougall, *Outline of Psychology*, p. 386.

how children who have learned some new fact seem suddenly to grasp its significance. What happens is that the new acquisition comes upon the appropriate elements among the older acquisitions to make apperception possible. A synthesis of the new and the old takes place, and the new becomes fixed in an assemblage of correlated facts. It is a process whereby we simplify and systematize our acquisitions and experiences by means of hitting on similarities or class concepts. McDougall refers to Newton's observation of the essential similarity between the motion of a falling body, and that of the moon around the earth, an observation which enabled him to formulate the law of gravitation. Apperceptive synthesis is a process of the utmost importance in memory. If we can gather up our new acquisitions in assimilation to the older ones, there is a far greater likelihood of our retaining them and being able to recall them, than if they are isolated fragments bearing no meaning in relation to the other elements of experience.

The apperceptive process depends fundamentally on the ability to form helpful associations. Association is by no means the magical formula that the associationists thought it to be. It does signify, however, that certain linkages or bonds are formed in consciousness owing to existing similarities or contrasts or to contiguity in space or time which create a tendency for one experience or one idea to lead to the recall of another. What occur together tend to recur together. When we study the details we see that there is a great variety of possible ways in which associations may be built up, such as whole and part relations, genus and species relations, analogies, similarities and contrasts of the whole or parts in respect to a great variety of qualities, temporal contiguity, spatial contiguity, and so forth. In remembering, associations are useful in that one memory may be of service to another. In all the machinery of remembering there is nothing that is comparable to the association-forming tendencies as labour saving devices. There is an old pedagogical maxim which says, 'proceed from the concrete to the abstract.' We do not begin to teach the processes involved in adding by getting children to juggle with abstract numbers, but by letting them see that two beans put together with another two beans make four beans. In other words, we build up memories for addition by means of association processes. The same thing applies to the other arithmetical processes as well as to other subject matter of teaching—geography, history, language, etc.

A further problem which concerns economy in learning is as to whether it is more advantageous in trying to memorize a long passage to study the lesson as a whole, or to divide it into parts and study the parts separately. Here again experimental work has been done and observations made, so that we are not left to a mere theoretical consideration of the problem. Woodworth[1] records the observations of Pyle and Snyder and of Pechstein. Pyle and Snyder's observations were of a young man memorizing passages of 240 lines length, in the one instance by memorizing 30 lines daily till the whole was acquired, and in the other instance by reading the entire passage thrice daily until it was acquired. The results showed that it required a total of 431 minutes when memorizing in parts, and only 348 when memorizing as a whole. Here the economy is 83 minutes, or nearly twenty per cent, by using the method of memorizing all as compared with parts.

Pechstein introduced another factor, viz. spacing, into this problem, and his results show that, though Pyle and Snyder's observations are usually applicable, there are exceptions under certain circumstances. Their experiment was with learning to trace a maze with a pencil. The maze was divided into four compartments which could be learned separately, and the entire arrangement was hidden from the subjects by means of a screen. They divided their subjects into four groups, each of which learned the maze in a different way. Groups A and B learned the maze as a whole; groups C and D learned it by parts. Groups A and C learned it by spaced trials at the rate of two daily; group B learned the entire maze at a single sitting, and group D learned a part daily for four days and on the fifth day learned to combine the parts. The results are indicated in the following table from Pechstein:

[1] Woodworth, *Psychology*, pp. 343 ff.

Part and Whole Learned, Spaced and Unspaced, in the Pencil Maze

	Spaced Trials	Unspaced Trials
Whole Learning	A 641 seconds	B 1250 seconds
Part Learning	C 1220 ,,	D 538 ,,

The results indicate that when the trials were spaced, it was more advantageous to study the maze as a whole. But when the trials were unspaced part learning had the advantage. And of all four methods the advantage was quite distinctly with unspaced learning of parts. The results, however, show how unsafe it is to jump to any conclusions as being applicable to all situations.

In memorizing material such as poetry, the consensus of opinion on the basis of experimental observations seems to favour whole learning. Probably most children, unless specially directed otherwise, would go about memorizing a poem by memorizing each stanza separately. The difficulty that follows from this method is that they sometimes experience difficulty in maintaining the order of the stanzas. There is the lack of a bond between the conclusion of one stanza and the beginning of the next, which is formed when the poem is memorized in its entirety. In cases of this kind teachers must direct the work of children, because whole learning requires less repetition and insures greater accuracy and security in retention.

Pedagogically we are especially interested in the practical aspects of the matter. It will be of value to indicate some of the factors of importance.

1. The first is interested attention. Any teacher can substantiate from his own experience the conclusion that the boy or girl who attends interestedly to a passage being memorized will acquire it more rapidly and more accurately than one whose focus of interest is elsewhere. Unfortunately, there are too many cases where children are made subservient to curricula and examinations. But one desideratum in an educational system is scope for the teacher to study the child's individual interests

and abilities, which would enable teachers to avoid making memory and other educational tasks disagreeable to the child.

2. The second factor is practice. McDougall describes an experiment[1] which he and an assistant conducted in the learning and relearning of rows of syllables. From their observations they were able to conclude that relearning showed a greater rate of improvement than learning through practice. From that he concludes that retentiveness is improved by practice. This is another way of describing the factor of use. We tend to forget what we do not use, and to remember what is repeatedly put to service. The value of drills and revisions is that they keep putting the children under the necessity of using their acquisitions, and that must assist them greatly in retention.

3. The factor of recency comes into account in normal processes. Ordinarily a person will recall more readily what has happened most recently. But it is precisely the opposite in cases of amnesia, in which the more remote elements of experience are recalled at the expense of the more recent.

4. A fourth factor is logical. It is the rôle played by meanings in remembering. Experiments show that significant words and meaningful passages are much more readily memorized and retained than nonsense syllables and disconnected words. Where there are meanings, logical associations are possible. Furthermore, unless for experimental observations, the memorizing of syllables, words or passages which carry no meaning to the subject is a laborious and wasteful expenditure of time and energy. A proud father once brought to me his little girl that I might hear her recite Sanskrit poetry. She had memorized, so he said, hundreds of high-sounding stanzas, scarcely any of which could have carried any meaning to her. The father was burdening her with laborious tasks which could have no meaning or interest for her, while he was not letting her attend school where she might acquire something interesting and helpful.

One of the services which the psycho-analysts have rendered us is to show that forgetting is not merely a passive and negative process, in contrast with remembering. True, it is the opposite

---

[1] W. McDougall, *An Outline of Psychology*, p. 297.

of remembering. But it is more than passive. One of the essentials for good remembering is to understand what is significant and what not significant. We need to cultivate the art of forgetting the non-essentials, and that is a process of inhibition towards particular groups of stimuli. But, unhappily, there is also another kind of forgetting in which the significant is forgotten. This is explained as caused by some form of repression which may be due to any one of a number of factors, but primarily to a focussing of one's interests on other things. Mr. T. H. Pear has made a provisional classification of forgotten experiences under the following headings :[1]

1. Embodied experiences, which include
    (a) apparently insignificant experiences, and
    (b) those which are significant, but completely congruous with one's personality.
2. Exiled experiences are those which are retained, but forcibly barred from everyday consciousness.
3. Superseded or retired experiences are those which have been unconsciously retired as the developing person unconsciously sloughs the past.

Teachers ought to be vitally interested in the forgetting of children as well as in their remembering. One thing to remember is that the child's personality, and the nervous system itself, as James said, may be made an ally. It may be made an ally in providing for the gradual disappearance of certain elements as personality unfolds. Forgetting is not necessarily a defective memory, but should be cultivated with discrimination, so that consciousness will not be burdened with the insignificant.

[1] T. H. Pear, *Remembering and Forgetting*, pp. 166 ff.

LITERATURE

W. McDougall. *An Outline of Psychology*. Methuen, 1924.

C. H. Judd. *Psychology*. Scribner's, 1907.

J. B. Watson. *Behaviour*. Henry Holt, 1914.

J. B. Watson. *Psychology from the Standpoint of a Behaviourist*. Lippincott, 1919.

E. L. Thorndike. *Educational Psychology*, Briefer Course. Columbia University Press, 1914.

G. M. Whipple. *Manual of Mental and Physical Tests*. Warwick & York, 1914-15.

T. H. Pear. *Remembering and Forgetting*. Methuen, 1922.

Beatrice Edgell. *Theories of Memory*. Oxford University Press, 1924.

H. Bergson. *Matter and Memory*. George Allen & Unwin, 1911.

CHAPTER IX

THE ASSOCIATIVE TENDENCIES

Definition — Associationism — Neural Associations — Association in the Various Mental Processes—Types of Association—Free and Controlled Associations.

The word association by derivation (ex Latin *associare* = *ad*, to,+*sociare*, join, L. *socius*, joined with, allied) simply means a union or connection. In psychology it has reference to a union or connection of ideas or images in the mental processes. It has been defined as 'a union more or less complete formed in and by the course of experience between the mental dispositions corresponding to two or more distinguishable contents of consciousness, and of such a nature that when one content recurs, the other content tends in some manner or degree to recur also.'[1]

The phrase 'association of ideas' was first used by John Locke, though the recognition of the principles of association goes back to Aristotle. In his treatise on *Memory and Reminiscence* he recognized the principle of association, and distinguished the various types as association by similarity, by contrast, and by contiguity. He wrote as follows:

'The occurrence of an act of recollection is due to the natural tendency of one particular change to follow another. If the sequence is necessary, it is clear that, on the former change occurring, the second will be summoned into activity, when, however, the connection is not necessary, but due to custom, the occurrence of the second process will take place only in most cases. It so happens that some people receive a greater bent from a single experience than others in whom the sequence has frequently taken place, and hence, in some instances, after seeing

---

[1] G.F.S. and J.M.B., article 'Association' in the *Dictionary of Philosophy and Psychology*.

the things once we remember them better than others who have seen them frequently. Thus, when we recollect, one of our previous psychic changes is stimulated which leads to the stimulation of that one after which the experience to be recollected is wont to occur. Consequently, we hunt for the next in the series, starting our train of thought from what is now present or from something else, and from something similar or contrary or contiguous to it.'

Associationism or Associationalism is the name given to a school of thought which regarded the laws of association as the fundamental laws of mental activity and development. Associationism as a theory 'starting with certain simple and ultimate constituents of consciousness, makes mental development consist solely or mainly in the combination of these elements according to certain laws of association. According to this theory rigidly carried out, all genesis of new products is due to the combination of pre-existing elements.' [1] According to a broad use of the term, Hobbes and Hume are included in this school, but strictly speaking the school is mainly represented by David Hartley (1704-1757), James Mill (1773-1836), John Stuart Mill (1806-1873), and Alexander Bain (1818-1903).

At times, Associationism has run off at a tangent in some peculiar direction as in the Mind-Stuff, Mind-Dust or Composition Theories, for these are practically reducible to one theory, under various names, which proposes that all mental states are compound or composite, assuming that they are brought about by the correlation of smaller states. This composition or mind-stuff theory is the result of a structural rather than a functional way of looking at mental phenomena. It assumes that the ultimate units of composition are of unitary type. William James, in his larger work,[2] deals at length with the theory. He points out that the theory is the outcome of the earlier school of evolutionistic psychology which was hampered by its metaphysical presuppositions. These men did not understand the unity of the psycho-physical organism as it is understood today.

[1] Baldwin's *Dictionary of Philosophy and Psychology*
[2] James, *Principles of Psychology*, vol. i. chapter vi.

They believed in a dualism between the physical and psychical. Tyndall, e.g., said, 'the passage from the physics of the brain to the corresponding facts of consciousness is unthinkable.' Consequently, the smooth working of the evolutionary hypothesis in their judgement demanded that consciousness in some degree be present at the very beginning of things. The mind-dust theory postulates the existence of particles or atoms (dust) of mind everywhere in nature, the concomitants of material atoms. These atoms or particles or mental-dust constitute the stuff of consciousness under specific circumstances. Baldwin rightly describes it as a sort of 'psychological atomism'. Herbert Spencer represents this particular school of thought.

Psychologists of today do not use the principles of association as explanatory principles for the mental process in the wholesale fashion that characterized the associationist school. One reason is that the whole approach to psychological problems is different. The transition from a physical to a biological point of view is evident in the accompanying transition from a faculty to a functional treatment of mental processes. This means that mental processes cease to be treated as though they were capable of being brought under mechanical laws, as the associationists believed. They are to be considered as functioning in a unified organism which is in process of development. At the same time there is a good deal in the description of the types of association which the modern psychologists find to be suggestive and valid in the writings of the older school. But today association is thought to be a synthetic process whereby the elements of mental life are organized. Indeed, analysis and synthesis are the two phases of mental activity which are constantly interplaying, and the associative tendency is implicit in analysis as it is explicit in synthesis.

There is general agreement today that the functioning and persistence of association processes have their basis in the nervous system. The associative tendency is to be regarded as physiological rather than anatomical. The connections that are established between images or ideas involve physiological correlates. 'The process by which the activities proper to several centres of the central nervous system are brought into a state of mutual influence or interdependence ' is called a nervous association. A process of neural association is involved in all mental processes more complex than the simple sensory presentations.

The higher mental processes, such as judgement, conception and reasoning are vitally related, then, to the complex associational processes in the cerebrum. Sometimes these cerebral processes involve a most elaborate organization or reorganization of the matters presented in stimuli. These neurological processes involve large areas in the central nervous system, and are incapable of localization in any specific sense, such as in the case of simple sensory presentations. The point of difference in the case of the associational processes is that they are not direct sensory processes, but involve a reorganization of simple material.

The word *association* is used by neurologists to connote higher types of correlation which are characterized by plasticity and modifiability. The word distinguishes these more complex responses from the simpler reactions of the mechanically determined reflex. In association, adaptability and modifiability are the dominant features, and on that account the exact nature of the response cannot be predicted with any degree of certainty, because of the fact that it is not determined by purely mechanical law. The correlation and association centres are developed in the posterior portions of the brain and spinal cord, although the distinctions, as already noted, are physiological rather than structural, and other parts of the central nervous system may be involved, while on the other hand the dorsal parts may at times be involved in the simpler processes.

Experiments on decerebrate animals have proved that the cerebral cortex is involved in the association processes. Certain experimenters have removed the cerebral hemispheres, either partially or completely, from animals of various species from fishes to apes, carefully observing the behaviour of the animals under these conditions. There is not a unified type of action in the case of all animals. In the case of decerebrate frogs, they were able to perform the ordinary types of reflexes, but associations, even of the simpler kinds, were impossible. In the case of monkeys reflex responses to stimuli of the optic, auditory and tactual kinds were performed, but there was poor control over movement.   Prof. Herrick reports the case of a boy who had lived for three years and nine months, and whose brain on post-mortem examination revealed the absence of a cerebral cortex, though there were no other significant defects.   This boy showed no ability to develop sensory or motor power.   'The infant fed when put to the breast, but showed no signs of hunger, thirst, or any other sensory process.   It lay in a profound stupor and during the first year of life made no spontaneous movements of the limbs.'   The observations, if we may generalize on such meagre data, seem to show that in the case of the human animal there is much more cortical control of reflexive and instinc-tive reactions than there is with lower animals.

The phenomena of aphasia throw a good deal of light upon the neural associations.   The word ordinarily signifies a defect of speech as the result of a cortical injury, but has latterly been extended to signify 'any loss or defect in symbolizing relations of things in any way'.[1]   Aphasia is to be distinguished from primary sensory defects, such as blindness or deafness, and from motor paralysis.   In this case the injury is to a part of the cortical regions which are integrated with a sensory process, so that the result is apparent in defective associations.   Aphasia in connection with speech does not necessarily involve dumbness, but the person loses control over the enunciatory movements, with the result that the sounds are disorderly.   Aphasia of the visual type does not involve blindness, but loss of visual memory, so that the sense of familiarity in connection with what has been seen before is absent.   The effect is inability to recognize objects which have been previously cognized.   Parallel situations arise in connection with auditory and olfactory aphasia. The images which recur in consciousness fail to elicit any cogni-tion of having occurred before.   They appear to be on each occasion perfectly novel.   Aphasia is thus a nervous disorder which effects a concomitant functional disorder in the processes of association, particularly of memory, but also in some cases of motor control.

[1] Herrick, *Introduction to Neurology*, p. 325.

The problems involved in conditions of aphasia are difficult because of the impossibility of definitely localizing the physiological mechanisms concerned in each case, so that the cause of the defect is not always apparent. In general it has been ascertained that the condition may be the result of one of three injuries, (a) injury to a sensory association area near the primary projection centres of the visual and auditory types; (b) injury to a motor association centre near the motor projection centres connected with the muscles of speech; (c) injury to any of the association tracts which connect these association centres. One point to be remembered is that cortical functions involve the discharge of nervous impulses and energy which need not necessarily be confined to one specific area. But the physiological process is one that involves the entire cortical areas, passing from one association centre to another, and establishing what has been called 'some sort of nervous equilibrium which finds its expression in a definite motor act or an idea'.[1]

That a pathological condition in the cortical centres disturbs the processes of association may be illustrated in many ways. A hemorrhage, e.g., will have that effect, and when it has been cured the equilibrium may be restored. I knew the case of a medical doctor who was confined in a hospital for the insane, the cause of the insanity being unknown. One day while walking in the corridors, another patient with clenched fist struck him a fearful blow on the back of the head, as a result of which he was rendered insensible. To the amazement of everybody, when he regained consciousness, sanity had been restored. It was found on examination that the blow on the head had scattered a clot of blood at the base of the brain, disturbing the normal association processes.

Similarly, what we call in psychology the association of ideas without doubt involves, on the neurological side, a discharge of nervous energy in the cortical regions between two groups of neurones which have in some past experience been brought together in a cortical response. This may be readily illustrated from the ordinary experiences of life.

[1] Herrick, *Introduction to Neurology*, p. 327.

Previous experience has made a connection between two systems of neurones, has established, be it never so faintly, an association tract, which tends to be revived with the stimulation of one of the original component elements. Of course, it must be admitted that this explanation is, in the nature of the case, theoretical, but it seems to explain the observable facts in the most satisfactory way. As Stout has pointed out, 'only part of the cortex has been mapped out into sensory and motor areas with definitely localized functions. Of the rest we can only say that it consists of neurones and groups of neurones which supply, in immensely complex ways, lines of communication with each other and with the sensory and motor areas.' It is to these portions of the cortex that we give the name 'association centres'.

There have been those who have attempted to state the neural correlates of associational processes in the form of a law. It has been stated thus: 'The passage of a nervous impulse through a chain of neurones leaves that chain more or less permanently altered, in such a way that its resistance to the passage of the impulse is in some degree diminished.'[1] But the defect in this statement is that it offers no explanation of the restriction of the nervous impulse to the particular passage that it selected on the original occasion. Though we have to confess our ignorance in regard to the formation of neural habits, it does seem to be clear that the simultaneous or successive stimulation of two groups of neurones makes it easier for a nervous impulse to be discharged from the one to the other on a future occasion.

The conscious processes have been compared to a stream, ever flowing and yet preserving its identity. So consciousness involves a continuous change and yet at the same time it is ideationally a continuum. Prof. James described it in his practical way: 'Consciousness, then, does not appear to itself chopped up in bits. Such words as "chain" or "train" do not describe it fitly as it presents itself in the first instance. It is nothing jointed, it flows. A "river" or a "stream" are the meta-

---

[1] Stout, *Manual of Psychology*, p. 89.

phors by which it is most naturally described.' The conception of consciousness as a continuously flowing stream, according to James, involves two things: first, that even where there is a time-gap in the conscious process, 'the consciousness after it feels as if it belonged together with the consciousness before it, as another part of the same self'; and second, that the changes which occur 'from one moment to another in the quality of consciousness are never absolutely abrupt'.[1]

The formation of an ideational continuum involves memory processes more or less definite, which in turn implies associations. So that ultimately the continuity of our conscious life has its basis in the capability which we have of combining various natural and mental processes into a unity. Were it not for this power we should be unable to appreciate the inter-relationship between the various presentations that come into the field of attention. Each presentation would stimulate a response, and that would constitute a whole bit of experience. We must say that the apparatus of association affords a conservation of neural and mental energy, and in that way enables us to make conscious progress.

The significance of association as related to consciousness involves the question of attention. Now the focussing of consciousness upon a particular point involves a process of analysis and selection, a dissociation relatively speaking of the specific thing on which attention is fixed from the field of other possible objects. But the analytical aspect of attention involves also an awareness of a synthesis of elements which it is proposed to discriminate in the field of consciousness. But not only does attention recognize the fact of association as a preliminary process to itself, it further recognizes it in the very process itself. For the different distinguishable elements which are discriminated when attention is so focalized are definitely and deliberately fixed into a unity. We see that in this way the process of attending is an analytical-synthetic process. Both dissociation and association are present.

The activity of discrimination involves not only analysis but also comparison and classification. It involves a perception of

---

[1] James, *Principles of Psychology*, vol. i. p. 237.

certain elements as similar to certain others, and dissimilar to still others.   If we say, e.g., that the taste of a mango is like that of a strawberry, but unlike that of an orange, we are including all of these acts, viz. discrimination, analysis, comparison and classification.   Now the making of comparisons and of classifications, it will be readily seen, involves the making or the recognition of associations, the fusion of experiences, and this is the outcome of focalizing attention.

It is very true, as has been frequently noted, that every act of attention involves the synthetic feature of association, for the very proposal to dissociate elements is a virtual admission of some sort of existing association.   This is sometimes spoken of as ' simultaneous association '.   Angell refers, e.g., to the discrimination of the colours on a postage stamp.   Now this is not merely a process of discrimination, though it is that.   ' It is also quite as truly one of association, for the qualities must be experienced together, must be mentally synthesized, that this special kind of discrimination may occur at all.' [1]   There are, moreover, as the same author shows, certain types of simultaneous association where the act of attention finds it difficult to separate the blended elements, as, e.g., when two harmonious notes are sounded together.   We may strike two notes on a piano which blend so perfectly that the sound produces upon us the effect of a unitary auditory sense-perception.   Yet we are aware that we have sounded two notes.   It is quite possible that, in an analogous way, despite our close attention, we may not be able to dissociate ideas and images which are fused in experience.

We may speak of attention as a process involving successive elements.   In other words, it is a process in which a succession of elements are synthesized, a process of ' successive association '. So we must admit the presence of the factors of association in some form or other whenever consciousness functions.   Ward states this matter in a very decisive way.   After approving of Bain's remark that ' so far as the mind is concerned, the generic fact is succession ', he proceeds, ' whereas it is easy to think of

[1] Angell, *Psychology*, p. 107.

instances in which the associated objects were attended to successively, and whereas too we are all well aware that the surest—not to say the only—way to fix the association of a number of objects is by thus concentrating attention on each in turn, it seems hardly possible to mention a case in which attention to the associated objects could not have been successive. In fact, an aggregate of objects on which attention could be focused at once would either be already associated or would simply be a whole as yet psychically unanalyzed.'[1]

The mental processes are carried on by means of manipulations of images. For images are the mental tools with which we carry on all our thinking. It might be even truer to experience to say that images constitute the thinking-stuff itself. To think is to have a stream of images in process in consciousness. Now, images are of varying degree of complexity and of abstraction. In their simpler forms they are reinstated sensorial experiences, and follow the types of the usual sensorial experiences, visual, auditory, tactual, etc. An image functions for us as a symbol. It may be a faithful representation for us of the concrete experience, in which case it is a memory-image. Or it may be composite in character, and lacking in any reproductive detail which may be referred to a single source experience, yet withal owing its structure to various concrete sources. The conclusion is that all of our mental processes, be they never so abstract or complex, are composed of images which are constantly flowing, and which are organized in accordance with the associative tendencies. Since the basis of all imagery is experimental, it means that the thought processes deal only with materials, which in the last analysis come to us out of experience.

This fact may be easily illustrated by reference to any field of thought. Applying it to religious thinking, it is apparent that our religious ideas are symbolic in character, are made of image-stuff which is referable to past experience. Religious conceptions take their rise in concrete situations, and are the outcome of our responses to social stimulation. In fine, the only way in which religious thinking is possible is by using imagery, the matrix of

---

[1] Ward, *Psychological Principles*, p. 194.

which is experience. A Neptune could have no significance except for seafaring peoples. A god of thunder would be only possible among people who had an experience of thunder. A tiger god could only be of meaning and worth for people who know tigers, a Ganesh for people who knew elephants. Mars could only have significance for folks practised in the arts of war, Mercury for people engaged in commerce, Baal for agricultural peoples, and so on, *ad libitum*. If the data were sufficiently full and accurate, it would be possible to show the connection in every case between the gods of religion and the social experiences of the folk.

Perception is a psychological process of considerable complexity, involving factors of familiarity or representation and novelty or presentation. It will be apparent that it is essentially a process of classification and identification. It is the least complex type of the combination of mental factors into a whole. The identification of the presentation involves a combining of it with represented elements, called up from past experiences in time, either simultaneously or successively. This is true of even the simplest perceptual experiences. In this respect, perception always involves imagination in the wider use of the term.

If association functions in the perceptual processes, it will be all the more apparent in the conceptual processes. William James has given us this definition: 'The function by which we mark off, discriminate, draw a line round, and identify a numerically distinct subject of discourse, is called conception.' The conceptual processes, like all mental processes, are dynamic rather than static. They involve two features, the creation of new concepts and the enrichment of older ones. In either case there is clearly a grouping operation in process, even more markedly than in the case of perception. The word etymologically means 'to take in' and so refers to the procedure of mentally consolidating or grouping factors common to a number of experiences in an ideational way. So, the concept is itself a symbol or token of an associative process that has taken place. It is an association of experiences in an idea which we can manipulate and utilize in further experiences. It is a case of the image-combining tendency whereby meanings are symbolized in order that they may be employed in communication with one another.

The reasoning process has been defined by President Angell as 'purposive thinking'. Elementary thinking is indeed involved in all the mental processes, simple and complex. But as conciousness develops, it is manifest in the various stages, in perception and conception, as we have seen, and in memory, imagination and judging. Reasoning occurs when we are confronted with problematic situations where it becomes necessary to manipulate ideas for the purpose of attempting to find solutions. But it does not imply newly created processes of manipulation, for these processes are dependent on our acquired habits of thought. Now these ideas that are so manipulated are nothing else than the concepts of which we have spoken, and reasoning is thus a process of dissociation and association of concepts, even as concepts are of more elementary images. We permit certain ideas, which we have selected in accordance with the particular view that we take of the problem, to be connected in association with other ideas which past experience teaches us to relate to the problem under consideration. The adequacy of our reasoning then rests on our correct apprehension of the problem and on our ability quickly and accurately to associate such ideas as will serve the experienced need. A particularly appropriate illustration of the usefulness of associative processes in reasoning is at hand in the use of the analogy. Where reasoning has to deal with problems of an abstract, speculative type, it is of immense assistance to be able to associate by similarity other problems to which solutions have already been found. Indeed, the perception of relations in any form, such as we have in reasoning, is an indication of the functioning of the associative tendencies.

Reasoning is inextricably linked with the judgement. To decide which is foundation and which superstructure, which is original and which product, is like the old enigma of the hen and the egg. Logically, reasoning is a process of judgements, but we are left wondering how the first judgement could have been formulated, save by a procedure of reasoning. Baldwin says that 'the essential feature of the judgement is that it sets forth, in a conscious contemplative way, the actual stage of the thought movement'. It involves the presence of an existence value and an existence predicate or reality. On the other hand, reasoning is thinking in logical form, whether it be correct or incorrect.   It is a process in which the reasoner is conscious that a judgement, the conclusion, is determined by another judgement or other judgements, the premises, in accordance with the general laws of thought.   The agent may not be able to formulate these laws in a precise way, though he tacitly approves of them and makes use of them in analyzing his meanings, and reaching his conclusions.

The judgement when it is expressed is a combination of concepts, involving in its simplest form a subject and a predicate. The logician calls it a proposition, and the grammarian a sentence. Even in its most simple form the judgement is an association of a predicate with a subject.   And in the more complex forms, the associative steps may be very intricate.   Judgements are sometimes classified into the analytic and synthetic forms.   But the same argument which was presented above in connection with 'attention' holds here also, namely that the processes of analysis and synthesis are interactive, the one presupposing the other.   So that the analytic and synthetic forms of judgement are really two phases of a unified process, based on the mental association of concepts.

The judgement functions as a bearer of meaning, a recognition of relationship.   This is primarily a combining procedure. It involves discrimination in a greater or less degree, differentiation implied or expressed, a manipulation of the data of experience in a primitive or developed form, and a positing of existing relations. The judgement represents consciousness functioning in the organization of the data of experience, and of course that involves both analysis and synthesis, dissociation and association, processes which, as we have observed, interpenetrate each other.

The syllogism represents a definitely organized form of association.   Here we see explicit what is probably implicit in many of our judgements.   The major premise and the minor premise and the conclusion in the proposition are all logically associated phases of a unitary judgement.   Now, the syllogism presupposes both types of reasoning, namely, the deductive and the inductive.   But, as Angell has convincingly shown, these processes are by no means separate and distinct, but rather phases of a common process.   'The actual procedure by which we assure ourselves of the tenability of an induction consists in comparing mentally each new instance with previous similar instances. In this operation the old experiences practically occupy the place of general principles, under which we array the new case. So that the deductive characteristics are evidently present in an unmistakable way in inductive forms of reasoning. Conversely, when we apply a general principle, or infer that a special consequence will follow an event, because of the general class to which it belongs, we inevitably avail ourselves of inductive methods, in so far as we label the new fact.'[1]

The Associationists spoke of the *laws* of association, indicating that their conception was that the functioning of association was static and structural. But in recent times the word *law* has been superseded by such words as *tendency*, *form* or *group*, in view of the more dynamic and functional interpretation that prevails. Dr. Ward, in commenting on the change in terminology, has this to say: 'The new terminology is illuminating: the substitution of *forms* for *laws* marks the abandonment of the old notion that association was by "adhesion" of the contiguous and "attraction" of the similar. We are thus left to find the cause of association in interested attention,'[2] a factor which we have seen is constantly, shifting.

The classifications of the associative tendencies by different psychologists show certain divergences which appear at first sight to be wider than they prove to be on closer examination. Some writers speak of five types, namely association by contiguity, association by similarity, association by contrast, cause and effect, and the whole and a part. It is quite easy to see that one could go on quite indefinitely listing possible types of connection. To cause and effect, and the whole and a part one might add genus and species, material and spiritual, substance and attributes, structure and function, and so on, *ad libitum*. But the question arises as to whether or not some of these relationships are not capable of subsumption under a more general form. Most psychologists affirm that to be so. So others reduce the

---

[1] Angell, *Psychology*, p. 289.
[2] Ward, article 'Psychology', in *Encylopaedia Britannica*.

types of association to three, contiguity, similarity and contrast. Still others effect a further reduction to contiguity and similarity, pointing out that contrast and similarity are simply the reverse and obverse of the same process. And others proceed to a still further reduction, and explain association on the one fundamental principle of contiguity which functions in accordance with the principle of habit.

Stout states the form under which contiguous association functions, as follows: 'If B has been perceived or thought of together with A, then, on a future occasion, the perception or idea of A will tend to call up the idea of B. In other words, the sequence of ideas follows the order in which their objects have been attended to in previous experience. The underlying principle is that mental activity when partially revived tends to repeat itself; it can only repeat itself if its original direction and order are reproduced.'[1] Stout goes on to say that this statement of the principle is valid enough so far as it goes, but it covers only temporal contiguity which is not a sufficiently broad compass. 'The truth is that the most important condition of association is not mere contiguity in the strict sense of temporal continuity of attention, but also continuity of interest. Where continuous interest pervaded the whole original process, the stronger this was the more selective is the revival apt to be, links being dropped out which are relatively unimportant to the general trend of mental activity.'[2]

Examples of the operation of this type of association are readily obtainable. A saddle reminds one of a horse, an ink bottle of a pen, a tin of petrol of a motor car, a hospital of an illness, a friend of a visit, and so on. Sometimes associations of this form attain a great degree of complexity. Dr. Mark, in *The Unfolding of Personality*, gives an instance from his personal experience. When young, a familiar family experience was to have tea in a summer house, when new bread and fresh fruit were usually served. About ten years later when walking in the Forest of Dean, he heard the clatter of cups and saucers which brought back to his consciousness the flavour of new bread and

---

[1] G. F. Stout, *Manual of Psychology*, p. 557.   [2] Ibid., p. 558.

red currants as though they were actually in his mouth. Using symbols, he practically represented the original experience, as S (summer), E (evening), O (out of doors), CS (cups and saucers), F (flavours.) The images were represented by small letters, s e o cs f. Ten years later, S E O CS recurred, and their functional indentity with the earlier experiences made them call up the s e o cs of the earlier experiences, but not those images only. There came associated with them by contiguity the 'f' also.[1]

It should be quite apparent that contiguity must not be interpreted as of any one type. That has already been pointed out in Stout's warning. There may be contiguity in time, or in space, or, as Stout shows, in interest. The association of two or more impressions may be made on the ground of their connections in time or in space or in interest. Association by contiguity obviously implies three elements, viz. (a) the fact of an external order, the presentation; (b) the fact of an internal order—the appearance or the occurrence together of the corresponding images; and (c) the connection of the images resulting from this.

Association by temporal contiguity may be of two types, viz. the connection of contemporaneous events and that of successive events. 'Any primary presentations whatever, occurring (1) together or (2) in close connection, tend to grow together or to cohere, in such a way that when any one recurs it tends to revive the rest as secondary presentations.'[2] The fact is that the element of succession cannot entirely be dismissed, even from the so-called simultaneous associations, for to exclude duration would be to reduce the whole experience to instantaneousness.

Another type of association is that by similarity. It is a familiar experience to all of us that we are constantly reminded of objects previously presented by objects similar to them now present to consciousness. The question arises as to whether, on that basis, resemblance ought to be regarded as an independent form of the associative tendencies. Some psychologists, e.g. Stout and Angell, are inclined to treat it as such. Angell

---

[1] H. T. Mark, *The Unfolding of Personality*, p. 41 f.
[2] Ward, *Psychological Principles*, p. 192.

illustrates the operation of the form in this way: ' The brain activities involved in thoughts of two similar things are in part identical, and consequently we have in their suggestion of one another a further instance of the principle of cortical habit.   The brain processes x and y, having the similar thoughts x^1 and y^1 as their concomitants, possess a common brain activity, z.   When x is active there is thus a chance that the excitation of z may stir up y, to which z also belongs.'[1]   It is of interest to note that the operation of association by similarity is often a delayed type of reaction.   For example, we meet some one who reminds us of an old acquaintance, but it may be only after some hours or days that we can recall who it is of whom the new acquaintance reminds us.

Association by contrast, may be taken as a modification of association by similarity, and as such of contiguity, if we accept Ward's position.   The truth is that we have no interest in associating objects by contrast unless there be an element of resemblance which leads us to desire to associate the similarity and dissimilarity together.   For example, we may know of twin brothers who are in many points alike.   But we fix on some dissimilarity by which we can distinguish them, such as complexion, height or any other characteristic that will serve as a contrast.   And the force of the association by contrast ultimately rests on their fundamental resemblance to one another.

The functioning of association depends on many different factors, but three stand out as of distinct importance, viz. frequency, intensity and recency of associative connections. Here the operation of these factors is the same as in the formation of habits.   The more frequently two ideas or situations have occurred together, the greater probability there is of them recurring in association.   An example in point is the association of Gandhi with the non-coöperation movement in India.   Again, the intensity or vividness of an experience with which some idea is associated will tend to make the connection relatively permanent.   Many of the experiences which soldiers in the Great War had, were of so

---

[1] Angell, *Psychology*, p. 213.

intense a character that deep association pathways, never to be forgotten, have been made. This factor accounts to a considerable degree for the associative tendency that frequently holds between an idea or experience and its affective tone. Recency is another factor that makes an association more likely to recur, because the images in association still have a good deal of their original freshness. That accounts for the fact that in dreams we frequently re-enact experiences of the previous day.

There are few actual associations in which one factor alone functions. Most of the actual experiences that we have of associations are more or less complex. There may, indeed, be elements of all the operative forces in a single association. At times the attempt to analyze an association opens up great difficulty. For example, Stout tells of a most peculiar type of association in his own experience. A line in his Latin Grammar which runs, 'Tum pius Aeneas umeris abscondere vestem', invariably calls up by association for him a notice in St. John's College, Cambridge, 'Smoking is not allowed in the courts and grounds of the College'. At first sight this association seems an enigma. But Stout explains it on the ground that he later observed that the form of both was that of a hexameter verse.

Associations may be classified on the basis of the control exercised. Some associations are altogether controlled or con- strained. In the process of trying to recall some name or object for practical purposes, we are accustomed to control our associa- tions as much as possible by reference to the desired end. Experiments have been performed by many investigators in this field, putting the stress on different features. Whipple, in his *Manual of Mental and Physical Tests*, records many of these experiments and the results. Their value is that they give an opportunity of investigating introspectively the associative functioning of consciousness, and thereby enabling us to define the types and factors which enter into it.

Other associations carry on without control or restraint. These are 'free associations', by which it is meant that no limit is placed upon the association in any way, the reactor being left quite free to allow the stimulating object or idea to call up whatever response it may. Experimental psychologists have also carried on investigations in this field with illuminating results as to the tremendous breadth of possible associations. Whipple summarizes the results of four investigations in American colleges and finds a fairly general agreement among them as to the type of objects, words or ideas that are called up by free association. I have totalled the responses of the four investigators and give the results in the table below.

TABLE SUMMARIZING THE RESULTS OF EXPERIMENTS IN FREE ASSOCIATION WITH INDIAN AND AMERICAN STUDENTS

TYPES OF ASSOCIATION	NUMBER AMONG INDIAN STUDENTS	SERIAL No.	NUMBER AMONG AMERICAN STUDENTS	SERIAL No.
Abstractions	2497	1	823	5
Political terms	2442	2		
Adjectives	2369	3	1285	1
Proper names	2046	4	745	9
Educational terms	1919	5	512	15
Functional terms	1700	6		
Geographical terms	1486	7	605	11
Vocational terms	1448	8	270	23
Verbs	1407	9	1284	2
People	1171	10		
Religious terms	1144	11		
Buildings	972	12	675	10
Amusements	822	13	272	22
Mercantile terms	819	14	119	25
Animals	664	15	1202	3
Vegetables	608	16	596	12
Parts and the whole	584	17	459	17
House furnishings	581	18	784	6
Kinship	562	19	130	24
Stationery and books	558	20	353	19
Implements and utensils	501	21	758	7
Transportation	468	23	306	20
Minerals	426	24	408	18
Arts	417	25	293	21
Sex terms	381	26		
Foods	374	27	535	13
Wearing apparel and fabrics	348	28	746	8
Meteorological terms	331	29	469	16
Analogies	111	30		
Other parts of speech			517	14
Miscellaneous	471	22	850	4
TOTALS	29,627		14,996	

The benefit of an experiment of this type is that it affords a means of discovering what interests are dominant.   In a process of free association where control is at a minimum the tendency is for the dominant interests to assert themselves.   With a view to finding out which interests are dominant among Indian students, I have tried the same experiment in Madras which Whipple records.   During the last four years I have tried it with sixteen groups of students, and secured 29,627 associations which were classified in the same way as those in the American groups, excepting that it was found advisable to add certain classes. Among American students, political and religious terms did not occur frequently enough to be treated separately, whereas they are both prominent among Indians.   During 1921-22 the political associations among Indian students proved to be particularly dominant, as it was the period when the non-coöperation movement was at its height.   During 1924-25 such associations were much less prominent.   One suspects that if the experiment had been performed on American students at the height of a presidential election campaign, the result would have been otherwise. The table sets the results of the American and Indian investigations side by side, though not with the notion that comparisons are of great value.

A number of other experiments have been tried in association by analogy.   One of the most interesting features of the previous experiment was the comparative fewness of associations by analogy in free association.   This seems very damaging evidence for the psycho-analytic hypothesis that analogical associations are very prominent in free association.   One would have expected that in a country, where analogical reasoning has been accepted as a valid logical process, the numbers might have been greater. In the West there are certain stock associations between concrete objects and qualities which they suggest.   Every group of people and every language area have their own characteristic analogies.   The experiments showed the following to be in use in South India, most of them in common use:

Object	Associated quality
lion ..	.. courage, majesty, ferocity
donkey ..	.. stupidity, patience

OBJECT	ASSOCIATED QUALITY
monkey	mischievousness, curiosity, imitativeness
dog	faithfulness
river	fluidity
lotus	beauty, purity
gold	worth, brightness
honey	sweetness
baby	innocence
bear	cruelty, ugliness
snail	slowness
lightning	rapidity, brightness
steel	hardness, strength
tiger	ferocity
jackal	cunning
blood	redness
iron	hardness
peacock	beauty, pride
bee	industry
watch	punctuality
rope	strength
crystal	clearness
bank	safety
crow	blackness
ocean	vastness
mountain	bigness
margosa	bitterness
owl	ugliness, gloom
bat	double-dealing
buffalo	stupidity, sluggishness
jungle	danger, thickness
ant	industry
milk	whiteness
elephant	large size
goose	stupidity, silliness
tamarind	sourness
deer	nimbleness
pumpkin	stoutness
brinjal	shortness

The wealth or poverty of one's associations are one of the best indications of intelligence. One evidence of feeble-mindedness is the poverty of one's associations, and conversely wealth of associations is an indication of superior intelligence. There are a number of intelligence tests successful responses to which depend on the functioning of associative tendencies. Stating differences between concrete objects from memory, the opposites tests, and the analogies tests are examples in point. Success in reasoning, in remembering, in artistic creation and in motor manipulation all depend in some sense on the functioning of these tendencies. One of the achievements of education ought to be the enrichment of one's stock of associations, so that in the hour of need it will not be necessary to hunt for the appropriate association as one would look for a needle in a haystack. The child must be trained to make observations of similarities, contrasts and other contiguities, so that building up of bonds is a constant, though relatively unconscious process.

LITERATURE

Wm. McDougall. *Physiological Psychology.* Dent, 1905.

H. C. Warren. *A History of the Association Psychology.* Constable, 1921.

G. M. Whipple. *Manual of Mental and Physical Tests.* Warwick & York, 1914-15.

C. G. Jung. *Studies in Word Association.* 1919.

E. L. Thorndike. *Educational Psychology*, Briefer Course. Columbia University Press, 1914.

T. H. Pear. *Remembering and Forgetting.* Methuen, 1922.

G. B. Stout. *Manual of Psychology.* University Tutorial Press, 1913.

H. T. Mark. *The Unfolding of Personality.* University of Chicago Press, 1912.

A. G. Tansley. *The New Psychology.* George Allen & Unwin, 1920.

CHAPTER X

THE PERCEPTUAL PROCESSES

THE reactions of the organism have been classified broadly as native and acquired. On this basis we must consider perception as belonging to the acquired group. The most elementary type of mental reaction is a sensory process whereby we are conscious of qualities. Perception is the next process in simplicity, but in this case we have the consciousness of objects. Those who analyze mental reactions in terms of levels place sensation as the first level, perception as the second, concept-forming as the third, and judgement and reasoning at the top. But we must guard against supposing that this means sharp lines of division between the various levels. The divisions are created in the interests of our theoretical descriptions and explanations, and do not exist in actual experience. The truth is that perception is integrated on the lower side with sensory processes, and on the upper side with the conceptual. While we perceive objects and sense qualities, still the objects that are perceived are not perceived apart from qualities, and the qualities which we sense are always attached to objects. Again, while we perceive objects and form concepts of classes of objects, we can neither form concepts apart from the process of perceiving various objects, nor do we perceive many objects without associating them with concepts of classes which enable us to identify them and name them.

William James described the mind of the child as a 'big, booming, buzzing confusion'. He is fairly surfeited with experiences, many of which are quite novel and do not admit of

grouping with anything in the past. The senses in which he
can employ the past tense are very meagre, and consequently he
does not understand many things that happen to him and about
him. The development of the mental life, however, carries with
it a gradual growth in the accuracy of the perceptual process. Our
knowledge of the details of the environment is constantly expand-
ing, and with it the capacity for identification and classification.
Though we may never achieve a complete reduction of life's
perplexities and confusion to order, still we can recognize a
steady tendency in that direction. To begin with, even the
sensory processes are by no means as accurate in infancy as
they become later on. For one thing, children are unable to
localize sounds and are insensitive to low pitched sounds during
the first four months of infancy, owing to the presence of mucus
in the ear. Development of accuracy is evident in most of the
sensory processes. There are exceptions, however. In some
respects, children exhibit a greater degree of sensitivity than
adults. Æsthesiometric tests with compass points show that
children are more sensitive to two-point space discrimination
than are adults. Perhaps it may be due to the fact that in the
smaller bodies the cutaneous spots are closer together. However, admitting possible exceptions, on the whole the growth of
the organism is characterized by increasing sensitivity.

The responses made to tests of intelligence give us definite
information in regard to the growth of perceptual ability in
certain respects. As an example, we may refer to the picture
tests. In the Binet tests the enumeration of three outstanding
objects is all that is expected at three years of age. When the
child reaches six years, he is expected to be able to enter into a
simple description of the picture, whereas at twelve years
interpretation is anticipated. Take the example of the picture
of the potter[1] which has been adopted in the Indian revision of
the Binet pictures. A three-year-old child would be expected to
enumerate three objects from among the men, woman, child,
wheel, pots, house, fire and trees. A six-year-old would be
expected to describe the scene in some way, such as, 'It is a

[1] Given on p. 221 of the author's *Psychological Tests of Mental Abilities*.

pot-maker's house, and they are making pots. The little child is crying, and the woman is standing at the door.' But at twelve years we expect some reading of meanings into the scene, such as, 'The potters are at work. One man is pouring water on mud evidently to get it ready, and another seems to be turning out a pot on the wheel, while the fire must be to burn the fresh pots. Probably the child has dropped a pot and broken it, because there are pieces lying about, and he is crying, while one of the men, maybe his father, has his hand pointing as if he were scolding.'

In this case we are not working with hazards as to the development of the perceptual processes. It has been ascertained, after examining many thousands of children that these are the ages at which the various stages emerge. If a child at six or seven years exhibits no ability in description, and a child at twelve is unable to interpret, we take these as indicating deficiency, and check the results with other tests to discover whether these facts are really symptomatic of defectiveness or not. But that is a matter of intelligence. Our interest in this connection is in the fact that the responses give us definite information as to the manner of unfolding of the mental processes. In the earliest stage we observe the perception of objects, but have no evidence that their relatedness is perceived. In the second stage we observe the perception of relationships between objects in a larger whole, namely the picture. In the third stage the perception of relationships is still further developed, and extended to past experiences, so that the child perceives meanings.

The perception of relationships and the perception of meanings develop side by side. It is the way in which the child learns to associate the novel with the familiar. As already noted, the little child has a very meagre past with which to associate present experiences. But as his stock of experiences grows, there is more variety, and hence many more different sorts of things with which present facts can be compared. Every complete perceptual process involves elements of both the novel and the familiar. Inasmuch as this particular process occurs now for the first, or for the only time, it is new. But in the measure that we draw on the past to get the data for identifying present facts, we are making use of the familiar. This process whereby we synthesize the new and the old, is frequently called apperception. The senses furnish us with the data of present experiences, our concepts supply the system of nomenclature for the objects, and memory brings to bear suggestions from the past, whereas in perception there is a combination of these elements into a living and meaningful whole. The significance of this for the educative process must appear on the face of it. Education embodies the integration and organization of the various elements of experience, and the unfolding of the self through that process. The more the child learns the relationships between the various facts which he perceives, the better is he educated. And the teacher has a splendid opportunity of guiding him in the process of integrating the elements of perceptual experiences into meaningful wholes. Nor is that to be accomplished by merely telling him that such and such relationships subsist. He must be led to a process of discovering them for himself.

We have referred to sensation as the first, and perception as the second response to a stimulus, the response in the former case being to qualities and in the latter case to objects. The perceptual process itself is slightly more complex, and the perceptual product is also more complex than is the case with sensation. This is due to the fact that in perception there are further facts associated with the stimulating object than in the case of sensation. True, we never see redness but only red objects, such as a red cloth, and never taste sweetness but only sweetmeats or other sweet objects. Nevertheless, we make a difference which is of theoretical value between the experience when it is centred in the redness or the sweetness, and the other experience which assimilates redness with softness and other qualities in a red cloth, or sweetness with hardness, etc., in a sweetmeat. The more elementary type is sensory, the more integrated is perceptual. But there is much to be said for keeping the thought of their fundamental unity before us through the term 'sense-perception'.

Another difference which sometimes emerges is to be found in the time required for the two types of reaction. Sensitiveness to qualities incites a prompt response, but there may be a delay in the functioning of perception.   During the interval between the first sensory responses to the qualities of the object and the final act of perception, there may be a process of trial-and-error in the attempt to establish relationships and identify the object. That may be observed by asking children to name various geometrical figures, pictures of which are shown.   It is frequently possible to observe a lagging of the perceptual process, if the child is not familiar enough to identify them without ideational comparison with past experiences, embodied perhaps in definitions. There is, moreover, neurological reason why the perceptual process should require more time than the sensory.   There requires to be an association of sensory elements to complete the perception.   That involves brain processes which are adjacent to, but slightly beyond the limits of the sensory areas.   I may hear a musical note from a *veena*,[1] but unless other sensations or past experiences come to my help, I am not able to identify the sound.   I am simply conscious of a musical sound.   But if I see a man playing an instrument, which I have learned is called a *veena*, I bring together a sound quality, visual qualities, and a memory image to form my *veena* percept.   Obviously, it takes more time, be it ever so little, to combine these elements than to experience any of them singly.

It has been said that the sensory facts are combined with memory images in certain perceptual experiences.   That raises the problem of the relationship between perception and imagination.   The difference between the two processes has been stated thus: while perception is the consciousness of objects present to sense, imagination is the consciousness of objects not present to sense.   When the object is present there is no difficulty in accounting for the stimulus.   It is created by the impact of the various qualities of the object on the sensory apparatus.   But in imagination there is a marked difference.   There is no object present to make any impressions on our sensory apparatus. Instead of being sensorially aroused as in perception, the process of imagining is ideationally aroused.   What shall we call that mental creation which enables us to represent to ourselves sights

---

[1] An Indian stringed instrument of the zither type.

and sounds, odours and tastes which are not being actually
experienced ? The name usually given is the 'image', or 'mental
image' to distinguish it from the 'sensory image' which is
experienced when the object is present. For example, the actual
image which is formed on the retina when we see an object
is a 'sensory image', while the mental portrait of that object
which we get in the absence of the object is a 'mental image' or
'memory image'. In imagination, as the term is employed in
the narrower sense, we experience a mental image in which
various elements of previous sensory products are fantastically
or creatively combined. In the wider sense, however, imagining
is any process wherein images are employed, whether it be a
memory process or a fantasy, such as the products of creative
art.

In either case the materials are of sensory origin. In
perception the combination of sensory elements is obvious; in
imagination the sensory elements are of somewhat more remote
origin, but it is plain that we have no other channels through
which they could have come.

There are certain differences between the products of these
two processes, which will be apparent when we consider that in
the one case the object is present and in the other case absent.
The first is a difference in intensity. An image is less distinct
and realistic than a percept. The image called up of the face or
voice of an absent friend does not possess the vividness and
aggressiveness that is characteristic of his actual face or voice.
The imagined odour or taste of an orange is much less satisfying
than the real thing. The nervous mechanism seems to be unable
to hold an image minus the sensory detail with the same striking
quality which characterizes the original experience. Furthermore, the absence of the object as a stimulus in imagination
results in a diminution in steadiness. The image is much more
fluctuating than the percept which is held steady by the presence
of the object. You may wonder whether your friend was wearing
a hat or a cap the last time you saw him, but when you are with
him there is no occasion for hesitation between the two. Ward
has compared the process of imagining to the flickering of a gas
jet, but remarks that ' there is not this perpetual flow and flicker

in what we perceive '.[1] It is superior in steadiness as well as in vividness.

Another difference is that percepts are experienced as objectively originated, whereas images are experienced as proceeding subjectively. Stout has put it, 'in actual sensation we are relatively passive and receptive, because impressions are determined by a factor which is not psychical at all—the stimulus. What the stimulus does for us in perception, we have to do for ourselves in the case of free ideas.'[2] Dr. Stout has stated an important fact in unfortunate language which seems to suggest that there is no stimulus for images or ideas. If he had used the phrase 'the stimulating object' instead of 'the stimulus' it would have been better. In perception the stimulus is without—an object; in imagination it is within—an idea or a feeling. This difference can be otherwise described by stating that a percept may be, and indeed is, continually confirmed and supported by sensory context, whereas an image not only cannot be so confirmed but may conceivably be contradicted by sensory context. The sensory elements which are reinstated in the image are detached from their original sensory context, and when a comparison is subsequently made it sometimes appears that resemblances are rather meagre.

Another distinction is that the percept is related to our motor activity, whereas the image is less so. If we see a motor car approaching us, the perceptual process leads to appropriate motor activity to avoid a collision in which we might get the worst of it. But the imagining of a score of motor cars need not involve a single step to the right or the left. To be sure, exceptions sometimes occur, particularly in abnormal experiences such as hallucinations. An hallucination is an image that is mistaken for a perception, and consequently the person who experiences may express himself in motor ways, but if he does the fallacy of his activities will very soon become apparent. The practical significance of perception is thus more immediate and probably

[1] Ward, article 'Psychology', *Encyclopaedia Brittanica*, 11th edition, vol. xxii. p. 569.

[2] Stout, *Manual of Psychology*, p. 545.

greater than that of imagination. We are unable to utilize the
image and act upon it as we can the percept. But perception of
an object is often a preliminary step to doing something with it.

The functions of perception will have been made more or
less clear in the process of differentiating it from sensation and
imagination. It will be clear that it is a type of response in
which we have both isolation and integration. The object is
perceived as a unit in differentiation from its environment. At the
same time that very act involves a selection and integration of
certain sensory elements. These processes are neural as well as
mental. Indeed, the mental process of perception may be said to
be the conscious concomitant of certain sensory-motor circuits.
Perception is often the intermediary between acquaintance with
an object, and appropriate action with reference to it. The
pathways in the nervous system connecting sensory receptors
and motor effectors lead through the association centres.
Perception is one type of associative process, and prepares the
way for a still further association of the sensory and motor.
Further, it enables us to combine, as we have seen, the novel
and the familiar, present sensory experiences with past experiences, and thus helps in the organization of life.

Perception is an elementary form of the cognitive process.
Some psychologists, such as Ward, speak of it as a type of
presentation, sensation being the more elementary type, and
perception belonging to the more complex. Perception, though
relatively complex as compared with sensation, is relatively
elementary as a cognitive process. It is the simplest form in
which the past and present are integrated for obtaining knowledge of a new object. 'The perceived thing', as President
Angell puts it, 'is not simply the physically present vibrations
of atoms and molecules which we call light, or sound, or what
not ; it is these vibrations, as they are interpreted by a psycho-
physical organism, which exposes to them a nervous system
already affected by past experiences, that enable it to get
only specific kinds of results from the present synthesis.'[1] The
word 'synthesis' is important, for truly perception is a synthetic

[1] Angell, *Psychology*, p. 170.

12

process, a unifying agency in which colours, sounds, forms, odours, tastes and other qualities are integrated and presented to us as definite wholes. Since perception is a form of the cognitive process, it is a definite form of learning. Mr. Kennedy-Fraser describes the stages in the process of perceptual learning as (i) the stage of selection, (ii) the stage of differentiation, and (iii) the stage of classification.[1] The selective stage is the first step away from the confusion of infancy. It would be exemplified in the little boy who calls everything to drink ' water ' and everything edible ' rice '. But gradually he comes to relate things by noting similarities and differences, and a process of differentiation is begun. At this stage he knows milk from water, and curry from rice, and often revels in the use of his newly formed percepts. This perception of relationships continues to grow, both analytically and synthetically, and the child begins to group his experiences. At this stage we observe perception merging in the concept-forming process. The child gets his concepts of food and drink, and begins to inquire to what classes and kinds of things various perceived objects belong. In that way he builds up an increasing body of knowledge.

The second great function of perception is the part which it plays in conation. The purposes of knowledge are not merely theoretical, but life's practical tasks. ' Science for its own sake ' or ' knowledge for the sake of knowledge ' are phrases sometimes used in trying to stir people up to dis-interested work. But in reality these phrases call for a psychological impossibility. The cognitive interests are never so compartmentalized in actual life. Dr. Ward has described the unity of the cognitive, affective and conative elements in this way: ' Broadly speaking, in any state of mind that we can directly observe, what we find is (1) that we are aware of a certain change in our sensations, thoughts or circumstances, (2) that we are pleased or pained with the change, and (3) that we act accordingly.'[2] The cognitive processes are thus definitely

---

[1] Kennedy-Fraser, *The Psychology of Education*, p. 95 f.

[2] Ward, article ' Psychology,' *Encyclopaedia Brittanica*, 11th edition, vol. xxii. p. 551.

and functionally connected with the active processes. The motto is not ' knowledge for knowledge's sake ', but ' knowledge for the sake of life '. We perceive, we acquire knowledge for the enrichment of life, deliberately planning to do something with what we acquire. In the struggle for existence, we seek to extend as far as possible our control, and one function of perception is to provide us with invaluable material for that end. For the purposes of control we need first to be able to identify an object —a perceptual process—and then we govern our course of action accordingly. Children learn through perceptual experience to act appropriately in regard to fire, scorpions, boiling water, quinine, castor oil, sweetmeats, kittens, coffee, jasmine and all the other countless things that enter their fields of experience. Our conclusion about those who fail to make use of their perceptions for purposes of control is that they are subnormal, and we treat them accordingly.

We have referred to perception as an elementary type of cognition. The question then arises as to the forms of cognition which it takes. Different psychologists have given different analyses of the forms of perception. McDougall, e.g. in his *Outlines*, classifies them as perceptions (i) of qualities, (ii) of time, and (iii) of space. The difficulty with this way of classifying is that the first group is likely to be confused with sensation in which there is consciousness of qualities. Of course, we must recognize that ' pure sensation ' is a myth. We are never merely conscious of qualities, but that criticism does not relieve the situation very much. After all, our differentiation, as repeatedly urged, is for theoretical ends, and has value for purposes of analysis. The same remark is applicable also to the perception of time and space. Neither of them has any existence in itself. What are perceived are things in temporal and spatial relations to one another. So also æsthetic perception is not the perception of an isolated beauty, but things which are beautiful, and social perception is the perception of persons in social relations. And the perception of meaning is the perception of objects in certain relations which we associate with past experiences of a similar nature that carried other co-ordinations. Strictly speaking, we should not speak of the consciousness of meaning as a perceptual process, as it requires a more complex mental mechanism involving conceptual thinking and reasoning.

The perception of time is the perceiving of objects in temporal relations. The types of experience which are included are simultaneity, successiveness, intervals, duration and rhythm. In a process of attention we observed the predilection of the organism for the element of change. Now of course change or process imply facts which succeed one another, and it is through our awareness of earlier and later facts or experiences that we form a notion of time. Hearing is usually considered to be the most accurate of the sensory processes for registering impressions of successiveness. It is more difficult to state which of two adjacent objects in a field of vision was seen first than to identify the earlier of two sounds which occurred close together. Some have thought that temporal perception must have originated in a sense of rhythm connected with breathing or the beating of the heart, but there is no conclusive evidence to bear that out, and our perception of time need not be disturbed by either respiratory or circulatory disturbances.

In the perception of time we ordinarily distinguish the parts into past, present and future. James added another point, and made his divisions the obvious past, the specious present, which he said had 'a vaguely vanishing backward and forward fringe',[1] the real present, and the future. Knowledge is clearly always a present experience, including knowledge of the past or the future. And knowledge of the present is always mixed with that of the past and the future. That is simply to say again that it is a process. Any time of which we can be conscious has duration, and hence James calls the perceived present 'specious'. The divisions which we make grow out of experiences of contrast, which is sharpened through practice. Time that is occupied by experiences of variety and interest seems to pass rapidly but seems long as we look back on it, whereas uneventful experiences drag as they pass but appear brief in retrospect. The more remote the

---

[1] James, *Principles of Psychology*, vol. i. p. 613.

past or the future, the more difficult is it to realize it clearly, and we ordinarily have recourse to symbols to help us.

The perception of temporal relations, like other forms of perception, grows in accuracy with experience, and the teacher has abundant opportunity to observe and stimulate its development in children. Very young children have quite vague notions of time. The word 'day' may simply connote the period of light in contrast to the darkness of night. Weeks, months, and years are very often confused completely in the child's mind. I have referred elsewhere[1] to some such cases of confusion. One case was that of a young girl who gave her age as fifteen years, and a few minutes later with equal assurance gave it as two months. Another was that of a boy of eleven years who regularly, and with no sense of absurdity, gave his age as thirty-five. A third was a child who, when asked to name the days of the week, continued without a pause to name the months, and ended with ' seven days in a week, and twelve months in a year '. Such errors are due to a failure to perceive the temporal relations involved in the periods mentioned, and unless they can be explained by some unusual circumstances are likely to be symptomatic of defectiveness if they appear in a child of from seven to eight years onwards. It is one of the things which teachers require to investigate so that avoidable errors can be corrected, and children be stimulated to develop along right lines. Certain subjects, such as music, typewriting and physical culture, have decided value as means to the development of temporal perception. But other subjects can be utilized quite well by associating certain tasks with definite periods of time.

The perception of space is acquired through all of the sensory channels. We can localize a colour in a cloth, a sound in a gramophone, a taste as in the mouth, an odour as in a rose, hunger as in the stomach, and so on. Yet some of our senses give us more accurate information than others in regard to location. We may not know with accuracy whence a sound or an odour is proceeding, but we usually know where a thing is when we see it, and we get accurate knowledge of the location of anything that we touch.

---

[1] Woodburne, *Psychological Tests of Mental Abilities*, pp. 46, 47, 52.

However, localization is only one form of spatial perception, and our other senses are important sources of information in regard to other spatial matters, whereas the accuracy of vision and touch varies under different conditions. Two-point space discrimination, for example, is far more accurate on the lips or hand than in the centre of the back, where the pressure and pain spots are much farther apart.

Size is one of the spatial categories concerning which the perceptual processes give us information. Vision and touch are obviously useful for this purpose. Sound also helps. The explosion of a big shell makes more noise than a small one. But 'a big voice' sometimes belongs to a small man. Our most accurate perceptions of size come through comparing the information which we get through the different sensory processes.

The perception of distance is another form of spatial perception. It is possible to measure the distance between two points in a visual way, by standing in a position of prominence so that we can see both points. Distance is also sometimes measured by calculating how long it requires for a sound to travel. It is possible to watch the flash when a gun is discharged, and calculate how long it takes for the sound of the explosion to travel. Then, allowing for the fact that light travels 186,000 miles per second while sound travels only 1,100 feet per second, the calculation may be made. Still another way is to walk the distance, and calculate it on the basis of kinæsthetic sensitivity. It is clear that our perception of distance may involve any or all of these factors.

Form and dimension are also types of spatial knowledge which are obtained perceptually. The eye and the hand are particularly useful in giving us this kind of information. An image of the object is formed on the retina of the eye, and in addition we are able to handle objects. Certain tests in the Binet system are designed to enable us to observe how far children have developed this type of perception. The recognition and reproduction of geometrical figures, and the form-board tests are particularly useful in discovering how well that capability is developed. The handling of cubes and blocks, and construction involving their use, such as that which Madame Montessori recommends, serve well to develop perceptions of this type. Perception of movement is also an aid in developing this capacity, and may be associated with both temporal and spatial facts.

There are two facts, analogous to one another, which are of interest in this connection, viz. binocular vision and binaural audition. We see with two eyes, and each retina has its own image of the object, and yet if vision be normal we are conscious of experiencing but one sensory image. So also each ear receives its own stimulus from the impact of sound waves, and has its own complete receptor apparatus, yet we are conscious of but one sensory experience. These two facts serve to show how delicately the organism is adjusted. In each case there is a re-enforcement of the sense-perception of which one may be only vaguely conscious in case of some disease or defect to one of the eyes, or one ear. Furthermore, the two corresponding organisms, one on either side of the face, serve to balance one another, and enable us to perceive spatial facts with an accuracy that would be otherwise impossible. A man who is deaf in one ear finds it much harder to locate the direction of a sound than one who hears equally well with both ears. And the person with two normal eyes maintains the capacity of perception more accurately than the person with one defective eye.

Various attempts have been made psychologically to deal with æsthetic reactions. Some speak of æsthetic sentiments, others of æsthetic feelings, and still others of æsthetic emotions, while perhaps the most satisfactory classification is to deal with them in the sphere of attitudes. The problem which concerns us in this connection is the part played by perception in these reactions. It is clear that the facts which we interpret æsthetically are given to us through the process of sense-perception. True, people differ immensely in the interpretation of these facts, and we have to reckon with an important subjective element in the perception of beauty. There is, indeed, no attitude in which the subjective factor functions more largely than in this. Furthermore, the social background is one of the important determinants of the attitude, though here and there appears an artistic genius who simply breaks over all environmental barriers, both in appreciation and in creative power.

Symmetry is one of the facts of foremost interest and importance in the perception of beauty. There are some[1] who explain all the facts not only of æsthetics but also of affective and conative life by that category. Symmetry of sound is harmony, and is the outcome of a periodicity in the sound waves. There are very few people living who do not prefer consonance to dissonance, or musical tones to noises. There is a smoothness and agreeableness, as Helmholtz pointed out, which characterizes those tones the vibrations of which do not interfere with one another, but rather blend. When tones harmonize with one another, the total impression upon us is one of relative unitariness rather than diversity, and the effect upon us is affectively pleasant. But where the air-vibrations are of mixed or rapidly changing rates, the effect is unpleasant. No really satisfactory explanation of the facts has been forthcoming, but the fact remains that the perception of harmony is pleasantly toned, and discord is unpleasant.

Similar observations may be made with respect to the perception of coloured objects, and combinations of colour. We speak of certain colours as 'blending' or 'going together' well, and of others as 'clashing'. The success or failure of a painting depends in some considerable measure on the harmony which the artist secures in his colouring. Primitive peoples and children seem to show a preference for the more intense hues. The ability to name the four primary colours is regarded by Terman and Burt as a test of five-year-old intelligence. Indeed, all those who have investigated intelligence, and tried to measure it, have regarded æsthetic perception is a contributing factor. In the tests for five-year-old mentality Terman also places the test of comparing three pairs of faces, one of each pair of which is decidedly more beautiful than the other. Psychologists are in agreement that if ability in æsthetic comparison is not a factor of intelligence, it at least develops parallel to it. It is decidedly lacking in the mentally deficient. In this latter test it is symmetry of form which makes the appeal. As a rule, curved lines possess a grace that appeals more than straight

---

[1] e.g. Sir Charles Walston, in *Harmonism and Conscious Evolution*.

lines and angles.   Figures that lack in proportion are not pleasant.
But proportion, harmony, symmetry, have the effect of resting us,
and contenting us with things as they are.   Asymmetry and
discord produce upon us the feeling that we want to do something
to change the situation, the characteristic conative tendency of
disagreeableness.   There are other factors the perception of
which also affects us æsthetically, such as intensity, definiteness,
and obstructions.   Either extreme of intensity is æsthetically
disagreeable, and things which are indefinite frequently fail to
arouse the sense of beauty.   Rhythm is much more appealing
than are impeded and obstructed stimuli.

Whether one tries to make æsthetics a basis for explaining
and organizing life or not, all are ready to acknowledge the
analogical value of the categories of harmony and symmetry.
The educational end was described by Herbert Spencer as one
of inducing harmonious relations between the external and the
internal.   Harmony between one's own motives and attitudes is
also desirable in the unfolding of life.   There is something
deficient about the person to whom the contrast between harmony
and discord makes no difference.   The teacher ought to use
music, drawing, painting, folk-dancing, and such other means as
may be at his disposal, to develop the perception of harmony and
æsthetic appreciation.

There are certain facts of social significance which we
perceive through sensory channels.   There are several social
reactions, such as anger, fear, sympathy, love, etc., which are
made evident to us by gestures, the appearance of the eyes, or
the general physical attitude of the person.   Even the lower
animals learn to get much information by such observations.
A dog very readily diagnoses the friendliness or unfriendliness
of a person by perceiving the indications of the attitude.   Children too are constant observers of the little signs which afford
keys to the intentions and temperaments of other children and
adults.   The ability to form judgements of other people develops
through social perception.   It is not always safe to be too certain,
however, on such data, for sometimes people feign expressions
contrary to their real attitude.   But on the whole we know that
certain gestures and facial expressions are expressive of certain
social attitudes, and we are safe in acting accordingly.

Perception may be social in the sense that we sometimes share in other people's responses. That is one of the effects which the social environment has on the individual person. He comes to see with the eyes of the group, and hear with the ears of the community. Its responses become his responses, and its attitudes his attitudes. He appreciates its humour, enters into its sorrows, and shares in its appreciation of what is beautiful. In an analogous way we may put down a good many differences in perception to social differences. Some things will never have the force to attract the attention of an Englishman because he is socially habituated to them, whereas a Tamilian would perceive them at once through the contrasts to his own way. The perception of different styles of dress or of wearing the hair well illustrates the matter under discussion.

The divergence in social perception was recently illustrated by an incident which took place in Japan. In recent years, returning the compliment paid by Western artists a generation ago, the Japanese have been studying European art. An exhibition was recently held in Tokyo for which the committee in charge obtained from the French Government the loan of several pieces of modern French sculpture, including Rodin's famous *Le Baiser*. When this was unpacked it became the centre of interest, but unhappily not as a work of art. In Japan kissing is among the acts which are socially taboo. The arrival of the Rodin statue created a serious problem for the Chief of Police of Tokyo. The solution which he arrived at was to permit the statue to remain on its pedestal in the exhibition. To do otherwise would have been an act of discourtesy to a friendly nation. But around it was erected an impenetrable fence of bamboo. Only a select few were permitted the doubtful privilege of admission within the screen. The incident illustrates the cleavage in social sanctions in two parts of the world. In France the exhibition of the naked body is disapproved, whereas the exhibition of naked statues as works of art is quite all right. On the other hand, the Japanese, who are without prudishness about the naked body, are unable to approve of naked statues. The responses of a Frenchman or a Jap to the same stimulus are thus widely different, and the difference is due entirely to social sanctions.

It is a strange coincidence that a good many people of defective mentality have quite good social qualities. The result is that unskilled observers often reach conclusions which are perceptual errors. It sometimes occurs that a young woman with beautiful features and certain social charms is brought before a court for moral delinquency. The psychologist who has examined her knows that she is feeble-minded, but the judge regards such expert opinion as pedantic show, and sets her free, only to give her a further opportunity of getting into trouble. As Woodworth says, 'apparently the only way to perceive intelligence is to see a person in action, preferably under standard conditions, where his performance can be measured'.[1]

The teacher ought to know something about the various kinds of errors of perception. It is usual to call them ' illusions ' but that must not be confused with the metaphysical conceptions of *maya* with which the people of India are familiar. Here we use it only in the psychological sense of a false perception in which a real sensory stimulus is present, but the fact of which it is supposed to be symptomatic is not there. Various classifications of erroneous perceptions have been offered by different psychologists. James had three groups, viz. (i) those due to movement, (ii) those due to a feeling of convergence, and (iii) those due to a feeling of accommodation. Perhaps the grouping which Woodworth suggests[2] is as good as any. He distinguishes (i) those due to peculiarities of the sensory apparatus, such as visual after-images, (ii) those due to preoccupation or mental set, such as the suspicions of the insane, (iii) those due to analogical responses, such as the ' proof-reader's illusion ', and (iv) those due to imperfect isolation of the fact to be perceived, such as the well-known ' barber's pole illusion '. The chief concern which the teacher has with facts of this type is to know in general the kinds of error to which the perceptual processes are liable, so that he may direct children to avoid them and correct them. The matter has been studied with considerable care, so that we know the relative limits within which errors of perception are possible

---

[1] Woodworth, *Psychology : A Study of Mental Life*, p. 446.
[2] Ibid., pp. 451 ff.

in normal persons. Weber's law states that equal relative differences are equally perceptible. That does not mean that different sorts of perception have equal facilities for discerning differences. Visual perception is keener than tactual, and tactual than auditory. A difference of one-fiftieth in seeing the length of a line is perceptible; one-tenth in lifting a weight, and one-third in the loudness of a sound.

One of the tests of intelligence which finds a place in the Binet-Terman scale is the discrimination of weights. In the five-year-old tests it is the ability to differentiate between two weights of three and fifteen grammes of identical external appearance. In the nine-year-old tests five weights are given—3, 6, 9, 13 and 15 grammes—which are to be arranged in order. The feeble-minded child usually begins in earnest, but soon resorts to playing with the weights, an indication that the kind of perception demanded is an element in intelligent processes. The intelligent child will also show his intelligence by auto-criticism of his errors. Some errors of perception will soon become evident to the child as errors, and he will proceed to correct the mistakes. It is much more desirable that he should develop the capacity and the habit of making his own corrections than that he should have them done for him by his elders. The increasing ability to perceive and to criticize one's own mistakes is one of the sure results of the educative process.

LITERATURE

T. H. Pear. *Remembering and Forgetting*. Methuen, 1922.

G. F. Stout. *Manual of Psychology*. University Tutorial Press, 1913.

H. C. Warren. *Human Psychology*. Constable.

C. H. Judd. *Psychology*. Scribner's, 1907.

E. B. Titchener. *Textbook of Psychology*. 1919.

Wm. McDougall. *Outlines of Psychology*. Methuen, 1924.

C. Spearman. *The Nature of 'Intelligence' and the Principles of Cognition*. Macmillan, 1923.

E. B. Thorndike. *Educational Psychology*, Briefer Course. Columbia University Press, 1914.

A. S. Woodburne. *Psychological Tests of Mental Abilities*. University of Madras, 1924.

CHAPTER XI

IMAGINATION

FOR a long time imagination was conceived as a sort of 'no
man's land' in mental geography. There the mental processes
roamed about at pleasure, and acknowledged allegiance to no
power whatsoever. Imagination was the field of fantasy and
unreality, a realm of mental life fraught with lurking dangers
everywhere. That point of view was reflected in the way in
which children were treated who were tempted to be imaginative. The child who could entertain itself by living for an hour
in an imaginary world was feared to be showing indications of
deceptiveness, and warned against it. 'Building castles in the
air' was a phrase implying opprobrious comment. One of the
benefits which it was hoped education might confer was that of
bringing the mental processes under discipline, so that 'flights'
of imagination might be curbed and the child might be steered
clear of the shoals.

The great reversion against this old point of view, which
characterizes modern education, is due largely to a more clear
understanding of the psychology of imagination. It is understood now as a more normal process, having a definiteness of
function hitherto unappreciated. Furthermore, it is seen to be
integrally united with the processes of memory and reasoning, and
consequently to be indispensable to the mental life So that the
practical problem of our day is not how best to overcome wild
imaginative tendencies, but how best to train and develop these
processes to be of the largest service to the person. Instead of
throwing cold water on the imaginative disposition of the child,

the present-day educator studies the best methods for its development, recognizing in it some of the finest possibilities of creative personality.

In the discussion of the perceptual processes there were certain points brought out concerning the nature of imagination in contrast to perception. It was pointed out that whereas perception is the consciousness of objects present to sense, imagination is the consciousness of objects not present to sense. That is really the meaning of McDougall's defining of imagination as 'thinking of remote objects',[1] for with him the word 'remote' means 'beyond the range of the senses'.[2] This distinction involves another, namely that perception is objectively aroused, whereas imagination is subjectively or ideationally aroused. This means that it is possible to confirm the perceptual detail by reference to the stimulating object, whereas no such confirmation is possible in the case of imagination. Further, the perceptual experience has a striking quality, a vividness which is lacking in imagination. And the perceptual process is superior to imagination in the matter of steadiness. Again, imagination is less related to motor activity than is perception. Finally, perception is a process of presentation, and imagination involves representation. In the most elementary kind of imagery, we picture to ourselves the object precisely as we originally perceived it, whereas in the more complex forms we picture something which is a combination of material that was perceptually presented in the first instance.

If we characterize imagination as reinstated perceptual experience, it is plain that there are several different forms. Memory is one type, and the content of the memory process we speak of as a 'memory image'. But that is a sufficiently important type of imagination to deserve separate treatment. Another is the anticipatory type which is sometimes called pre-perception. A third form corresponds to the word 'imagination' when used in its narrower connotation as designating the creative combination of elements of previous presentations. Strictly speaking reasoning may also be taken as a process of imagination, as it is

---

[1] McDougall, *Outlines of Psychology*, p. 284.   [2] Ibid., p. 207 n.

one in which images are combined with reference to particular problems or purposes. McDougall has suggested another basis for classification into (i) reproductive or representative imagination, (ii) constructive imagination, and (iii) creative imagination.[1] But it is a doubtful procedure to maintain that the constructive and creative forms are separate types. Of course, he acknowledges that these forms are inextricably mingled in actual life. It would seem, however, that construction were better regarded as one form of creativeness.

Imagination is always reproductive. Inasmuch as the image is a reinstated sensorial or perceptual experience, the possibility of such an experience rests on the previous experiencing of the perception. In the case of remembering, the effort is to recall the images as far as possible in precisely the same relationships to one another as the original perceptual elements stood in. A great deal of the usefulness of a memory process depends on maintaining the correct temporal sequence, because temporal sequence is often a clue to causal relations. By far the largest number of people remember by the aid of visual images. They picture the event as it happened 'in the mind's eye'. They tell us that they can close their eyes, and see a scene just as if it were really present. Some people are unusually gifted with the ability to visualize and to describe scenes, so that others can call up images in response. This is surely an obvious case of imagination, though the imagining may be quite true to the details of the original experience. In the same way, there are people who can recall auditory images very well; others, kinæsthetic images; others, olfactory images; and others, images of taste or touch. In the psychological sense, an image thus has a much wider connotation than in popular usage, in which it is largely confined to reinstated visual experience. But in all cases it is reinstated or reproduced, that is, has reference to the past.

While imagination always has an element of reproduction, some of the processes concerned have also a creative or productive factor. The castles that are built in the air are always built with bricks obtained on the ground; nevertheless, they may not

---

[1] McDougall, *Outlines of Psychology*, p. 291.

correspond to any castle hitherto erected. Our dreams by night and our day dreams also usually involve new combinations, sometimes very fantastic, of the stuff of past experience. Inventions of new devices and instruments are the products of men of imagination and foresight, and unless they had first of all been born in someone's consciousness they would probably never have taken concrete form. The scientific hypothesis too is the work of creative imagination, the imagination of someone who has been able to view a problem in a new light and propose a solution as the result of the creativeness of his thought combinations. The work of art, whether it be a poem, a painting or a sculpture, is a most patent illustration of the work of creative imagination. True, it contains no detail that is not the gift of past experience, yet those details have been woven together as never before, so that the product is truly an artistic creation. It is the presence of such a strong creative element in so much thinking that is worth while, that compels us to realize how essential it is that we should be careful to encourage the development of the imagination in children in the interests of their futures.

The imaginative tendencies of the child are one of its great assets. Who has not watched a little child at play, imagining companions, situations and problems which are not there? One cannot but be struck by the realism of that imaginary world of the child. The adult who has not enough of the child mind remaining in him to appreciate the reality of the child's experiences is impoverished indeed. Yet how often such tragedies occur! Sometimes when it is meal-time or bed-time the stern, unimaginative parent will call the child to put away his playthings and come, and will be surprised to be told by the child that he is in the midst of some important enterprise, building a bridge across the river, conducting a procession through the village, or what not. At a time like that the parent or elder brother or sister who fails to enter into the child's imaginings and treats his playthings at their face value only will be doing a great injustice and perhaps a serious injury to the child. Who knows but that the keen imagination of the child is the forerunner of a novelist or a poet, a painter or a sculptor? Surely this is a gift that is to be encouraged and not dampened. Instead of throwing cold water on such tendencies, parents and teachers would do well to be on the lookout for means of discovering them and fostering them. The imagination may be the master-key to the child's future, the indicator of his finest ability. It should be watched and tended as carefully as any other element in the child's life.

A psychological examination of school subjects will disclose the presence of certain subjects which are especially well designed for developing the child's imaginative ability. Obviously, drawing and colouring with paints should be useful in enabling one to discover ability to draw and paint. The literature classes may serve to discover and develop imagination along literary lines, such as poetry and good prose writing. Very often it is possible to combine historical and literary lessons, and that affords an excellent opportunity under wise direction for drawing out ability in histrionic directions. It is very often found that natural sciences, and even the physical sciences, can be turned to good account, inasmuch as the observations made present appeals to the imagination, both in the appreciation of beauty and in the solution of problems. The play hours also offer exceedingly valuable material for judging of and encouraging certain imaginative tendencies, and that is precisely one of the reasons why play should be directed and observed just as mathematical or any other operations. The teacher who pays no attention to the play of his children is depriving himself of one of the best sources of information about them, as well as one of the best means for obtaining their confidence. That leads to an observation which applies all along the line, viz. that the usefulness or otherwise of any subject in the development of the imagination depends to a great extent on the teacher. A good teacher will discover means for developing such tendencies in what to another might seem the most prosaic of occupations.

There are certain typical operations and attitudes which illustrate the functioning of imagination. The first of these to claim our attention is play. Play almost invariably involves an element of imagination. The game-situations are calls upon the child to imagine himself in a rôle or in a place quite different from the existing facts. One of the great things about the child is his

13

readiness and ability to do that realistically. In many instances the child's play involves imagining even the materials with which he is to play. But even where he is given instruments, they are not regarded as of value in themselves. The worth of the toy is instrumental to the play ; it is a plaything which often represents something that functions in adult life. A doll represents a real baby, a drum or a horn are imitations of real band instruments, a wooden horse stands for a real horse, and so on. One of the values of the plaything is its incentive to the imagining of the real things for which they stand. Very often it is possible through the child's manipulation of the plaything to discover outstanding abilities in predispositions towards certain types of activity. Imagination becomes a guide to ability.

The new attitude towards play is closely linked with the new attitude towards imagination in general. Play is no longer merely tolerated as a necessary evil, the sooner over the better. It has come to be appreciated as worth while for its own sake. Some psychologists would include play in their catalogue of the instincts, and though some of the play reactions may be considered too complex to be so classed, nevertheless the tendency to do some things just for the fun of doing them, without any considerations of survival value, is surely an instinctive tendency. The play responses, since they are so natively characteristic of the organism, have definite purposes to fulfil in the developing life. One is the development of the varied forms of motor manipulation. Another is the opportunity for the unfolding of character in such a way as to include the elements of comradeship and fair play. Still another is to offer scope for the development of certain phases of the imagination not only in relation to motor but also mental manipulation, with reference to purposes which will bring satisfaction. 'There is no one single "play instinct" that furnishes all the satisfaction,' says Woodworth, 'but conceivably every natural and acquired source of satisfaction is tapped in one play or another.'[1] The value of play is positively apparent in the satisfaction and thrill that accompany the various play responses.

---

[1] Woodworth, *Psychology: A Study of Mental Life*, p. 488.

Play is regarded so much as a diversion or a relief from work that it is refreshing to find a new movement to make use of play as an active method of learning. This new movement is described as ' The Play Way ' in a book with that suggestive title by Mr. H. Caldwell Cook. There are, of course, some of the more orthodox who view with suspicion any attempt to put the play attitude into school work, but one of the best replies to their criticism is to point to the participants and the attitude which they display towards their work. Woodworth makes a distinction in the case of art, saying that to the producer it is work and to the consumer play.[1] This would seem to be an unwarranted distinction. When a person enters his artistic work with the joy of creation, the distinction between work and play may very well disappear. So is it with children in a school where the play way is utilized as a method of instruction. There is no subject in the curriculum that cannot be made more interesting by appealing to the imagination of children. How much more appealing and sensible it is, for example, to teach the multiplication processes by some such methods as playing at a shop in which various numbers of articles and various quantities are purchased and bought at given rates. It links the operations with real life, and makes the school seem more like a game. There is no doubt that the success of the Project Method in arousing interest and holding attention is due to this very fact, that the spirit of play is put into the work of the school. One of the best illustrations of a successful use of the Play Way, as Prof. John Adams has pointed out, is in the Boy Scout and Girl Guide movements. Some splendid practical lessons are learned, social virtues are developed, and various kinds of motor manipulation are acquired through scouting. It has a most alluring appeal to the boys and girls, who respond by throwing all the energies of the play spirit into the difficulties and tasks which confront them. And even disagreeable things are done with willingness and spirit, because this spirit dominates. It is a real preparation for vital living problems, the whole strength of which is through its appeal to the imagination.

A second type of mental function which illustrates imagina-

[1] Woodworth, *Psychology : A Study of Mental Life*, p. 517.

tion is the dream. A dream is the experience during sleep of a succession of images or fantastic ideas as present, and a modified form of the experience sometimes occurs even in waking consciousness, which is called the day-dream. Dreams are the most elusive of mental experiences, both in the experiencing of them and in the attempt to describe and explain them. That is doubtless due to the fact that they occur when the major portion of conscious processes is at rest. Yet it is obvious that all the processes are not at rest, or we should not even have dreams, for they are one form of mental activity. Which processes then are at rest, and which of them are active? Various attempts have been made to answer that question. Prof. Rignano, e.g., attempted to account for dreams[1] on the basis of the absence of the affective element of consciousness. On account of its absence, absurdities, doubts, fears, antagonisms, surprises and the sense of shame are not experienced. But many persons object that they do experience feelings which sometimes last for a long time after the return to waking consciousness. It would seem to be dangerously upsetting to our understanding of the unity of the organism. Cognition, affection and conation cannot be induced to function separately when we are awake, and there is no good reason to suppose that they will do so even when we are asleep.

Dreams are constituted by a conglomeration of images from past experiences. Nobody today thinks of dreams as the formless, contentless, mental materials that were evidently in the mind of Shakespeare, when he wrote

> ' I talk of dreams
> Which are the children of an idle brain,
> Begot of nothing but vain fantasy ;
> Which is as thin of substance as the air ;
> And more inconstant than the mind.'[2]

We are assured that no image can ever be formed that has not been born of perceptual parentage. Even the wildest, most impossible dreams are made of a great deal of detail which originally had perceptual content. On the other hand, it is very seldom that dream images conform in content or temporal succes-

---

[1] E. Rignano, *A New Theory of Sleep and Dreams*, in Mind, July, 1920.

[2] Shakespeare, *Romeo and Juliet*, act I, scene iv.

sion to the actual experiences which furnished the details. True, sometimes dreams are re-enacted perceptual experiences, but seldom without some additional content or distorted combination of images. Is it possible to discover any meaning out of this complexity of imagery? Has it any relation to mental life in the large? This is one of the questions in which modern psychology has been particularly interested.

The people of India have always been interested in dreams, and have done much to keep alive the belief that they are meaningful experiences. Indeed, dream interpretation is almost a *sastra*[1] in this country, and interpreters of dreams are consulted as authorities much in the same way as physicians and scientists are looked to as authoritative in their own fields. It is not possible in a brief reference such as the present to deal at any length with this particular lore, and from the point of view of scientific psychology there would be little to be gained. The approach to the subject is rather pre-scientific and magical than psychological. Like other magical interpretations, dream interpretation has followed largely the logic of *post hoc ergo propter hoc*.

An example will help to make it clear. A student sent the following written query to my desk recently. 'A friend of mine recently dreamed that his brother, who was then in good health, died. The following day his brother suddenly fell ill and died. Please explain.' My reply was first to give a counter query: 'A friend of mine recently dreamed that his brother, who was then in good health, died. The following day his brother did not fall ill and die. Please explain.' The point is that the person who has the magical attitude lays undue emphasis on chance occurrences of temporal succession, and argues from them to logical succession, quite neglecting the scores of exceptions that there may be. Even if he were to dream a thousand times of a death which never took place, he would not be so much impressed as he would be by one occasion when the dream came true.

Psycho-analysis has, within the last twenty-five years, done an immense amount of work in seeking to understand and explain

---

[1] Sanskrit, science.

dream experiences.   It was in 1900 that Dr. Sigmund Freud published his *Die Traumdeutung* (The Interpretation of Dreams), and that really marks the beginning of the new interest in the subject.   There are two fundamental postulates from which Freud begins: (i) that mental experiences can be explained in mental terms, and (ii) that mental experiences as well as physical are definitely caused and not mere chance happenings.   It is the belief of Freud that much of the material of dreams was hidden from conscious-ness in the unconscious.   It is, of course, nothing new to say that all dream imagery is in a sense memory imagery, though the combination of images may be new.   Freud thinks that this combination is in accordance with definite principles and for reasons of biological significance.   Many dream images, according to him, are symbolic, and one problem of the psycho-analyst is to discover the key to the symbolism.   The method most commonly in vogue for discovering the nature of the symbols is to utilize tests of ' free association '.   If the conative control is removed as far as possible, the dominating interests and influences have a tendency to assert themselves.   That is why a free association is like a dream.   Control is at a minimum and latent images have an opportunity of asserting themselves.   Some of the materials in the unconscious are there as the outcome of repression for moral or other reasons.   This very fact of repressing a problem instead of settling it in one way or another, is frequently the cause of complexes which are emotionally disturbing.   If by a process of free association it is possible to get at the root of the disturbance, and that often involves an interpretation of dream symbolism, then the subject may be relieved of his anxiety.   It is not necessary for our purpose, which is to show the place of the dream as a function of the imagination, to indicate the various schools of psycho-analytic interpretation which have arisen.   The similarities in their points of view are much more significant.   The main consideration has been well stated by Prof. Pear :

' The dream, therefore, appears to be a mental structure the constituent mechanisms of which are not different in kind from those which characterize the mental events of waking life.   It is the reciprocal interplay of these mechanisms, the altered emphasis

which each of them receives, and their comparative freedom
from the dominating directive tendencies of the day-time which
combine to make the dream the *enfant terrible* of the well-
ordered personality, and the delight of the modern psychologist.'[1]

A third type of mental activity which illustrates the functioning of imagination is that which culminates in invention. By
invention is meant that process whereby some original contri-
vance is created to meet some need. It involves working in the
direction of an end, and criticism of work done with reference
to the purpose in view. It is a process of adjustment with
reference to the materials in hand to make them serviceable to
the end. Thus the inventor must carry on a process of manipulation which he does in a real spirit of play. The inventor is so
keenly interested in the solution of his problem, and the manipulation of his materials to that end, that he becomes absorbed in
interest and enthusiasm, and sometimes has to be reminded of
the physical need for food and sleep.

The successful inventor is one who is skilled in imaginary
situations. Having realized his problem, he pictures to himself a
possible way or ways in which it might be solved. Then he
goes on imagining how it would be possible so to manipulate his
materials as to bring about the end he has in view. That is to
say, his motor manipulation is preceded by mental manipulation.
Such mental manipulation is a characteristic of intelligence, and
one of the foremost traits that the intelligence tester seeks to
find. Some of his tests are especially well adapted to discover
such ability. Take, e.g., some of the form-board tests. A
child of superior intelligence does not have actually to try each
block in the different recesses until the correct one be discovered, but he manipulates them mentally and reaches his
conclusions before he actually handles them. Again, the completion tests call into play imaginative ability together with self-
criticism of the imagined complete sentences. The same sort of
mental operation is involved in solving puzzles. It requires
ability in imagining situations, and seeing into the puzzling

---

[1] T. H. Pear, *Remembering and Forgetting*, pp. 117 ff.

element. That experience of sudden 'insight', which so often leads to the successful solving of a problem, is always due to ability in imagining situations.

This reminds us of the close affinity between reasoning and imagination. For reasoning, like invention, is a type of mental manipulation. Valid reasoning is the work of one who keeps his imagery clear, so that he can compare and classify and set into proper relationship the various images. To be able to study a problem carefully it is necessary that one should be able to look at it from various angles and scrutinize it on all sides—a process of manipulating mental imagery. The endeavour to call up elements which will help towards a solution of the problem is a still further form of image manipulation. An invention whereby the inventor hits on the device which will meet the need to which he is giving his attention is thus a special form of the reasoning process. In reasoning it is common to think of the problem as mental and the solution as mental; in invention we often think of the problem as concrete, and the device which solves it as material. But the distinction is superficial, and we all recognize that it is so when we use such phrases as 'inventing a plan', 'inventing a scheme' or 'inventing a reason', where obviously the invention is arrived at mentally by a process of reasoning.

In inventive reaction we see the creative factor of imagination in full function. The problem may be quite an old one, and the material to be manipulated perfectly familiar, but there is a breaking away from the *mammul*[1] ways of reacting. It is essentially the same spirit which we see in the little child learning to walk, who for the first time gets sufficient courage to go without support. It is the creative spirit again which characterizes the educated young Indian who breaks from certain caste traditions and treats his wife as a companion rather than a servant. It is the young man who dreams dreams and invents inventions. An imaginative turn of mind that is not developed in youth has little chance of unfolding in later years.

We may refer to the scientific hypothesis as a fourth type of

[1] Anglo-Indian, custom.

imaginative functioning, and one which, like invention, is very closely akin to reasoning. The hypothesis of the scientist is an explanatory device, and the sciences are always interested in casual sequences. How is it possible to discover the explanation for a phenomenon or event that is not known? The trial-and-error procedure is to assume a certain explanation or postulate it, and then try it out in the laboratory. If it proves inadequate, a fresh trial is made, and so on, until a satisfactory 'hypothesis' is discovered. It is not infrequent that a hypothesis appears to satisfy the facts for a long period of time, and then some fresh facts are brought to light which cannot be fitted into the accepted scheme. A familiar example is the Ptolemaic astronomy which satisfied the demands of cosmogony and navigation for centuries. But the discovery of the sphericity of the earth proved that the old astronomy was inadequate, and Copernicanism grew up to satisfy the new needs. When an exception to a hypothesis is discovered, it is a scientific challenge to find a new hypothesis which will be big enough to account for the old rule and the newly discovered exception.

Prof. Creighton, in his *Introductory Logic*, has this to say about the formation of hypotheses: 'Hypotheses are not received from without through sense-perception, but are made by the mind. They are the creations of the imagination. A good theorizer, like a poet, is in a certain sense born, not made. The man to whom "nothing ever occurs", whose intellectual processes are never lit up with a spark of imagination, is unlikely to make any important discoveries. It has been by a flash of scientific genius, by imaginative insight which we may almost call inspiration, that great scientific theories have been discovered.'[1] The author goes on to quote from Tyndall's essay on *The Scientific Use of the Imagination*: 'With accurate experiment and observation to work upon, imagination becomes the architect of physical theory. Newton's passage from a falling apple to a falling moon was an act of the prepared imagination. . . . Out of the facts of chemistry, the constructive imagination of Dalton formed the atomic theory. Davy was richly endowed with the imaginative

[1] J. E. Creighton, *Introductory Logic*, p. 182 f.

faculty, while with Faraday its exercise was incessant, preceding, accompanying, and guiding all his experiments. His strength and fertility as a discoverer are to be referred in great part to the stimulus of the imagination. Scientific men fight shy of the word because of its ultra-scientific connotations; but the fact is, that without the exercise of the power, our knowledge of nature would be a mere tabulation of co-existences and sequences.'[1]

Tansley speaks of the successful scientific investigator as one in whom the egoistic instinct, the instinct to attain mastery, is well developed. There is the continual effort to keep in touch with the whole environment, 'to avoid surprise, by constant exploration, continual testing and re-testing, extreme ultra-conscientious thoroughness, and the greatest caution before taking a step in advance'.[2] It is, of course, possible to have this spirit in excess, and even to become neurotic as a result of an ego-complex. Nevertheless, when not in excess, it is 'a necessary part of the scientific equipment'. A man must have enough self-assertiveness, enough confidence in himself, to believe that he can discover a solution to his problem, or he will never be a successful scientific investigator.

It is the work of the imagination to bring the relative facts together which bear on a problem under investigation. It is the task of imagination to explore every possible avenue for facts which will throw light on the dark places. It need scarcely be said that a scientist has always to have his feet on the ground. Imagination harnessed to facts, or better still imagination controlling and directing facts, is the key to scientific progress.

There still remains for discussion a fifth type of creative imagination, viz. æsthetic imagination or art. A thorough psychological investigation of æsthetic facts would carry us far afield, for art seems to have to do with the entire mental life—sensations, perceptions, feelings, emotions, imaginations, expressions, sentiments and attitudes. In discussing the perceptual processes we pointed out how the perception of beauty is one of the funda-

[1] Tyndall, *Fragments of Science*, p. 104, quoted by Creighton; ibid., p. 283.

[2] A. G. Tansley, *The New Psychology*, p. 213.

mental forms of perception. And we indicated that probably the
most satisfactory psychological account of art is to place it with
the attitudes, an attitude being defined as a tendency to some
characteristic action. But though that be granted, it is tantalis-
ingly difficult to describe the attitude. It is really going around
in a circle to say that the æsthetic attitude is the tendency to
appreciate and create beauty in the environment, for that would
leave the term 'beauty' undefined, and we would be likely to
think of it as that quality which our æsthetic nature appreciates.
Fortunately, most people understand what is meant by beauty in
spite of inability to define it. It may be contended that people's
ideas of beauty vary immensely, and that is partly true. Nevertheless, there is a fairly common agreement about the meaning
of beauty, though wide divergence as to the objects which can be
characterized as beautiful.

Imagination is essential to the æsthetic attitude, both as
regards production and consumption. The basis of beauty cannot
be delimited to objective characteristics, but is found within ourselves, and is determined in our experience by our attitude towards
and relation to the object whose beauty impresses us. As Hume
said : 'Beauty is no quality in things themselves ; it exists merely
in the mind which contemplates them.'[1] There are some
people who consider such a description as one of opprobrium,
because of a certain prejudice against the subjective. But, as
Santayana has pointed out, 'a judgement is not trivial because it
rests on human feelings'.[2] Even the appreciation of artistic products of other people or of beauty in nature demands an imaginative turn of mind that will enable one to discover what is present.
The word 'empathy' carries the meaning of the experience.
Empathy means 'feeling into' an experience that is characteristic
of æsthetic appreciation. A child may imagine himself an eagle
soaring above the limitations of his playmates, and his imagination takes on the character of reality in proportion to the
empathy he puts into it. The history of art affords many stories
which illustrate this matter. For example, there is the story of

[1] Hume's *Essays*, xxi.
[2] George Santayana, *The Sense of Beauty*, p. 4.

Turner and the woman to whom he had been showing a gorgeous painting of the setting sun which he had just completed. ' But,' she said, ' Mr Turner, I never see colours like that in the sunset.' ' Don't you wish you could ? ' was the significant reply. She lacked empathy. It is to empathy that one must credit the appeal of beauty, and empathy is conspicuously an experience induced by imagination. It would be a mistake to try to confine the work of imagination to cognitive elements only, and empathy is a good example of imagination working with affective elements also.

The creative side of art still more obviously illustrates the play of imagination. If the feeling element is important for art, so also is expression. Bosanquet has stated this in connection with the social view of art. He says, ' the festal or social view of art will help us here. Suppose a tribe or a nation has won a great victory ; " they are feeling big, and they want to make something big," as I have heard an expert say. That, I take it, is the rough account of the beginning of the æsthetic attitude. And, according to their capacity and their stage of culture, they may make a pile of their enemies' skulls, or they may build the Parthenon. The point of the æsthetic attitude lies in the adequate fusion of body and soul, where the soul is a feeling, and the body its expression, without residue on either side.'[1]

Imagination sometimes makes use of symbolism. A symbol is anything which stands for something else. It may be an object, either animate or otherwise, which is taken as emblematic of a moral or intellectual quality, as the jackal is a symbol of cunning, or it may be simply a representation, as when the word ' horse ' calls up the idea of a horse. Symbols are far more common in experience than is popularly supposed. The analogy is a case of reasoning through symbolism, and in the Nyaya school of Indian philosophy is taken as one of the methods of logical proof. But the analogy is significant psychologically rather than logically, and like other symbols is a bearer of meaning. From this point of view all language is symbolical. Words have no intrinsic value, but their worth is instrumental to the communication of ideas. That is ever the case with the symbol, whether

---

[1] B. Bosanquet, *Three Lectures on Æsthetic*, p. 75.

in language, in the dream, in art, or in religion.   Its value does
not attach to itself *per se*, but to itself as a bearer of meaning.
That mental process whereby one image calls up another,
materially quite different, is imagination.   It involves a process
of comparing images, discovering the common elements, and
classifying them accordingly.   It is a process through which we
discover and communicate meanings.   So that the function of
the symbol is of immense pragmatic value to the imagination
and to the mental life as a whole.

Some authors classify artists into two schools, the realists and
the idealists.   The former are said to give realistic representa-
tions of what they have experienced in Nature, whereas the
latter idealize their subjects so that they do not quite correspond
to anything in Nature.   It is questionable how satisfactory such
a classification may be considered.   It would seem that there is
an element of the ideal in all art.   Really great art is not content
with merely copying, but is the expression of a creative mind.
Art is like religion, in that it pictures an ideal world, and also in
that it believes in the possibility of making the ideal world a
reality.   Again it is like religion in that it often offers a means of
escape from the disagreeable and the ugly to a kingdom of
beauty and God.   The materials with which the artist sets to
work may be quite concrete or historical, but as his creative
imagination works with them, they become refined ideals, ideal-
ized persons, places or events.   Thus the mind operates through
imagination, pursuing and exploring the possibilities suggested by
the facts of experiences, heightening the emotions, remodelling
personalities and rebuilding the past as an ideal structure.

So far the reference of imagination has been largely to the
past.   But though the images come to us out of the past, their
manipulation is with reference to the future.   It is more important
from the practical point of view to be able to anticipate the future
than to recall the past.   It is possible to conserve a good deal of
human energy by anticipating the course which events are likely
to take, because it enables us to avoid wasting effort in useless
endeavours.   'One thing at a time, and that well done' may
be quite a good motive for the perceptual processes, but
a good deal of success in thought and action depends

on being able to look ahead several steps and consider our opinions and actions before the moment of necessity arrives. There is a very real sense in which 'anticipation is greater than realization'. The laurels for success in business, in education, in science and even in games usually go to the good visualizers who can imagine the possibilities which the future holds, and build their structure of conduct accordingly. Life is always moving forward, and imagination helps it to move in the right direction.

The variety of situations in which the imagination functions is an indication of the important place which it occupies in the mental life. It is of foremost value in the creation and appreciation of beautiful objects. But it also has immense pragmatic value as in invention and the hypothesis forming of the scientific imagination. It is also the backbone of a reasoning process in which images are controlled and manipulated with reference to problematic situations. Reasoning has been described as 'mental exploration', and the field of exploration is the sphere of mental images. Again reasoning has been described as 'purposive thinking', which is another way of saying that the mental imagery is directed to a certain end. Plainly, one of the functions of education is to develop the abilities of children to such ends. Life for the most of folk is made up of an unending succession of problems. As has been said, 'we live by problems rather than by solutions'. Reasoning is that mental process whereby we acquire the habit of manipulating images so as to bring them to bear on such problematic situations. The school, by training the child to face certain typical problems, and find his own way to a solution, tries to develop an attitude and an ability which will stand the child in good stead throughout life.

LITERATURE

J. R. Angell. *Psychology*. Constable, 1908.

Wm. McDougall. *Outline of Psychology*. Methuen, 1924.

G. F. Stout. *Manual of Psychology*. University Tutorial Press, 1913.

James Drever. *Introduction to the Psychology of Education*. Edward Arnold, 1923.

A. G. Tansley. *The New Psychology and Its Relation to Life*. George Allen & Unwin, 1920.

T. H. Pear. *Remembering and Forgetting*. Methuen, 1922.

John Adams. *Modern Developments in Educational Practice*. University of London Press, 1922.

S. Freud. *The Interpretation of Dreams*. George Allen & Unwin, 1900.

J. E. Creighton. *Elementary Logic*. Macmillan, 1916.

G. Santayana. *The Sense of Beauty*. Constable, 1896.

CHAPTER XII

THE WILL

Consciousness Active—Sensori-Motor and Ideo-Motor Action—The Development of Control—Is the Will Free?—Some Physical Limitations of the Will in Children—Pedagogical Warnings.

'How to train the will' was one of the problems which concerned the educational psychologist of the past generation. Although the phrase is suggestive of an approach that is no longer tenable, we are still vitally concerned with the problem of volition. We might characterize our modern age as one which has emphasized the will in opposition to the rationalist seventeenth and eighteenth centuries which emphasized the intellect. The new emphasis harks back to Kant indeed, for it was he who first studied it critically, and did justice to the 'practical reason' as set over against the 'pure reason'. He was particularly concerned with its bearing on ethical judgements. 'Nothing can possibly be conceived in the world, or even out of it, which can be called good without qualification, except a Good Will.'[1] Kant has exercised a profound effect on the pragmatic school of thinkers, of whom William James was one of the founders. This movement is marked by an element of voluntarism which we see in James himself, whose chapter on 'Will' in his *Principles* is so suggestive, and who also wrote that famous essay on 'The Will to Believe'. It was his conviction that the will through faith may lead us into paths that give us valid knowledge which would be unattainable by intellectual processes. Another and altogether different type of voluntarism we see embodied in Nietzsche, who was disgusted

---

[1] I. Kant, *Fundamental Principles of the Metaphysic of Morals* (trans. Abbott), p. 9.

with what he regarded as the effeminacy of modern civilization, and preached the doctrine of a ' will to power '. These are some of the striking evidences that are characteristic of the modern emphasis. Since the will is a psychological conception, whatever may be said about it ought to be checked by what psychology discloses in regard to it.

There are some who begin the study of the will by a definition. A good deal may be said for James' contention that desire and will are experiences with which everybody is so perfectly familiar that definitions are superfluous. Nevertheless, the words *will, volition* and *conation* are used by different writers with varying degrees of latitude, and we cannot be quite indifferent to the matter of definition. In this chapter we shall use these words, unless otherwise indicated, in the broad sense as standing for the theoretical active phase of consciousness. We shall recognize, however, that there is a legitimate narrower usage as referring to the active manifestations of that phase of consciousness. A very straightforward definition is that which Tansley gives of conation : ' the general term for mental set or tendency to action : one of the three aspects of the " complete mental process ". Concretely " a conation " is the mental tendency of striving to do something.'[1]

It need hardly be reiterated that we must regard the life of the organism as a unity, whether of the conscious and subconscious, the mental and the motor, or the cognitive, affective and conative factors. The distinctions which we make may be serviceable for theoretical science, but in actual life there are no disintegrations such as they suggest. The organism is characterized by tendencies to awareness, to feeling and to action. As Angell has put it : ' The whole mind active, this is the will.'[2] So that our study of the will is virtually a study of consciousness in its active phases. We are fundamentally motor, and the primarily observable phenomena are what we do, i.e. acts. The psychologist begins his work by observing acts, and the teacher who is a student of human minds and mental processes begins by

---

[1] Tansley, *The New Psychology*, p. 299.
[2] Angell, *Psychology*, p. 437.

watching what children do. So that from the beginning to the end we are intensely interested and vitally concerned with the conative factor of life.

We observed at the outset that there are two groups of organic reactions, viz. the native and the acquired. This gives us a clue to our approach to the present inquiry. Other classifications have been made of actions, such as into involuntary and voluntary, or impulsive and determined, or sensori-motor and ideo-motor. It does not matter so much what terminology we follow, so long as we understand the significance of our classification. The terms 'native', 'involuntary', and 'impulsive', suggest that group of activities which we are able to perform and do perform without learning, using the equipment of nerves, muscles and glands with which we came into the world. The terms 'acquired', 'voluntary', and 'determined', suggest a development which has taken place since birth, by which we are able to do certain things which we could not do without learning to make certain adjustments and co-ordinations that were not naturally ours. It is that something which has intervened and enabled us to perform what are more than reflexive or instinctive activities, to which the name 'will' or 'volition' is given, when the word is used in its narrower connotation. Conation, as the word itself signifies, involves all tendencies to strive, all tendencies to actions. But within those tendencies we may distinguish the two classes, the native or impulsive, and the acquired or determined.

The other classification that is sometimes used is into sensori-motor and ideo-motor actions. The former group includes motor reactions which are the result of sensory processes, and the latter those which are the outcome of ideational processes. This classification serves a useful purpose so long as the sensory and the ideational are not taken to be static, but are understood to be processes. There are many processes, particularly the impulsive or native, which are aroused to activity by sensory presentations. We see a snake and we run. The stimulus is a sensory process of the visual type; the response is motor. But those responses which we ourselves regard as higher and more complex are for the most part aroused by thought processes.

We think of a visit to a friend for fellowship, or to a temple for worship, and we act accordingly. Here the moving stimulus is ideational, whereas the response in the first instance is motor. It will be apparent that the ideo-motor reaction is a case of substitution of ideational for sensory excitation in the stimulus. Originally the movements involved in going to a friend's house or to a temple were aroused by sensory excitation, perchance the sight of them, or else hearing about them from somebody else. But now the ideational process is substituted for the seeing or hearing, because it calls up an image which reinstates the latter part of the former sensori-motor process. The idea re-arouses the nervous centres associated with the former sensori-motor circuit, so that, unless otherwise inhibited, similar motor responses follow. The beginning of the conation is in this case an idea, whereas in the more primary experience it was sensory.

The question arises as to how it comes about that we acquire the ability to substitute ideational for sensory processes, determination for impulse.

That is really a long story in the development of the race and of the individual. In the earlier stages we observe that the majority of movements are random and uncontrolled. Little by little control and co-ordination are effected with reference to the appropriate reactions for various types of stimuli, until eventually the child is able to determine what responses he will make instead of reacting aimlessly, or at least impulsively. In the case of the human infant it requires a period of about two years before all of the rudimentary motor responses can be effected as determined. The intervening period from birth until this control is at last realized is a transition period of first-rate importance in the evolution of conation. Voluntary control is gradually built up by a process wherein the unco-ordinated native reactions are organized and systematized with reference to ends. In general, the larger muscles are first subdued, and later on the smaller ones, the control of which requires greater nicety of adjustment. The child will attend to now one group and now another, until the desired co-ordinations are effected. We have all been observers of those two typical adjustments and controls being attained as children learn to walk and to talk. We have seen how uncertain the first attempts are, and how gradually uncertainty gives way to firmness, and errors are eliminated. Incidentally, it may be pointed out that we have good examples of the operations of the trial-and-error method of learning.

Bringing the glands and muscles under control and producing desired co-ordinations effects a marked conservation of energy. In the learning stage, when the child is making the transition from random to controlled movements, there is much energy diffused. There is always in a healthy child a certain amount of energy ready for use, and the desire of the educator is to see that such energy is not wasted, but utilized for the development of the child. All learning and the formation of habit is with a view to directing energy into right channels, acquiring as many co-ordinations as possible, and setting free energy for the formation of new bonds. At first the movements are random. But here and there an accidental success is attained, which is accompanied by a feeling-tone of pleasurableness. This leads to repetition of the successful, satisfying response until control is effected in that direction. Another result is the deliberate elimination of those movements which have proved useless and unsatisfactory. Thus, deliberation is finally substituted for random trials, and energy is directed to desired ends. In the measure in which development proceeds, we can thus observe an increasing tendency for the child to make use of ideational processes instead of blindly or impulsively following the lead of sensory processes. In short the development of the self is a development from the sensori-motor to the ideo-motor, from impulse to deliberation.

The development of the conative processes is not always along a smooth pathway. There are many outposts to be conquered, many rough places to be levelled. Difficulty arises sometimes because unconsciously useless movements, by means of repetition, become fixed and it is difficult to eradicate them. Most of us have acquired little 'mannerisms', which are often useless movements which have not been eradicated. Some men constantly use gestures with hand or head in conversation. Others interject grunts as others are speaking. Many Indian students get the habit of reading all of their work aloud, thereby wasting time and energy. If these useless movements are allowed to be continued long enough, it is very difficult to bring them under control later. Another difficulty arises through the competition of stimuli. Which stimulus shall we respond to first, and to which response shall we give the preference? It is not always easy to determine. If our response be impulsive, it will be determined by the pressing needs of the organism, its instinctive tendencies and dominant interests. But sometimes we determine that some other interest or need shall dominate, and determine to inhibit certain impulses while we select other ways of acting. Such control is only gradually effected as the self develops. Many times, if we responded purely from impulse, we should yield to bodily fatigue and sleep, when we actually determined that we must read a while longer until a certain task is completed. An adult may lose an entire night's sleep to watch by the bedside of a sick friend, where it would be impossible for the child who is more largely under the direction of impulse. Teachers should never forget that the conative processes are developmentally conceived, that control is only gradually attained. We cannot expect the same serious concentration in the elementary school pupil that we anticipate in the college student. Neither do we look for as much control in the little child running about the village as when he begins to attend school. The kindergarten is a practical recognition of the transition period from the sensori-motor to the ideo-motor. It straightway appeals to the child's impulsive tendencies with the object of helping him to bring his movements little by little under control, until he is at length able to select and inhibit for himself. Conflict and obstruction are facts which belong to the everyday experiences of life. The development of conation should involve the securing of harmony, perhaps by the eradication of the undesirable, and perhaps by a combination of competing tendencies in a higher conation, a process of integration, like Hegel's synthesis of the thesis and its antithesis. Some conations are quite incompatible, and disturb the equilibrium of the mind, giving rise to complexes which may be emotionally disturbing. The child will learn in time that life is full of such conflicts, and that the smoothing of the rough places depends very much on himself. But teachers and parents may, without laying undue stress on disagreeable facts, direct the child's development so that he will develop his own abilities of self-determination and self-direction to the end that life may unfold with a maximum of harmony and a minimum of unhappiness.

'The will', says Hobhouse, 'is not to be regarded as an additional impulse, or as a force existing outside impulses and operating upon them. It is rather the system or synthesis of impulses, the broad practical bent and tendency of one's nature.'[1] This is a fact which can scarcely be over-emphasized. In talking about the will, we are not concerned with a faculty distinguishable from knowing and feeling, nor yet with a sort of superimpulse. We are dealing with the entire personality in action. We see the personality as a whole, or at least its nucleus expressing itself in a determination to follow a certain course of action in preference to any other available course. The unfolding of personality is from impulse to voluntary choice, and the self is involved in all volition. The will is something greater than the experience of any one moment. It is the self on its active side. That is the reason why a consideration of the will is of ethical as well as of psychological significance.

The functions of the will are four: constraint, restraint, persistence, and the organization of life. Constraint and restraint are obviously correlative terms. Selection always implies inhibition. The determination to make a certain response is equally a negative determination with respect to other possible responses. Nowhere is this double character of the will better illustrated than in the phenomenon of selective attention in which, as we have seen, consciousness is focussed upon a particular object and deliberately turned away from other competing stimuli. The wise teacher will direct the educative process as far as possible by appealing to the child's positive tendencies and interests which, if they dominate sufficiently, will automatically work their own restraints. No healthy personality can be developed out of restraints alone. 'Don'ts' and 'Thou shalt nots' are expressions for the policeman rather than the educator. Children need positive guidance, that will enable them so to build up the desir-

---

[1] L. T. Hobhouse, *Mind in Evolution*, p. 350.

able linkages that the undesirable will have no chance. To be sure, there is truth in the admonition that one needs to be able to say ' No ' at the proper time. But that, too, depends on having built up such a set of positive co-ordinations that certain negations are unavoidable. Building up positive habits of fair play through games and competitions, will do far more to insure the desired conduct in after years, than all the preaching in the world about the evils of cheating.

The ability to persist in one's efforts, even in the face of obstructions, is an important phase of conation. The very homely expression ' stick-to-it-iveness ' has a very plain meaning. There are times when it is necessary to keep our attention upon subjects that are boring, and conscious effort is needed to maintain the process. For example, many students of psychology find it difficult to attend to discussions involving the details of the nervous system. Individual temperaments and interests differ in this regard, and the objects to which some attend almost spontaneously require a good deal of effort on the part of others. Of course, continuity of attention is much more readily secured where we study to make a subject appeal to the interests of children, and a good deal may be accomplished in overcoming monotony and tediousness by efforts to make the subjects of the school curriculum interesting. But it must be admitted that there are some tasks, both in school and out of it, that require attention, despite the fact that they are not interesting, because of their subsequent usefulness. Children need to learn to persist even in the face of distractions and obstructions. Then, again, there come times when we are called upon to make decisions which involve a careful consideration of a very complex situation. Young men come to the time when they have to think through the problem of their life's work, and that involves weighing a great variety of interests and possibilities. There is a good deal of tension involved in holding the mind on the problem to weigh all the complications and reach a decision. Experiences which present moral issues make similar demands upon us, and the more severe the temptation the more effort is required to make the necessary decision. In all of these cases we may observe the will functioning in enabling us to hold fast to the task requiring our attention and effort.

The will functions also in the organization of life. It should not be identified with any momentary experience, but with the whole self on its active side. McDougall traces all conations, desires and aversions to the operation of the self-regarding sentiment which sets free motives for the attainment of controls. Whatever name we may give to the tendency, it is evident that there must be an operating principle in the organization of life. Without some systematizing of our desires and tendencies, life would be pretty much helter-skelter. Conflicts have to be settled. Dilemmas have to be resolved. Where that is not done, the result is the arising of emotionally disturbing complexes. This organization of the various tendencies and desires of life into an integral unity is one of the most fundamental functions of the will. It is, indeed, personality active in the task of harmonizing and organizing life. No teacher would be so foolish as to suggest to his pupils: 'Go to, let us organize our lives.' But in a thousand ways he may indicate the ways in which harmony may be brought out of apparent discord, and difficulties made to disappear. The child will be led to organize his life, not by word of command or threat of punishment, but by direction in the ways whereby he can solve his own problems, make his own adjustments and relieve his own tensions. Successful education is that which teaches a child to act for himself, to become a self-directing personality.

> 'Self-reverence, self-knowledge, self-control,
> These three alone lead life to sovereign power.'

Are our conative tendencies free to go in any direction whatsoever? Do we really decide each course of action on its own merits when the time comes for action? This question is one over which there has always been a considerable difference of opinion, some holding that the will is free to determine the directions in which effort shall be put forth, while others claim that in the last analysis the entire gamut of behaviour is explicable in terms of mechanical causation. If it were to be proved that all behaviour is mechanically caused, then the moral life becomes a mockery and the science of ethics a mere dialectic performance. Since education is concerned with the development of moral character, this question is one which vitally concerns us.

We want to know whether the end of our striving is after all a phantom goal, or whether we can do anything creatively to contribute to the unfolding of personality.

Psychology has felt the influence of the mechanistic tendency which has characterized modern science to some degree. The behaviouristic school in particular follows that bent. It has felt the influence of biological mechanists, such as Jacques Loeb, who declare that they know that living organisms are nothing more than chemical mechanisms. For them there are no sensations but only sensory processes, no percepts but only perceptual processes, etc. While acknowledging their service to science in emphasizing the dynamic element, and in encouraging research, we need not commit ourselves to their extravagance in ruling introspection out of court, and in reducing mental processes to discharges of nervous energy. Their solution of the problem of body and mind, by reducing mind in effect to body, is too simple. Psychology must recognize the very intimate connection between the mental and the neural, but can find the unity in an organism that is at once mental and neural better than by a reduction of one to the other.

The other extreme is to declare that the will is absolutely free. There are those who, on moral or religious grounds, declare that nobody has any right to throw the blame for their actions upon anything or anybody but themselves, that in the last analysis they themselves have chosen their courses of action, because they must have so determined what to do before any action could take place. The freedom of the will is at once man's glory and the source of all his unhappiness.

If we approach this problem psychologically, we shall have to admit that man is neither a machine-like creature, a victim of circumstances, nor perfectly free in every particular. There are influences which play important parts in determining his conduct, limits to his freedom, restrictions to his possibilities. These influences are partly social and partly individual. We shall discuss each of these in brief.

The chief of the social influences on human nature and conduct is the folkway. All along from primitive culture to our more complex civilizations, we find man determined very much in his individual actions by the group's way of doing things. Nowhere is that more clearly observable than in South India with its tyranny of *mammul*,[1] dominating the economic, the caste and the religious life. The Telugu proverb that asks, 'if your father dug a well, would you have to drown yourself in it?' is a thrust at the oppression of custom. Now it is only when we experience a sense of crisis that we realize that we have been so rigidly determined by the group in our conduct. But there are innumerable ways in which we follow the way of the folk without so much as observing that it is a socially determined habit. Explain this fact by the herd instinct or anyhow you will, the fact remains that many times we show no evidence of freedom in what we do.

McDougall points out three groups of social influences in determining the activity of the individual—imitation, suggestion and coercion. Imitation appears both individually and socially. We find the little child imitating the sounds of its elders, and the ability to imitate is so much stronger in infancy that languages learned in childhood are much more like a native tongue than those acquired in later years. Baldwin has described conscious imitation in the sense of a persistent endeavour to copy models which have been set as the real beginning of volition. But there is a good deal of unconscious imitation also that is socially originated.

It is not possible to draw hard and fast lines between imitation and suggestion. They are very intimately related, and often work conjointly. Imitation may be due to suggestion. In the social life there are many instances of large groups of people attempting to follow in the footsteps of a leader. The way in which thousands of Indians today take their cue from Mahatma Gandhi is common knowledge. Why are many spinning, and many weaving *khaddar*[2] who did not do so before? Why have such phrases as 'non-co-operation' and 'passive resistance' become current coin? Are they not due in no small measure to the suggestion of a magnetic personality? Suggestibility is a characteristic of child nature of which every teacher ought to take full

---

[1] Custom.   [2] Homespun cotton cloth.

advantage. At the same time he should guard against the disadvantages which arise from it, for his unconscious, undesirable manners may possess quite as much power of suggestion as the model bits of behaviour which he is consciously emphasizing.

Coercion is obviously social determination. It is behaviour in accordance with rules and regulations which are enforced by the strong arm of a parent, a teacher, or a policeman. A certain amount of coercion seems to be necessary to protect society from those who would not do the desired thing on their own account. The tendency today is to make as sparing use of it as possible as a method of social determination.

These facts of imitation, suggestion and coercion make it evident that we are by no means always free to do as we incline. We cannot be members of social groups, and not be limited by the kinds of behaviour common to the group and approved by the group. The social character of personality involves inevitable limitations. Freedom is freedom within the group life. In emphasizing the element of freedom in the modern educative process, we must never lose sight of that fact. Much as we desire the child to have as much liberty as possible to develop his own personality to the fullest degree, we must not forget that pesonality never develops in a vacuum. It rather unfolds in constant contact with other persons who have the same rights to freedom. And this contact of personalities which characterizes the entire social life involves a degree of social limitation with which we must be prepared to reckon.

On the individual side there are also limitations that we cannot afford to underestimate. There are the limitations which are consequent upon the physical character of the organism. We have vision, audition, kinæsthetic ability, nervous energy, and so on, all of them within calculable bounds. In addition, many people suffer from physical defects of one kind or another, which place limits upon what they can do. More and more school authorities are realizing the responsibility which they bear in looking into the physical conditions of children. The development of a healthy will and normal intelligence is frequently frustrated by bad teeth, enlarged tonsils, the presence of adenoids, defective eyesight, under-nourishment, enlarged spleen, faulty ventilation or a tainted water supply. Regular medical inspection is not a luxury, but a prime necessity. In some cities in the West the school boards employ nurses and dental surgeons to look after those who require attention. It is sometimes due to poverty that children are neglected, and sometimes it is due to ignorance of the presence or nature of trouble.

A gentleman who today is one of America's outstanding scholars, recounted his own personal experience in my hearing. He was a young boy brought up in the country, and his parents used to send him towards evening to bring the cows home to be milked. Sometimes he would return saying that the wall must have been broken down somewhere and the cows escaped, because they were not to be seen. His father, returning from a day of hard work, would then go in search of the animals and find them where the boy was supposed to have looked. Of course, the parents thought the boy was being false and shirking his work, and used to rebuke him in a way which he knew was undeserved. Then he was sent to school, and the teacher discovered that he could not see unless the page were put almost in contact with his face. So they sent him to an ophthalmic doctor, and it was discovered that he had only one-tenth normal vision. When glasses were provided to correct the defect, it was soon found not only that he could do his school work, but that he could find the cows when he went to look for them. Here was an obvious case where willingness was being greatly limited by a physical cause.

Another case came under my notice when I was teaching in Kurnool. There was a small boy in the school, the son of a highly respected man, who was not only stupid in school but was developing tendencies to pilfer things belonging to other boys, and tendencies to tell lies shamelessly. It seemed to me to be a case for medical, if not surgical, treatment, and when I sent him to the district surgeon it was found, as I anticipated, that he had enlarged tonsils and adenoids. Here again was a case where the child's freedom to act as a normal child and develop as a healthy person was being hindered by a physical defect that was no fault of his own.

In addition to these physical limitations, there are others of a more psychical type. Each person has a characteristic temperament which determines the limits of his activities to a certain degree. If one be of a phlegmatic temperament, vivaciousness and abounding cheerfulness may be quite impossible to him, no matter how much he may admire them in other people. If one be excitable, he is dispositionally hindered from receiving surprising news quietly. To a certain degree, it is possible for us to alter our dispositions by continued effort, but anyone who has tried will realize that he is not as free as he would like to be in that regard.

Our conative life is also determined in many respects by unconscious influences, motives, interests, attitudes, prejudices, desires and complexes that have entered into the self so completely that they are part and parcel of us, and yet whose operations are largely below the threshold of consciousness. Psycho-analysis has done much to draw our attention to the influence of this unconscious part of the self. There are many hidden motives and desires, buried deep in our mental make-up, which nevertheless are capable of asserting themselves when occasions arise to call them forth. Is it not frequently the case that we experience certain likes and dislikes which determine the limits within which we are able to act, and the origin of which we are unable to account for? The source may have been in some experience of long before which gave rise to certain linkages, certain complexes of psycho-neural material, which continue to assert themselves through the years, though we are no longer conscious of their genesis.

Dewey has given us a psychological analysis of the freedom of the will. After pointing out that what men have struggled for is certainly not a metaphysical freedom, he indicates three elements of importance, viz. (i) the ability to carry our plans to fruition without the cramping and thwarting of obstructions; (ii) the capacity to vary our courses of action, and to experience change and novelty; and (iii) the capacity to desire and to choose between alternatives.[1] Freedom is not altogether a gift of nature. There is considerable fiction about the idea that all men

---

[1] Dewey, *Human Nature and Conduct*, pp. 303 ff.

are born free and equal, despite the declarations of democratic constitutions. In the first place, all men are born with certain limitations ; and in the second place, freedom is not all a natural gift, but some of it is achieved. It is achieved in a world of other persons, and achieved to some extent by mutual undertakings of give-and-take. Very often it seems that we agree to the curtailing of freedom at some points that it may be fuller and freer in other directions. Freedom we cherish and long for in preference to any other way of living. We would rather be free though we make blunders than be held in straights though we be led along perfectly correct paths. And so would a child. It is much bettter to let a child learn by the path of freedom though it entails mistakes than to chalk out his way so that he *must* go aright. 'He who never made a mistake', runs the proverb, 'never made anything.'

From the pedagogical point of view there are certain dangers which need to be guarded against in the education of the will. William James mentioned the 'explosive will' and the 'obstructed will'. Perhaps we might add to these the 'immature will' and the 'misguided will'. These phrases must be understood as simply pictorial ways of referring to dangers concerning which every educator needs to be alive. They are not entities which can be examined under a microscope, but types of mental behaviour which educationists agree are undesirable. So we must try to train children that worthy conduct may always be exhibited and undesirable conations avoided.

The explosive will is a type of character in which the response follows the stimulus so rapidly that there is no time for restraining suggestions to have a chance. We have all seen children, and adults too for that matter, who act precipitately with no thought of what is the appropriate thing to do in a given situation. They are hot-heads, always ready to explode with energy, who speak and act first and think afterwards. Such people possess the attractiveness which goes along with vivacity, but when we analyze it, we find it is due largely to failure to develop the capacity for inhibitions. In little children we see very little attempt to control impulses, a minimum of inhibitory power. But as development takes place, we look for more and more of deliberation and less and less of impulsiveness. When we find people who with advancing years have not developed the ideo-motor capacity, but still respond chiefly in sensori-motor ways, we must conclude either that they are defective in some way or that their education has been neglected. People who flare up suddenly and with little apparent reason are very likely to be feeble-minded, or they may be emotionally defective.

The obstructed will is the precisely opposite danger from the explosive will. In this instance the inhibitory tendencies are too strong, and the impulsive are sluggish. The result is that the person is characterized by a certain stubbornness or perversity. It is most difficult to rouse him to action, especially action of the kind desired. In some cases such obduracy is due to some defect or disease of the nervous system, while in other cases the thought processes may be quite clear. James mentions three examples of the obstructed will, the sluggard, the drunkard and the coward, and in none of these cases could it be said that the impulse to right action has been deliberately overcome. There is something wrong somewhere which prevents them from doing the right thing. We have met some insane people who always had to be invited to act contrary to our wishes if we were to get appropriate results. If you wanted the man to leave your compound, you invited him to come into the bungalow. Many others of more moderate types of perversity are not insane, but they are certainly lacking in healthy conative capacities. Most of the moral tragedies of human experience are due to people who cannot, or at least do not, form the proper links between stimuli and responses. They do not act in accordance with their own knowledge of what is right and true. Their will to goodness is obstructed.

The immature will is very much akin to the explosive will. It is very clearly illustrated in the feeble-minded individual, who remains a child in intelligence even after physical maturity is attained. Have we not often felt like depicting the conduct of grown men as childish? Here in India we see people of all stages of culture. There are a number of tribes in the jungle regions who are comparatively primitive and whose folkways seem to us decidedly childish. And in the hamlets, where we have largely non-caste illiterate folks, we get similar impressions. Immaturity may take the form of responses which are more becoming to children, or of explosiveness. Certainly, there is no surer cure for this type of ill than the school in the community. The more rapidly education spreads among our hill tribes and depressed classes, the less evidence will we have of immature volitions.

Misguided wills are in many cases the result of the wrong kind of education. We have in many of the elementary schools of the Madras Presidency teachers who have not the most rudimentary knowledge of mental processes. And yet they are trying to guide children in the way these processes should unfold. Is it surprising that some of the guidance should be misguidance? And yet it is probably better than children would get if they were left to run about the village or herd cattle. Scores of people do the wrong thing because they do not know the right. Again the salvation from this trouble is in the spread of education along intelligent lines.

It may have seemed to some that this discussion of the will has included a great many other things that are ordinarily considered under knowledge and feeling. It could not be otherwise. We have already pointed out that neither serious thought nor emotional experience is possible without effort or action. And we repeat, the entire personality in action is what is meant by the will. It is more than any momentary experience either cognitive or affective. It is the whole self in all of its relations, and so it is of the utmost moral as well as educational significance. The self which we are trying to educate is a moral personality. By the education of the will we can only mean the development of personality or of character. Whether we consider the end of life from the moral or the educational point of view, it matters not. Both morals and education agree that it is the unfolding of personality. And the will is personality in action.

LITERATURE

Wm. James. *Principles of Psychology*. Henry Holt, 1890.

J. R. Angell. *Psychology*. Constable, 1908.

W. McDougall. *Outline of Psychology*. Methuen, 1924.

W. McDougall. *Social Psychology.* Luce, 1916.

C. H. Judd. *Psychology.* Scribner's, 1907.

L. T. Hobhouse. *Mind in Evolution.* Macmillan, 1915.

J. Dewey. *Human Nature and Conduct.* George Allen & Unwin, 1922.

A. G. Tansley. *The New Psychology and Its Relation to Life.* George Allen & Unwin, 1920.

J. A. Hadfield. *Psychology and Morals.* Methuen, 1923.

G. A. Coe. *Education in Religion and Morals.* F. H. Revell, 1904.

T. Mark. *The Unfolding of Personality.* University of Chicago Press, 1912.

A. F. Shand. *The Foundations of Character.* Macmillan, 1914.

CHAPTER XIII

THE PSYCHOLOGICAL BASIS FOR INSTRUCTION

OBSERVATION OF MENTAL PROCESSES—THE PSYCHOLOGY OF THE CLASS—
PAEDOCENTRIC INSTRUCTION—THE MONTESSORI METHOD—THE DALTON
PLAN—THE HOWARD PLAN—THE GARY SYSTEM—THE PROJECT
METHOD—BUILDING WITH DOMINANT INTERESTS—FREEDOM AND
DISCIPLINE.

THE practical teacher looks upon his work as primarily that
of instruction. Presumably he has acquired a body of knowledge
which he aims to impart to those placed in his care, and which
he aims to impart in such a way that the pupils' intelligence and
personality will be developed in the process. It is quite obvious
that, in order to accomplish his aim, he must understand the
psychological basis for instruction. If he has a thorough-going
knowledge of the fundamental factors, in the development of the
mental processes, and of the relationship between the various
subjects being taught and those processes, he will surely be able
to understand and adjust his teaching to his pupils. Speaking of
the teaching of Latin, Prof. John Adams says: 'It may be
legitimately maintained that the teacher cannot, by any possibility,
do real teaching at all if he neglects either John or Latin.'[1]

It ought to be apparent to every teacher that, to do his work
well, there is demanded of him an almost colossal amount of
knowledge. There is still a good deal of the popular impression
abroad in South India that anybody who has passed through a
certain number of classes himself ought to be fitted to instruct
others. Let us not be so feverishly hasty to get schools in every
village and hamlet, desirable as that may be in itself, that we
become willing to commit the task to raw youths with themselves
only a smattering of knowledge, and with absolutely no know-

---

[1] J. Adams, *Modern Developments in Educational Practice*, p. 12.

ledge of the nature of the mental processes to be developed, or of the psychology of the subjects to be taught. The seat of our problem is in the training schools and classes. Happily the educational authorities in the Madras Presidency have at last realized that too much time was being occupied by training schools in supplementing the subject-matter of the elementary and secondary schools, and too little in teaching young men how to teach, and the whole training school curriculum is being revised with a view to remedying that defect. A really good teacher must be a sound psychologist. The whole foundation of the educational structure is psychological, and the plain reason for so many curiously formed structures is due to carelessness or ignorance in regard to the foundation.

Instruction involves an instructor, subjects to be instructed, and subject-matter. The subjects to be instructed are, in the majority of cases, gathered together into classes, and very often the teacher has regarded the class, rather than the persons composing it, as the subject of instruction. The subjects for instruction are *actually* particular kinds of subjects, and *potentially* something quite different; and the teacher is just as fundamentally concerned with the potential as the actual. In other words, he must be constantly recognizing and reckoning with a factor of change, which exists and ought to exist. He wants so to teach that the child will retain what is good, and develop where improvement is possible. While giving due heed to the matter of development, it would be a mistake to think that implies perpetual change and nothing but change. If such were the case, what would become of one's achievements which are good and useful? The fact that there are certain elements which need to be preserved, and certain others that require modification with the unfolding of personality, means that the educational problem is one of considerable complication. Certainly, if any person needs to be as 'wise as serpents and harmless as doves' it is the teacher or parent who has to instruct and guide children.

Certain of the time-honoured pedagogic maxims are based on sound observations of the mental processes. 'Proceed from the particular to the general' or 'from the concrete to the abstract', are maxims which stand firm in the light of psychological development. It need scarcely be said that our mental processes naturally and normally follow that order. The lower animal's great disadvantage as compared with human beings is its lack of ability to learn conceptually. Its learning is almost entirely on the perceptual level. It can learn to react to some fairly complicated particular situations, but if put into similar situations is at a loss to know what to do. The learning of the rat in threading the maze is an example in point. Let the animal learn to run a maze until it goes through unfailingly with no errors, and then shorten or lengthen the runways, or shift the position of the maze through 90 or 180 degrees, and the animal is quite at sea. It has to begin again to learn how to adjust itself to the new situation. Young children are very much like animals in that their responses are particular and their learning perceptual. The younger they are the more difficult is it for them to carry over what they have learned in one situation to another and analogous situation. But the development of intelligence involves, among other things, an unfolding of the ability to generalize. The power of carrying over what has been learned in one situation and applying it in an analogous situation involves, of course, an element of generalizing. It means a grasping of the fundamental similarities, which is the first step in generalizing.

Any who have had experience in the use of intelligence tests with younger children will have had ample opportunity to obtain illustrations of this matter. In the Binet-Stanford tests for five-year intelligence, one asks for simple definitions of the words *chair*, *horse*, *fork*, *doll*, *pencil*, and *table*. Terman gives a few illustrations from his subjects, and these serve very well to indicate the perceptual character of learning in five-year-old children. The following are the examples of satisfactory responses which he quotes:

'*Chair*: "To sit on." "You sit on it." "It is made of wood, and has legs and a back."

'*Horse*: "To drive." "To ride." "What people drive." "To pull the wagon." "It is big and has four legs."

'*Fork*: "To eat with." "To stick meat with." "It is hard and has three sharp things."

'*Doll*: "To play with." "What you dress and put to bed." "To rock."

'*Pencil*: "To write with." "To draw." "They write with it." "It is sharp and makes a blue mark."

'*Table*: "To eat on." "What you put the dinner on." "Where you write." "It is made of wood and has legs."

' Examples of unsatisfactory responses are such as " A chair is a chair "; or " There is a chair "; or simply " There " (pointing to a chair).' [1]

A study of these simple definitions is illuminating, inasmuch as they show at the same time the particularistic character of the child's thought processes and the beginnings of the tendency to generalize. As intelligence develops we find an increasing ability to generalize, so that when the same type of test is applied as a measure of eight-year mentality, a greater ability in generalizing is demanded. In that test the words to be defined are *balloon*, *tiger*, *football*, and *soldier*. We may observe some of the examples quoted by Terman from his subjects :

'(*a*) *Balloon*.
> '*Satisfactory*. "A balloon is a means of travelling through the air." "It is a kind of airship, made of cloth and filled with air so that it can go up."
> '*Unsatisfactory*. "To go up in the air." "It's full of gas."

'(*b*) *Tiger*.
> '*Satisfactory*. "It is a wild animal of the cat family." "It is an animal that's a cousin to the lion."
> '*Unsatisfactory*. "To eat you up." "To travel in the circus."

'(*c*) *Football*.
> '*Satisfactory*. "It is a leather bag filled with air and made for kicking." "It is a ball you kick."
> '*Unsatisfactory*. "It is round." "You kick it."

'(*d*) *Soldier*.
> '*Satisfactory*. "A man who goes to war." "A man that walks up and down and carries a gun."
> '*Unsatisfactory*. "He fights." "He shoots." ' [2]

---

[1] L. M. Terman, *The Measurement of Intelligence*, pp. 167 ff.
[2] Ibid., pp. 221 ff.

When we come to the twelfth year, definitions of abstract terms are called for. In commenting on the test, Terman remarks that 'the reader may be surprised that the ability to define common abstract words should develop so late. Most children who have had anything like ordinary home or school environment have doubtless heard all of these words (*pity, revenge, charity, envy, justice*) countless times before the age of twelve years. Nevertheless, the statistics from the test show unmistakably that before this age such words have but limited and vague meaning. Other vocabulary studies confirm this fact so completely that we may say there is hardly any trait in which twelve- to fourteen-year intelligence more uniformly excels that of the nine- or ten-year level.'[1]

The use of the test not only confirms the validity of the well-known pedagogical maxims, but furnishes data of a character which enables us to understand with greater precision how the mental processes unfold. Five-year intelligence involves comprehension and the ability to define in terms of use. Eight-year intelligence shows an appreciable advance in the ability to generalize. Twelve-year intelligence marks the beginning of the definite ability to understand and form abstractions. The teacher has thus not only valid general maxims to guide him in the work of instruction, but he has definite indications as to the way in which mental development is related to chronological development, so that he may organize his system of instruction in accord with these facts.

The majority of us have received what the school or college has to impart to us through the medium of the class. Our visual image of the school consists in a number of rooms, each with a good number of desks. Those who are teachers think of the same sort of rooms only looked at from the front. In many cases the thought of the class calls to mind a number of children of approximately the same physical age, but with marked inequalities in mental capacity. There may be homogeneity along other lines also, with reference to such matters as caste, religion, or traditions. Now there is a great deal to be said for the practice

---

[1] L. M. Terman, *The Measurement of Intelligence*, p. 284.

of dividing children into classes, for purposes of instruction, foremost among the advantages being that of economy. With increase in the space and furniture, it is possible for one teacher using a single equipment of apparatus sometimes to teach forty children instead of one. Having one teacher to a pupil will be a most extravagant expenditure of energy and ability, when so much more may be accomplished by means of class organization. If the class be characterized by a sufficient amount of homogeneity, there is no reason why progress may not be very good indeed. That sort of homogeneity which is most important educationally is to be found where the members of the class are of like mental age and like attainments. If there be similarities in these matters, and in addition if the rates of ability to progress be approximately equal, you have an almost ideal homogeneity from the point of view of instruction. There are other matters of less importance which nevertheless help, such as the same status in society, similar social environment, a similar attitude towards sport and other like interests. The greater the degree of homogeneity, the more effectual can instruction be in a class.

A class is thus a social group and is capable of that kind of psychological analysis which is used with reference to any social whole. Psychologists have only comparatively recently turned their attention to studies of this type, and we cannot say that any unanimity of interpretation has yet been achieved. The problem which they have to solve has to do with the character of the unity which marks a social group. There is one point on which all are agreed, viz. that the unity is a psychological one. It is an inter-relationship between minds, and the inter-relationship is itself psychologically determined. It must be apparent to the student of social groups that there are marked differences in the degrees of unity attained, and surely we may say that this factor is dependent on the amount of homogeneity present. In a mob we get a unity that is due to a common object of attention, and it would sometimes seem easier to secure common attention to a destructive than to a creative task. Many social groups owe their unity to a community of attitude towards some particular object or problem. Congresses of scientists and politicians and conventions of members of religious groups are instances in point. The class in an organized school has common objects of attention in the curriculum which is to be covered, the examinations for which preparation has to be made, the promotions which are sought, and the education which is the object of endeavour. It is therefore possible for the instructor to secure a fair degree of attention to common enterprises and common problems. The greater the sense of community that is felt, the easier is it to secure concerted attention. This is what we mean by *esprit de corps*.

There are different interpretations current as to what is meant by the social unity. With some scholars, society is regarded as an organism, and is interpreted on the analogy of biological processes and structures. But psychologically this seems somewhat exaggerated, for there is not the evidence in the interplay of individuals comprising a social group of that delicacy and subtlety which mark the mutual adaptations of the various parts of an organism. There are others who think that society is characterized by a consciousness or mind which is something distinct from the individual minds of the members of the group. Prof. Dewey says of this theory, which has been championed by Dr. McDougall in his *Group Mind*, that 'it is difficult to see that collective mind means anything more than a custom brought at some point to explicit, emphatic consciousness, emotional or intellectual.'[1] It is always more easy, he argues, to get crowd activity where there is a near 'background of rigid and solid customs conjoined with the phenomena of a period of transition'.[2] This is quite as well illustrated in the India of today as the China and Japan to which Dr. Dewey refers. It is a unity that is the outcome of suggestion that appeals to a dominant emotional tendency and an inhibition of conflicting tendencies. A social group is thus a psychological unity and never a metaphysical unity.

The class illustrates another characteristic in common with other social groups, viz. a liability to disintegration. It is not an uncommon thing in political, scientific or religious gatherings to hear that people who had come together for a common purpose had broken up into smaller groups which were disputing with

---

[1] J. Dewey, *Human Nature and Conduct*, p. 60.   [2] Ibid., p. 61 n.

one another. Disintegration is due in some way or other to a breaking up of the unity of attention on a common object. That may be due to the emphasis coming on matters wherein opinions differ. Or it may be due to a factor of disturbance. It is apparent, for example, when a class is attending to a problem of common interest and the class in a neighbouring class-room bursts into a round of applause over some remark or incident there. A teacher or an orator is sensitive to any influences that tend to disintegrate the unity of his class or audience, and he is at once put on his metal to throw out such appeals as will re-establish the unity.

The most serious defect of the class, from the point of view of instruction, is its liability to disintegration. Such disintegration is sufficiently disconcerting when it is due to some disturbance either external or internal. But it is much more serious when it is the result of fundamental psychological differences. The presence of two or three students of decidedly inferior intelligence in a class of average high intelligence, creates a most serious problem for the teacher. If he goes at such a rate that the dullards can follow, the class as a whole suffers and makes nothing like the progress of which it is capable. On the other hand, if he sets his pace according to the average ability of the members of the class, the dullards will get practically nothing. The only alternatives seem to be to give up the class as a basis for instruction, or else to be much more scientific in the organization of the school, so that none need suffer to the advantage of others.

Many educationalists are coming to the conclusion that it is practically impossible to secure that homogeneity in a class that is necessary for effectual instruction. There ought to be community in the matter of attainment to begin with. Then, if progress is to be uniform, there should be fairly equal intelligence. Neither of these can be quite disregarded to the advantage to the other in the matter of school organization. But, as we saw in the third chapter, intelligence is made up of the ability to do a miscellaneous lot of things well, and in a class of pupils, even of fairly equal intelligence quotients, the various assemblages of abilities may have very marked differences. In one group linguistic ability may dominate, and in another mathematical ; in one group it may be mental manipulation, while in another it is motor manipulation.   Again there will be differences in physical endurance, and differences in temperament, differences in tastes, and differences in emotional emphasis.   Some are more submissive ; others are predominatingly self-assertive. Some are more egoistic ; others have a greater degree of altruism. It is a most difficult problem for the teacher to try to do justice to all, and do it through the medium of class instruction. For, in spite of the fact that the form of organization is the class, the subjects to be educated are individuals rather than the group.

The school is a social group, and the class is a smaller social group within the larger.   Human life is very largely social life. And the school has a most valuable function to perform in affording a training ground for children to prepare for larger social demands and opportunities.   We want young people to realize that there should be no conflict at bottom between individual interests and social interests.   One of the services of the class is to inculcate that idea.   At the same time, the social group should be a ministrant to the individual, and neither a class nor any other group is doing its best if it hampers individual development.   The centre of education is not an institution nor an organization, but personality.   We may very appropriately say of the class, what Jesus said of the Sabbath, that it was made for man, and not man for it.

'One of the most notable features of present-day education is the reaction against class-teaching,' says Prof. John Adams. 'The class has, in the past, been largely taken for granted, and its very existence tended to guide teaching method into certain definite lines.   Many modern teachers are dissatisfied with the limitations thus imposed on their freedom, and are in revolt against the whole system.   The wish being father to the thought, there is a rumour that the knell of class-teaching has been rung.   The question, "Who tolled the bell?" produces various answers.   There is quite a demand for the honour, but, on the whole, the evidence seems to point to Dr. Montessori.'[1]

Dr. Montessori certainly was one of the pioneers in a revolt

---

[1] J. Adams, *Modern Developments in Educational Practice*, p. 136.

against the older class instruction, and the result is slowly spreading. It is shifting the emphasis to the child. The important thing to know is not whether the child is keeping pace with the class, but whether the class is contributing sufficiently and efficiently to the development of the child. It is one of the results of the modern emphasis on personality which characterizes education as well as so many other sciences. Other methods have followed in the wake of that of Madame Montessori, some of them modifications of her plan, and others quite different. A brief survey of some of these methods will let us see the way in which increasing attention is being given to paedocentric instruction.

I. The Montessori Method

Madame Montessori is one of the pioneers in the work of modern educational method. She was a student of the Italian anthropologist, Sergi, from whose work she learned something of the way in which man develops and ought to develop. She realized that, if one is to engage in the work of educating individuals, the more we can know about them the better for our purpose. She also made a study of the results of experimental psychology, with special reference to their significance for education. The study of these sciences with reference to education led her to side with the view of Rousseau, that liberty is one of the fundamental concepts for pedagogy, and that it is a concept which has been practically unknown to educators. One may say that it is in respect to this new emphasis on freedom that Madame Montessori is most really a pioneer. All of the more recent developments in educational method have taken this leaf from her book. To be sure, some have misconceived the purpose of emphasizing freedom, and have taken freedom to be the negation of discipline. But it must be obvious to anyone who seriously observes personality, that freedom is a *sine qua non* to the entire moral and social life. An individual to whom freedom is denied descends inevitably to the level of a machine. Personality implies freedom to choose and to act and to think for oneself in a social situation. The criticism of the older pedagogical methods is not that they insisted on discipline, but that thay made the child subservient to the class and the curriculum.   There was too much tendency to treat all children as though they needed precisely the same kind of treatment to develop.   Madame Montessori set herself the task of remedying that defect by giving the school more of the atmosphere of the home, where the different members of the family co-operate in common tasks.

The Montessori method lays stress on the education of the senses.   Special sensory exercises have been devised and apparatus invented wherewith the child's special processes—vision, touch, hearing, etc.—are stimulated and developed.   It is accepted by all that much of the mental life is based on sense-perception, even as the more complex processes are based on the more elementary.   Herein lies the real worth of the new method, that the sensory and observational processes are given free scope for full development.   Dr. Montessori says : ' By means of our so-called " sensory exercises " we make it possible for the child to distinguish and to classify.'   That is, she deliberately planned the development of the higher mental processes through the more elementary ones.   The one question which some are inclined to ask is, whether the facts warrant the use of these ' sensory gymnastics ' for the attainment of the end in view.   Inasmuch as this method gives an opportunity for development through self-expression, it is unquestionably on the right lines.   In so far as it makes use of sensory processes for their own sake, it is one-sided.

Another feature of the Montessori system is the emphasis on the imagination.   The extraordinary imaginative activity of the child is characteristic of immaturity.   Madame Montessori says: ' An adult resigns himself to his lot, a child creates an illusion.' Now illusory imagination is based upon credulity, and tends to perpetuate a belief in the legendary and mythological.   But these are not the sorts of beliefs which it is desirable to have in the adult mind.   The time comes when we desire these beliefs to disappear.   The conclusion which she reaches is that imaginative activity ought to be based upon truth and reality.   She looks forward to the establishment of the positive sciences which will crowd out the myth and the fairy tale.   But she does not carry out the logic of her own position in actual practice, for she finds a real place for these things in the work of developing the æsthetic imagination. The method really needs the corrective which may be obtained from the place of the imagination in modern psychology as including memory processes, scientific imagination, æsthetic imagination, fantasy, and so forth. Giving the child a considerable portion of work of an exacting and definite nature will correct any abnormal tendencies which may be the result of wild imaginings, and imagination, if it be stimulated to function in creative channels, will produce some of the finest types of personality which the world needs. In imagination, as well as in sense-perception, the Montessori method is in advance of the Montessori theory.

II. THE DALTON PLAN

Education on the Dalton plan is a continuation and modification of the Montessori method. The origin of the name is simply due to the fact that the plan was first put into operation in Dalton, Massachusetts, the person to whom the credit of originating the plan is due being Miss Helen Pankhurst, a student of Dr. Montessori, who for some time was in charge of the interests of Madame Montessori in the United States. The plan is also known as the Dalton laboratory plan, from the fact that it aims to introduce, in a much more thorough way than any antecedent plan, the method of the laboratory into education. We are all familiar with the idea of laboratories for chemistry, physics, zoology, etc., but who ever heard of a laboratory for every subject in the curriculum? Yet this is precisely what Miss Pankhurst conceived as a working plan. Take, for example, the study of History. Obviously, it is possible to have a History laboratory by collecting maps, books, pictures, anthropological exhibits, and other materials such as would make the study more concrete and interesting. The laboratory method makes more serious demands for specialists in the various subjects of the curriculum, but it has the advantage that each teacher can centre his attention on the task of making one particular subject live for the pupils and has not to rack his brains in regard to a whole curriculum of subjects.

The laboratory method, which the Dalton plan emphasizes, is a further extension of the Montessori method of making the individual the centre of educational interest rather than the class. Professor John Adams refers to these new methods as ringing the knell of class teaching. The task of the educator is not so much that of teaching in the sense of instruction, as of guiding the pupils as they carry on their own work. Under the older methods, pupils went to school to acquire what the school had to offer in the way of knowledge; now the objective is the satisfaction of the need for self-development. Formerly judgement was passed on teachers, subjects and schools according to their disciplinary value; today self-discipline is regarded as much more fundamental. It is not difficult to see that where classes are kept small, the teacher has a much better chance for watching the development of the individual members. The difficulty arises when classes are large, and quite plainly the cost of education would be tremendously increased if small classes were made the rule. On the other hand, it is becoming increasingly evident that mass methods of education are more or less of a travesty on education. People are fortunately beginning to realize that there could not be any better investment of public funds than in the education of those who are to be the future citizens of the State. Where the emphasis is on class instruction, the dull child has very little chance of improvement, even according to his poor capacity, and the chance of discovering the genius is small. The Dalton plan offers a remedy for these defects, by combining individual teaching and education of fairly large numbers through the use of the laboratory method. In the laboratory a number of pupils may be kept occupied with tasks, and at the same time the specialist-teacher may pass from the one to the other, offering suggestions for the guidance of the individuals.

The Dalton plan carries on the Montessori method in the matter of freedom. Miss Pankhurst says, however, that we must not think that freedom means 'do as you like' or indiscipline. It rather means freedom to carry out a given piece of work in which one is interested. Psychology has made it very plain that the core of conscious development is in interested attention. The task of the educator is to arouse the interests of the child in the direction of those things to which we want to attract attention. The abolition of the time-table in the old sense, and of class-instruction, giving a greater amount of freedom for the child to determine the direction of study and to see larger opportunity for unrestricted self-development—these are outstanding features of the Dalton programme.

The Dalton laboratory plan regards education as it ought to be regarded—in the co-operative sense. Miss Pankhurst prefers to call it 'the interaction of group life'. Professor Dewey says that 'the object of democratic education is not merely to make an individual an intelligent participator in the life of his immediate group, but to bring the various groups into such constant interaction that no individual, no economic group, could presume to live independently of others.' If education be a co-operative task, it means that both teacher and pupil must have a clear conception of the task to be accomplished, and that it must be so accomplished that both teacher and pupil will have opportunities for the free expression of personality. The child must be trained to think of his school work as more than preparation for life, as life itself. He must be led to think of himself as a member of society to which he must make his own contribution. The curriculum on the Dalton plan is divided into tasks which pupils take on a contract system, a contract being equivalent to about one month's work. The idea of this plan is to deepen the sense of social responsibility and to make the life of the school seem more a part and parcel of real life. At the same time, the teacher who is a specialist gets a better opportunity for freer and fuller self-expression, inasmuch as he is not required to deal with a number of subjects but can concentrate on the object of his special predilection. Teaching is likened to taking a horse to the water. The horse must have freedom to do its own drinking.

In the Dalton system a graph device is used to indicate the progress which the individual is making in each subject. The one outstanding advantage which the plan possesses is that each pupil is permitted to make progress proportionate to his intelligence and energy. The gravest danger is that of immature specialization.

III. THE HOWARD PLAN

In the same way that the Dalton plan is a modification of the Montessori method, we may speak of the Howard plan as a modification of the Dalton plan. The originator of this method is Mrs. M. O'Brien Harris, D.Sc., who has described her system in a volume which bears the significant title, *Towards Freedom*, published by the University of London Press. The name of the plan is derived from that of the school where it was first put into operation, viz. the County Secondary School for Girls, Clapton, built on the site of John Howard's birthplace and unofficially known as the John Howard School. Dr. O'Brien Harris, like Miss Pankhurst of Dalton plan fame, was a student under Dr. Montessori, and both the American and the Englishwoman are happy to make acknowledgements to the Italian educationalist for inspiration. Dr. O'Brien Harris thinks that there is much more community between the Dalton and Howard plans than there is difference. The common element they owe to both their authors having taken Dr. Montessori's Training Course. The main differences Mrs. O'Brien Harris describes in a letter to Prof. John Adams as ' (1) the retention of class-teaching as an integral part of our work, and (2) the relief to the congestion of the time-table, by arranging that the number of subjects taken by a girl in any one term is (except in rare cases) less than the full number which she studies during the pre-matriculation period. The form system practically, though not necessarily, requires the full number each term.'

The general trend of all of the three plans mentioned is well described by the title of Dr. O'Brien Harris' book, *Towards Freedom*. This freedom is attained through various means. One method which all three plans have in common is a reformation in the school furniture which is used. The idea that each class should be supplied with a uniform style and size of desks or benches, illustrates the older emphasis on the class. Anyone who has observed even a little bit knows how absurd it looks, and some know how uncomfortable it feels, to have a uniform size of desks and benches for children who may vary in height by as much as a foot and in weight by forty or fifty pounds, for no other reason than that they happen to belong to the same class.

Another direction in which freedom is sought is the curriculum. Obviously, self-development must include individual curricula and time-tables if the child is not to be swallowed by the class. The modern psychological methods of measuring mental abilities confirm the wisdom of this method. We know that intelligence is made up of a number of abilities, and that it is not always the same combination of abilities that make children of approximately equal intelligence. A class system that regards them on a dead level does justice to no one. Furthermore, each child is ordinarily able to progress much more rapidly in some subject or subjects than he is in others, and a system of education which insists that progress in all subjects of a curriculum must be uniform, is doing an injustice to the individual and killing his interest in his school work.

The solution of the educational problem, according to Mrs. O'Brien Harris, is along the lines of auto-education. She quotes Ruskin : ' Education does not mean teaching people to know what they do not know ; it means teaching them to behave as they do not behave.' Self-education is not a new discovery, but it is receiving a new emphasis. Morally and socially there is no discipline worthy of the name but self-discipline. Digestion can not be carried on by proxy. So, too, children cannot be moral by proxy. They must be led to do for themselves what ought to be done, and to inhibit what ought not to be done. The auto-educationalist seeks to develop order and serenity within the pupils so that they will evolve self-mastery, æsthetic appreciation, and social responsibility.

The departure which Dr. O'Brien Harris has made in the way of school organization is that her classification is made vertically instead of horizontally, to quote Prof. Adams. The horizontal classification is into classes ; the vertical is into houses. In the house system members are of different ages so that the older may help the younger. Children remain members of a house not for merely one year but for a number of years, so that the influence of the mistress on the pupils is not cut short just when it is beginning to be most effectual, as in the ordinary school system. Like the Dalton system, an individual record is maintained on a card, and there is none of the older competition for

16

marks. Incentives are held out for the development of individual ideals, and for the children to compare their own progress with their ideals. The houses are given the names of certain European cities, Florence (the Geography room), Athens (the Mathematics room), Winchester (the room for English and Latin), Venice and Rome. The rooms are made as attractive and suggestive as possible, and a spirit of loyalty to the house is instilled in the minds of the pupils.

As was indicated, there is more place for class teaching in the Howard than in the Dalton plan. Class teaching is indeed an integral part of the work. At the same time, the work is so arranged as to enable each individual to have his own time-table and to go at his own pace. The work of the pupil is checked at various stages, the records being maintained on cards that are designed for that purpose. A larger place is made for the arts and the crafts than is usual in the ordinary school curriculum. This provides for the development of certain elements of personality, such as æsthetic appreciation and manual skill, for which the older school curriculum made inadequate provision. The Howard system possesses an elasticity that is commendable, and affords real scope for the initiative of the child, though it does not pretend to be a final solution of the educational problem.

IV. THE GARY SYSTEM

Gary is a city in the State of Indiana, only a few miles east of the city of Chicago. It is not yet twenty years old, and yet today has a population of over 50,000. The town is built on the famous sand dunes of the shores of Lake Michigan, and was planned by the United States Steel Corporation as a suitable site on which to erect their industrial works and build a town for their workers. Happily for Gary, there came to it as superintendent of its school system, early in its history, Mr. William A. Wirt, a man of 'poetic insight', as his friends say, and yet of practical genius in educational matters. The system which he installed in the mushroom city soon became the most talked-of educational system on the American continent. To be sure, Mr. Wirt had an unusual advantage in beginning his work, for he had no outworn traditions or well established customs to overcome. On the other hand, his task was by no means easy, for the steel industry employed at least two-thirds foreign-born children or children of foreign-born parents. Mr. Wirt came to the town when there was but one small school, and the system which has been evolved is largely his own building.

The outstanding feature about the Gary system has been said to be its school architecture. Mr. Wirt began by challenging the well-known pedagogical adage: 'A place for every pupil and every pupil in his place.' He did not believe that there must be just as many desks and benches in a school as there are children. The usual supposition on which school managements proceed is that no more pupils can be admitted than there are available seats. But in modern schools there are a great many additional features, such as manual training, drill, gymnastics, library work, etc. On every occasion when a class is engaged in one or other of these exercises its class-room will be left unoccupied. Mr. Wirt's plan was to make use of the class-rooms when a group was engaged upon manual training or some other occupation. Prof. Adams says: 'Mr. Wirt, like Nature, abhors a vacuum, and, like Nature, at once proceeded to fill one when he found it.' He therefore planned to provide accommodation for only half of the children, calculating that only about half of the school time would be spent in the class-room. This plan had a distinct appeal to the city fathers, because it offered an economy which they were glad to have. Accordingly, they extended to Mr. Wirt the freedom which he wanted for the development of his system according to his own ideas. As the system has developed, there was provision made for many extras, such as extensive well-equipped playgrounds, a swimming tank, laboratories, an art room, a conservatory, rooms for manual training, libraries and recreation rooms. The school day is made much longer than the ordinary school day, being seven hours, to provide for all the changes, and to allow time for all the classes to get in their required work.

The Gary schools are made an integral part of the city in a commendable way. There is a spirit of co-operation that marks the entire system. As one example, the town analyst is also the teacher of chemistry in the high school, and a good deal of the analytical work is conducted in the laboratories of the school. Periodical analyses of the town water and of the sweetmeats made in the various shops are made in the school laboratories by the pupils under the direction of the analyst.   Obviously, this gives the pupils the sense that they are actually engaged in the problems and tasks of life, and not merely in the business of getting ready for something serious which is to follow.   The Gary schools are in that way schools in citizenship, and the activities of the school revolve about the interests of the town itself, giving to the whole educational work a sense of communism, of partnership in real and worthful tasks.   Moreover, the Gary schools are perpetual centres of activity.   Many criticisms have been put forward against the system, because the schools have been made to function seven hours in the day and seven days in the week.   Is not so much school very soon going to make the children and teachers alike feel 'fed up' with the whole business ?   But these criticisms are very soon found to be superficial, when a closer examination of the system is made and it is seen that no teacher or pupil is kept busy all of that time. It is because the school is the centre of community activities that it is open so much of the time, and there must be a sufficient number of teachers employed so as to provide for shifts and enable all to have the recreation and leisure that they need.

The Gary system is in harmony with the Dalton and Howard plans in its emphasis on specialization. A splendid corps of specialists has been gathered in the Gary schools, so that the students have the advantage of the best of instruction in whatever branch of learning they may be engaged.   In addition to the regular teachers, there are supervizing masters who have charge of the different forms.   They teach English or Scripture, and thus are not divorced from the teaching work of the school.   Some of the form-masters are also specialists in some subject, but in their forms over which they have supervision, their work as specialists is made subservient to their work with their boys.

The longer school day which the Gary system provides enables a larger provision for choice on the part of the pupils. Thus the freedom which the Montessori, Dalton and Howard plans seek for in their own way is secured in the Gary plan by the extension of the school day so as to provide a much more varied programme and one that operates over a wider period of time. At the same time, each pupil must arrange his programme in consultation with the supervizing master, and no change is permitted without his consent. The Gary system may be said to be still in the experimental stage, but none can doubt that it is making a contribution to educational administration and method which, perhaps in a modified form, will persist.

V. THE PROJECT METHOD

The Project Method has been defined as the use of the purposive act in the educative process. In this respect it is in harmony with the whole emphasis of modern education. Pupils must be made to understand clearly why they do what they do. It is no longer possible for a teacher to conduct a school or a class on the principle of coercion. The pupil has a right to demand, and does demand, to know why he should study various subjects which are given a place on the school curriculum. It is quite admissible that some subjects may still be studied because of their disciplinary value, but even that is a purpose—the purpose of disciplining the mind for other tasks. But the whole trend of education is a recognition of the personal element as of paramount importance. Moreover, persons are not all alike, and what some need for self-development may be quite different from the needs of others. So the modern educationalist studies the purpose with reference to the person.

The Project Method gives a new significance to the word, 'problem'. It is considered entirely from the practical point of view. Dr. J. A. Stevenson says : 'A project is a problematic act carried to completion in natural setting.' That gives us the clue to the understanding of the method. Problems must be real problems, problems with meanings that are practical, that is, that are related to some concrete situation. Surveying a field and finding its area are mathematical processes, but they may obviously be taught as associated with some such practical task as dividing the field up into city lots to be sold as building lots for the erection of houses. Cubic measure may seem to the small boy an uninteresting process if it be taught abstractly, but if it be taught with reference to the number of yards in the wall of a house which has been built and has to be paid for at a given rate, the child will very readily see the meaning of the problem in practical projects. In this sense the Project Method is not something new, for any sensible teacher will teach mathematics with reference to practical problems such as have been given. But the Project Method, in the technical sense of the term, means not simply imagining a situation, but so far as possible making the pupils face the actual situation 'in its natural setting' and solving the problem with reference to the needs of the project. Even a miniature project carried through in the laboratory is not quite adequate. Let the pupils get beyond the school confines and work out the project. For example, a class of boys may be asked to undertake the project of building a house or cultivating a field. In that case, they are made to see the significance of every detail of the work, the need for arithmetical and geometrical processes, the need to know something about sanitation and irrigation, the need to study climatic conditions, soil, rainfall and other elements in physical geography, the use of a knowledge of chemistry in studying the soil and the action of lime, and so forth. It will make the boys realize, as they would not otherwise, the significance of much they are asked to study in school. They will realize its practical purposiveness in relation to real projects. A real experiment along these lines is being conducted at Moga, in the Punjab, and has attracted a great deal of attention on the part of those engaged in educational work in India. Mr. W. J. McKee is the genius who is behind the Moga project, and he is doing a great deal in making his students, and also other teachers, realize the practical element in the purposes of education.

The Project Method has one decided advantage from the point of view of modern psychology. It studies education from the angle of building up bonds between certain stimuli and responses. The emphasis is described by Prof. Kilpatrick as follows: 'The reader is asked to note (a) how a "set" towards an end means readiness in and action of pertinent bonds with reference to that end, (b) how this end defines success, (c) how readiness in the bonds means satisfaction when success is attained, and (*d*) how satisfaction strengthens the bonds whose action brought success.' The desideratum is to study the formation of the stimulus-response bonds in accordance with the laws of learning. These have been enunciated by Thorndike, as we have already observed, as the laws of Readiness, Effect, and Exercise.

Modern education lays a great deal more stress on the social element in the process than did the older methods. The Project Method is an attempt to remove any apparent conflict between the demands of the social situation and the interests of the child. It tries to make the child feel that he is a part, and an integral part, of the group. Our entire fabric of social institutions is an evolution from human needs and interests. They grew up as the group's responses to stimuli. Now the pupil is a member of the group, and by participating actively in the group's activities he is made to feel his integral unity with the group life. This is the proper foundation of the building up of moral character. The judging of a moral situation and the performance of the act which will be considered by the group as moral is made possible as the individual acquires the habit of responding appropriately to a given situation, until at last a bond is established between the stimulus and response. Children in school are themselves a society in miniature, and may be taught, under the guidance of a skilful teacher, to make their own discriminations as to the right and the good. A moral situation is social, and implies a sharing of purposes by the members of the group. The perpetual sharing of purposes, which necessarily characterizes school life brings about that attitude of give-and-take which is necessary for the moral life of society. The great contribution of the Project Method is precisely this development of personality in a democratic atmosphere.

It is commonplace to remark that instruction ought to appeal to the interests of pupils. There is not always a very definite connotation to the word 'interest' however. Our English word is simply the Latin impersonal verb, which means 'it concerns', and has come to be used in two distinct senses. It may be used with reference 'to *experience* or to *disposition*, to the conscious or to the unconscious. As referring to experience, " interest " signifies the fundamental affective factor, which is always involved and gives the experience what we call " meaning ". Feeling of value or " worthwhileness " probably expresses with sufficient clearness and concreteness this aspect of experience. When we speak of *an* interest, however, the reference is not to this affective aspect of experience, but to a structural feature of the mind itself, to a disposition.'[1]

In education, interest signifies the active identification of the self with any object. When a child is interested in his work it means that he has put himself into it, identified himself with it. There is no truth in the traditional idea of a diremption between interest and duty. To arouse a child's interest in any study or educational object involves a direct appeal to the self or the disposition. Interest is the active, moving side of the disposition, and therefore has a definite affective content. A child feels pleasurably in undertaking interesting tasks, and disagreeably in having to do things that do not appeal to its interests. Since interest is thus in large measure dispositional, it devolves upon the teacher to study the individual temperaments of his pupils. Where he finds certain interests to dominate his class in common, his task will be simplified. Where there are more individuals, he must give individual attention to the varying needs.

The teacher who builds with dominant interests and abilities will be much more successful than the one who is merely an instructor of certain given subject-matter. Such constructive instruction finds its basis in individual psychology. Experimental work such as the determination of intelligence quotients furnishes the technique wherewith the educator must assemble the information he requires. A beginning has already been made in the devising of character and temperament tests, and without doubt the future will see important advances in this type of work —work which will be of immense value to the teacher in determining the best methods for educational development.

There is considerable work being done in planning school work so that it will make a more direct appeal to the interests of

[1] Drever, *An Introduction to the Psychology of Education*, p. 125 f.

children. One of the devices is to make more use of the play activity of children. There is an old idea that play and work constitute a dilemma in actual life, a distinction which has undoubtedly done considerable harm in hindering people from making the pedagogical use of play that they might. They regard play as of less value, because it lacks the seriousness of work. It is characterized by an immediacy of end-enjoyment, in contrast with work which has some more ulterior end in view. 'Its value is a "make believe" value, and its world a "make-believe" world.'[1] This whole attitude, it seems to me, is based on a misunderstanding. Any one who has watched children at play must surely be impressed by the thorough-going realism of it all, and the absence of guile. It would be a more valid distinction to speak of play as arousing a *direct* interest, and work *indirect*. And surely there is good pedagogical reason for making appeals as directly as possible. The dramatic method of teaching literature and history is full of splendid possibility. The Play Way, like the Project Method, is intended not as a diversion or make-believe, but as suggesting an active and direct appeal to interest in learning.

There are some who look with suspicion on this method, as though it were an attempt to eliminate the uninteresting from the school curriculum. Prof. Bain, who holds to the old-time dilemma between work and play, says: 'Then comes the stern conclusion that the uninteresting must be faced at last; that by no palliation or device are we able to make agreeable everything that has to be mastered. The age of drudgery must commence: every motive that can avert it is in the end exhausted.'[2] Surely the teacher's task is not to alternate the interesting and the uninteresting so mechanically. Every one knows that there is a certain amount of knowledge, the attainment of which involves an uninteresting grind. But there is such a thing as so relating the uninteresting to the interesting that the mental strain will be reduced, and yet attention be held.

The conduct of a school ought to be viewed as a co-operative enterprise. Such a treatment is possible only as the teacher can

---

[1] Drever, *An Introduction to the Psychology of Education*, p. 101.
[2] Bain, *Education as a Science*, p. 184.

make his appeal to direct interests, and enlist the child actively in the work of the school. Certainly one of the paramount aims of education is the freeing of activities. The immediate object is the work whereby the mind indicates the activity which it is desired to execute. Courses of study and particular lessons are in that sense means for the freeing and directing of activities. This is, of course, in revolution to the old notion of a child as a passive receptacle into which given quantities of knowledge are to be poured. There is no better way to rouse the interests of children than to instil in them the sense of partnership in common enterprises. Give to them the sense of active creative co-operation rather than that of passive receptivity, and the energy they will put into their work will be vastly increased. The atmosphere of co-operation is much the most conducive environment for liberating activities and developing abilities. And these activities must be internally motivated by appeals to the subjects' interests rather than externally motivated by the authority of the teacher. It is this spirit of active co-operation that brings about real democracy in education.

The aim of instruction is not minds well stored with knowledge, but the development of moral personalities. Moral personality involves as a primary requisite an element of freedom. Without freedom to choose between alternatives no morality is possible. So that the educational aim is to train children in such a way that they will develop as self-conscious, self-directing and self-determining personalities. On the other hand, as a social institution, there must be an element of organization that harmony may be secured. The problem, then, is how to offer the pupil the opportunity for development as a free person, and still preserve the order of the school. This is what we ordinarily mean by the problem of discipline, though in its original and larger sense it means systematic training through education. The popular idea that freedom and discipline are fundamentally opposed to each other needs to be dispelled. Surely, systematic training, even under authority, need not be subversive of liberty for individual development. The authority of the teacher is not an educational authority when it follows the methods of the policeman. Preserving order in school is not the ultimate test of efficient instruction. There must be order, but the good teacher will secure it naturally and regard it as subsidiary to his primary end.

The relation between freedom and discipline resolves itself into a particular phase of the general problem of the relation between the individual and society. The school is founded on a belief that the interests of the individual and the interests of society are not at bottom in conflict. It has already been observed how the newer methods of instruction are endeavouring to give greater scope for the development of the individual. Occasionally one meets with a teacher with lack of perspective, who sees only one-half of the situation. If the half he sees be discipline, he is very likely to regard his children as so many receptacles. But if he is concentrating his attention on freedom, he may swing to the opposite extreme and let order go to the winds. It must never be forgotten that personalities have to be developed in social environments, that is, in environments of other persons. Freedom for Henry to develop must not be at the expense of David, Edward, Joseph, and all the other members of the class. There must be mutual give-and-take, a reciprocity of freedom and discipline. Only thus is a social organization possible. Only thus can the school fulfil its mission in a democratic environment.

LITERATURE

John Adams. *Modern Developments in Educational Practice.* University of London Press, 1922.

E. L. Thorndike. *The Principles of Teaching.* A. G. Sellar, 1916.

Wm. James. *Talks to Teachers on Psychology.* Longmans Green, 1920.

D. Starch. *Educational Psychology.* Macmillan, 1922.

W. C. Bagley. *The Educative Process.* Macmillan, 1905.

J. Dewey. *The School and Society.* University of Chicago Press, 1915.

F. N. Freeman. *The Psychology of the Common Branches.* Houghton Mifflin, 1916.

E. A. Kirkpatrick. *Fundamentals of Child Study.* 1903.

Madame Montessori. *The Montessori Method.* Heinemann, 1912.

Miss Evelyn Dewey. *The Dalton Laboratory Plan.* Dent, 1922.

M. O'Brien Harris. *Towards Freedom.* University of London Press, 1923.

John Adams. *The New Teaching.* Hodder and Stoughton.

T. P. Nunn.   *Education : Its Data and First Principles.*   Arnold, 1920.

H. Crichton Miller.   *The New Psychology and the Teacher.*   Jarrolds, 1921.

H. Crichton Miller.   *The New Psychology and the Parent.*   Jarrolds, 1922.

J. A. Stevenson.   *The Project Method of Teaching.*   Macmillan, 1924.

P. B. Ballard.   *The Changing School.*   Hodder & Stoughton, 1925.

CHAPTER XIV

THE OLD EXAMINATION *VERSUS* THE NEW

THE educative process is one wherein we profit by the
experiences of the past so that we may improve in the efficiency
of our responses to stimuli. It enables us to profit in the way of
using the knowledge and skill attained in previous reactions so
that we may adapt or modify present reactions. One of the
practical problems of the educator is that of discovering whether,
and to what extent, there is any improvement. To what extent
have our pupils learned to choose the more appropriate and
reject the less appropriate reactions to given situations? The
Law of Exercise in learning suggests to us that exercise so
strengthens the bond between a stimulus and its response, that
the teacher has the best of psychological reasons for seeing that
in the initial stages of learning the child does the right thing.
The Law of Effect re-enforces the Law of Exercise, inasmuch as
responses which are accompanied with satisfaction are likely to
be more firmly fixed in the organism. Instruction ought to be
given keeping these principles of learning unfailingly in mind.
But then comes the question, how is an instructor to know to
what extent he has succeeded?

It must be clear that the measure of a teacher's success in
instruction is the attainments of his pupils. So that any device
which actually measures the attainments of pupils is, at the same
time, measuring the results of instruction. Such is the *raison
d'être* of examinations. They are designed to test the child's
improvements, his attainments in various branches of instruction,
and in so far to be an index to the success or failure of the teach-

ing. There is, then, a valid psychological basis for the practice of having examinations. If we desire to know whether a child has acquired the ability of making an appropriate response to a given situation, the thing to do is to give him an opportunity of making it. We can find out whether Tom can play football by putting him in a game of football; and we can ascertain whether Margaret can cook palatable food by letting her cook and by trying the results of the cooking. So we find the degree of arithmetical, spelling, composition and other acquirements by the assignment of tasks which call into play the operation of the processes involved in appropriate responses. If the test be of such a character that the desired response, and that response alone, will achieve the desired result, it will be a good test. Take one or two examples from the simpler responses. In one of the primary grades the teacher discovers whether Jane knows the meaning of the number ' six' by calling for various manipulations of objects or digits that involve an understanding of that meaning. In a similar way he ascertains whether George has any class-concept ' book ' by exercises involving a practical use of it. The examination system has grown up as a sort of glorification of this elementary principle of testing attainments.

One of the most serious pedagogical problems is as to what extent examinations succeed in accomplishing their own object. Testing the results of instruction and learning is perfectly sound from the psychological point of view. But there are two questions to be asked : first, as to the scope of the educational process to which the examination method is applicable, and second, as to the success or otherwise of the examination method which has been in vogue. The first question is exceedingly important, though it may be easier to deal with than the second. But we must consider each one by itself.

The first question is the question of scope. Do examinations test the progress of the entire education, or of only certain factors? The end of the educative process is the development of a free and full personality, fitted to respond appropriately to a great variety of situations. As we shall have reason to see in the following chapter, personality includes a great many things other than intelligence and learning. It is very complex, and involves affective and conative elements as well as cognitive. The ordinary examination is a measure almost exclusively of cognitive elements, and does not appreciably touch either the affective or conative. The influence and results of teaching are thus something far more widespread than would appear from examinations. Among the aims of teaching may be counted the establishment of certain permanent interests and values, the fixing of a moral outlook which will dominate behaviour throughout life, and the cultivation of finer emotions and æsthetic sensibilities. The teacher tries to influence the moulding of personality, so that going morally wrong will be harder, and doing the right more normal. He endeavours to make the truth more compelling, the right more urgent, the good more attractive, and the beautiful more alluring. In short, all that is included in the achievement of high character is the aim of teaching—the inspiration of lofty ambition, the formation of noble ideals, and the achievement of moral power. Moreover, these are the more important of educational aims, and they are the types of results that examinations do not test, or, if they do, only to a limited degree. The profounder influence on ambitions and ideals often lies beneath the surface, to be disclosed only under the stress of a crisis or in the intimacy of friendship. The educational process is always seeking to build up and augment these hidden powers. But the sort of tests that indicate the effects of education in these regards are those experiences of life that demand a weighing of moral issues and the making of moral decisions. The ways in which the person responds to such moral situations may be very largely determined by the teaching he has received in school, and yet the schools have very inadequate means of discovering the results of its influence. Intelligence, as we have seen, can be measured, and the results give us quite valid results for comparative purposes at least. But character does not so readily lend itself to a technique of measurement.

It may be said, however, that a beginning has been made in the direction of testing character traits. Since the psycho-physical organism is so integrally a unity, it would not be possible to measure intelligence at all adequately without some measure of character. Investigations made by such men as Terman and Thorndike yield a positive correlation between mental ability and character traits. Even a superficial observation would show that there are certain moral qualities which, when present, help the student very much in intellectual affairs. Persistence, emotional self-control, physical self-control, adaptability, power for sustained attention, fortitude, freedom from inertia, assurance, venturesomeness, honesty, etc.—these are some of the moral qualities most closely allied to mental work. After all, the same person is mental and moral at one and the same time, so that there ought to be a positive correlation between such traits.

As one example of a test designed to be an actual index of certain character traits, mention may be made of the Downey Individual Will-Temperament Tests. The tests are such that they involve mental abilities, but the design of Dr. Downey is not to measure the mental abilities as such, but to observe the operation of certain moral qualities which are involved in the performance of the tests. For example, there are thirteen pairs of contrasting adjectives, such as *lazy* and *industrious*, *extravagant* and *thrifty*, and the subject is asked to check one word in each pair which is characteristic of himself. But the significant features are not the list of qualities so checked, but the speed with which the person makes decisions and the reasons for delays, if any. Various tests are given of writing according to different instructions as to speed, distractions, size, etc., and these are devised to test such qualities as the ability to inhibit competing stimuli, aggressiveness, patience, perseverance, etc. This indicates that a beginning has been made in a type of test for character traits, but we have to admit that it is only a bare beginning. Though it may be true that examinations call into play certain moral qualities, they do not measure them with a fine degree of accuracy. They may indicate the general directions in which character may be expected to develop and express itself, but there is a measure of artificiality about the situations they induce which make predictions rather hazardous. The chief difficulty is that sufficient data have not yet been assembled to pronounce on the validity of the tests. Our conclusion is that, as far as scope is concerned, examinations are inadequate as measures of the results of teaching, for they afford scarcely any indication of the more weighty matters concerned, on the basis of which the success of teaching ought to be judged.

The second question to be considered concerns the success or otherwise of the traditional examination method as applied to the subjects in which it is employed. Does an examination in History, e.g., really test the knowledge and ability of the examinees in that subject? A similar question may be asked of each subject to which the examination system is applied. Furthermore, is the examination system a reliable criterion by which to gauge the progress of a student and determine his advancement in school? The feeling that the examination system as it has been conducted for a long time is a failure has been growing in intensity for a long time. As far back as 1888 there appeared in *The Nineteenth Century* an article over the signatures of 400 very eminent persons protesting against what they termed the sacrifice of education to examinations. Since that time some progress has been made, especially in the sphere of elementary education, which has been largely freed from the former burden, but in secondary and collegiate education there has been comparatively little change.

The story of the beginnings of mental measurement is now quite a familiar one. In the present author's book on *Psychological Tests of Mental Abilities*[1] a brief historical account of the origin and development of the system was given. It will be recalled that there are a host of eminent psychologists, including Binet and Simon in France, Winch, Ballard and Burt in England, Newmann and Ebbinghaus in Germany, and in America Terman, Thorndike, Goddard, Whipple, Otis and many others, who have laboured indefatigably during the last two decades. One of the results of the work of these men is to show the advance of the method of measurement in application to all mental processes and mental products. The method of measurement includes the devising of tests and the arrangement of tests in scales which are graded in accordance with some accepted basis, such as age or school-grades. These tests and scales are put to thorough tests by application to thousands of subjects, and modifications are made wherever necessary, in the light of the increasing body of data collected. The mathematical technique

---

[1] Woodburne, *Psychological Tests of Mental Abilities*, chapter i.

of statistics, with its important methods for determining correlation, is rigorously applied to all of the data so assembled. To begin with, this method was utilized chiefly with regard to the study of intelligence, and, as we have seen, an altogether new and much more precise method of classification was secured on the basis of the intelligence quotient. But as time elapsed, it grew upon scholars who were at work in the field that it offered a method of rich possibilities in the field of mental attainments as well as capacities. So tests and scales of attainment began to spring up as a new type of examination, an examination which is really a measurement and not an award of marks nor a guess at attainments.

One of the outstanding advantages of this system is that the examination itself is scientifically examined before it is accepted as valid. When a number of tests have been tested, and arranged in a scale, it is possible for the examiner to eliminate the subjective element. His endeavour is to devise such a scale that each test will be scored by the same mark, no matter who may be the examiner. There should be only one possible correct answer, so that there need be no weighing of the response as to its merits. Each question calls for one meritorious response, without which it is valueless. In other words, the examination is rendered as much as possible fool-proof. It tries to prevent the examiner—not the examinee, as has been so traditionally supposed —from making a fool of himself—a characteristic, all will agree, of no small merit. To make the point clear, I may give an example of a question that is not fool-proof, and another that is. Of the former type, take as an extreme case the old question: ' Have you left off beating your wife ? ' It is presented in the form of an alternative which, for the majority of respectable people, is quite fallacious. Either of the possible answers ' Yes ' and ' No ' suggests a dangerous allusion. Of the fool-proof type, the following question may be taken as an example, for it admits of only one possible correct answer: ' Is coral obtained from mines in Burma ? '

Another defect with the older system of examinations was that it was often largely a test of writing an essay on the particular language of the examination. Very frequently it was deliberately made to serve that purpose, sometimes to the great disadvantage of the subject under examination. When I was teaching the Scripture class in the high school at Kurnool, South India, it was my practice to tell the students that I intended to use the class as an aid to teaching English by demanding clearly expressed answers to questions. There at least I can claim the merit of having let the students know what I was doing, but very often teachers in other classes follow the same practice without taking the students into their confidence in the matter. Dr. Ballard, in commenting on this practice, says:

'The modern examination is dominated by the essay. It is based on the essay; it is built on the essay; it stands or falls by the measurability of the essay. And by the essay, I do not mean a specially ambitious piece of writing; I mean anything and everything that may be called English composition—any "attempt", however trivial, to express ideas in discursive prose. Sometimes, as in the English paper, the whole test consists of one or two long essays and nothing else; more often, as in the History paper, it comprises from half a dozen to a dozen questions, to each of which the answer is a brief essay. Except in Mathematics and the Manual Arts, the essay—the putting together of words—dominates the whole procedure. And the question here under discussion is not whether the writing of English is a profitable school practice (that, I take it, is beyond dispute); nor whether it is desirable that our pupils should go out into the world endowed with the capacity to express their thoughts in clear and correct English (nobody in his senses would deny that); but it is whether the essay, written under the stringent conditions of the examination room, and assessed in our present ignorance of the science of marking, is a good and true means of measuring. And my scepticism', continues Prof. Ballard, ' goes further than denying that it is a good means of measuring the pupil's knowledge of geography, history and science; I deny that it is a good means of measuring anything—even his knowledge of the mother tongue.'[1]

There are some illustrations given in Dr. Ballard's excellent

---

[1] P. B. Ballard, *The New Examiner*, p. 52 f.

book, which serve to show that he had some quite good reasons for reaching his estimate of the essay method. One was the case of two students in an English training college, one an Englishman, named Smith, and the other a Welshman, named Jones. The principal was their teacher in English, and he demanded of them an essay on some appointed theme once a fortnight. They worked and consulted together and always sent in much the same type of essay, but each time Smith's was marked 'very good' and Jones' 'very fair'. Moreover, the principal was well known as a conscientious man, and there was much evidence that he read the essays with great care. One week the students played a trick. Each man copied out the other man's essay, and sent it in under his own name. The expected happened. The essay under Smith's name was marked 'very good' and that under Jones' 'very fair'.[2] The students had submitted the principal, unknown to him, to a psychological test, and had found, as they suspected, that there was an attitude or prejudice operating in his case, which was very firmly fixed, in spite of his desire to do the right thing for his students.

Another example recorded by Dr. Ballard was the case of an examination in History which was given at an American University in 1920. The papers were evaluated by six professors of History working as a panel. A student was required to get 60 out of 100 for a pass, and it was agreed that any paper to which any professor assigned under 60 marks should be circulated so as to ensure fair play to all borderline cases. One of the professors, who was exceedingly conscientious, began by writing out what he considered model answers to the questions, but inadvertently his model answer paper got mixed up with the papers of those which he had failed and were sent round to the other five professors for their appraisal. This paper was read by them as a *bona fide* answer paper, and some of his colleagues plucked him, the marks ranging all the way from 40 to 80.[1]

There can be no denying the fact that a teacher who has observed the performances and the progress of a student throughout a year is in a much better situation to form a reliable

---

[1] Ballard, *The New Examiner*, p. 54 f.   [2] Ibid., p. 66.

appraisal of his work than an examiner who has only one performance on which to judge him.   Probably there is none of us who
are teachers who could not give instances of injustices that are
directly traceable to the examination system.   Sometimes these
injustices are explicable, and sometimes they remain as mysteries.
Let us take the present Secondary School Leaving Examinations in vogue in the Madras Presidency, with their complicated
system of moderation of marks.   Every year there is a grand
chorus of complaints from various parts of the Presidency.   It
is said that the system itself affords the unscrupulous an
opportunity of manipulating school examination marks in such a
way as to procure advantages.   Now, of course, the best kind of
system would not be quite proof against immorality.   But
leaving aside the question of honesty, it is certainly desirable to
have a system that lends itself to more objective manipulations.   Then there are our University examinations.   The results
always contain many surprises.   Some who were expected to
succeed do not, and some succeed when nobody anticipated
that they would.   Failures are sometimes due to emotional
agitation, even when the student richly deserves to pass.   Others
are due to methods of working which put them at a disadvantage
in a public examination.   Sometimes the man who is verbose
and can rapidly organize his materials gets a second class, when
a slower worker who has a far wider comprehension of his
subject gets only a third.   The critical thinker, who is the more
intelligent and has attained more than the man who ' by-hearts '
text-books and professor's notes, is often at a disadvantage in our
public examinations because he is so critically anxious to express
himself correctly.   A system that lends itself to such variability
and such anomalies is psychologically a failure.   It is neither a
fair test of mental capacity nor of mental products.   It rates
both intelligence and progress on the basis of a chance performance, and the assessment is very largely made by men who have
no knowledge of the student.

   The traditional examination is not a failure only in regard to
essay-writing subjects.   It fails to examine even those subjects
which are characterized by precision.   A number of experiments
have been conducted by various educational psychologists into

the marking of examination papers in mathematics. Many are acquainted with the almost classic example given by Starch and Elliot of their experiment into the accuracy with which teachers mark papers in geometry. Reproductions were made of a question paper and an answer paper in plane geometry, and these were sent to the teachers of a large number of colleges and secondary schools, with the request that the teacher of geometry should mark the answer paper on the basis of 100 marks. One hundred and sixteen teachers returned the papers and the results were tabulated. Two of them gave marks over 90, and one below 30; twenty gave 80 or more, and twenty others 60 or less. Forty-nine teachers passed the examinee, and sixty-nine failed him.[1] In consideration of the definiteness of the subject-matter of geometry, one would have expected that there would have been a far greater approximation to unanimity in regard to the appraising of the paper. And if this is the type of result which obtains in such a subject as geometry, how much greater must be the divergences in subjects which involve the essay type of answer.

Bearing in mind the criticisms of the old type of examination, the practical question is as to how these are to be overcome. We have maintained that there is a valid psychological function for the examination to perform, inasmuch as it tests a person's ability to respond to a given situation by giving him an opportunity to respond. And we have seen that the traditional type of examination, from the psychological as well as the educational point of view, is a failure. The new type of examination is designed to achieve the legitimate function without falling into the errors of the old. Growing, as it has, in large measure out of tests of intelligence, it follows the methods adopted in these tests. Intelligence tests and scales are devised, on the principle that intelligence consists in being able to do a miscellaneous lot of things and to do them correctly. The tests are designed to call into play certain samples of the abilities at the individual's command, and these samples are selected in accordance with the variety of psychological processes which they call into operation.

[1] See Monroe, *Measuring the Results of Teaching*, p. 8 f.

On the same principle, the new examination or attainment test calls for sample performances. As a matter of fact, the old examination also called for sample performances, but in that case the samples were few and scattered. In this instance they are many, though they do not call forth such extended performances. It has sometimes been supposed that a sweeping question was more comprehensive in its scope than a number of smaller questions, but a great many smaller questions, carefully prepared as to the points which they involve and as to variety, are far more comprehensive as a test of one's knowledge of a subject, than a few questions of the more general type. This is the principle of the new examination. Instead of a few questions that call for answers of the essay type, a great many questions are asked, each of which involves a particular point and yet can be answered very speedily by those who know the subject. By means of this type of answer it is possible to give the student a much larger number of questions, cover the subject more extensively, and discover the student's attainments a great deal more thoroughly. Take, for example, the Alpha test used by the American army psychologists. There were 212 questions asked, and a total of twenty-three minutes and fifteen seconds was all that was allowed for completion of the answers. Of the 212 questions, any person who answered 135 correctly in the allotted time was considered of very superior intelligence. This was, of course, designed as a test of intelligence. In a psychology test, which I worked out on the basis of Woodworth as a text, my class was given 160 significant questions to be answered in the same length of time as is usually required for a paper of four or five questions demanding answers of the essay type, viz. two hours ; and there were no complaints about insufficiency of time. The examination was a far greater test of their knowledge of the subject, for there was an average of nearly eight questions on each chapter in the book.

The new examination possesses a much greater degree of validity than the old. The opportunity for chance factors to operate are very much fewer, since the knowledge required is a detailed knowledge of the whole field. It is quite possible with the old examination for a student to pay considerable attention to a few items which his instructor has emphasized, and thus to secure a very fair mark.   This gives the shrewd student an advantage.   If he has the penetration to gather from his instructor the particular topics which are emphasized, or if he makes a search of former examination questions to ascertain what the stock questions are, he may be able to get through with a minimum of work.   But that kind of preparation for the new examination will only serve to disclose the superficiality of the student's work.   The new examination serves two very desirable and closely correlated ends.   It first of all puts the careless and unprepared student at a disadvantage; and secondly, it enables the careful student to show the examiner with what precision he has prepared his work.   I can recall an instance from my own experience as a student.   For examination in English literature three poems were set to be memorized.   I had observed from the class lectures that the professor considered Keat's *Ode to Autumn* to be the most important, and altogether a better product of poetic art than the other two.   Consequently, I memorized that, and let the other two go.   Happily for me, my guess was right, but a wrong guess might have lost me ten per cent of the marks obtainable. Possibly there is some justification for a student scoring high who is keen enough to put emphasis where emphasis is due. The harm comes where the advantage goes to the student who deliberately plans to get through with a minimum of effort.   Dr. Ballard has summarized the matter very succinctly: ' The main advantage of a large number of questions is that they cover the whole field.   Instead of probing the mind at a dozen points they probe it at a hundred points.   The old examiner dips his hand a few times into the storehouse of the pupil's mind and brings up samples which he assumes to be fairly representative of the whole stock. . . .   The less " luck " there is the better; and the more questions are squeezed in the more luck is squeezed out. Thus the new examination gives the candidate a greater feeling of satisfaction than the old; a feeling that, at any rate, he has got his deserts—that the examiner has put his finger on his strong points as well as his weak points.'[1]

---

[1] Ballard, *The New Examiner*, p. 69.

One of the great iniquities of the old type of examination is that it encourages cramming. Cramming is sometimes the last resort of a student who has not been conscientious during the year. Sometimes it is the resort of one who wants to obtain high distinction at the final examination. People who cram usually consult former examination papers to ascertain which are favourite questions. The objection which some have preferred against the new examination is that it encourages cramming. A student may get possession of any of these standardized tests of attainment, and cram up the answers so that he can obtain marks when the examination is given. But the truth is that to cram for an examination of this type is to steadily and thoroughly prepare the subject. The questions are so designed as to cover the whole field. As already pointed out, the psychology examination which I gave to my class included 160 questions, or an average of approximately eight to each chapter of the text. It is clear that preparation for this examination, even should the student have the question paper before him, would involve covering the whole field of study and acquainting himself with the most significant facts of the entire course. For that reason, there is no need to worry even if the student has the question paper before him for his work of preparation. And there is a further reason for cramming being of no advantage, viz. that the determination of success and failure is based not on an *a priori* fixed standard, but on the median. The median is a statistical device, obtained by arranging the scores in order, and finding that score which is such that half of the examinees score above and half below it. The scores are divided into percentile groups which makes possible a convenient use of them. The use of the median instead of a fixed passing mark avoids all of the difficulties due to the uncertainties of different groups and of individuals who score either abnormally high or abnormally low.

It is not possible to give even a brief account of the different scales of attainment which have been and are being devised. Those who want a short account are referred to the published volume of my previous lectures.[1] In that short account

[1] Woodburne, *Psychological Tests of Mental Abilities*, pp. 148-81.

reference is made to tests of arithmetical abilities, reading abilities, spelling abilities, ability in handwriting, and ability in composition. On the basis of the scores obtained in different tests of attainment, it is possible to work out a computation of any individual's educational achievements which will be much more precise than that obtained from the old examination. The new instrument of precision for attainment corresponds to that for intelligence, and is known as the Educational Quotient (E.Q.). The method of obtaining it is to add together the scores of a child in various tests of attainment, and take the average of the same, since the scores are arranged on an age basis. Then this average is taken as the child's educational age. The educational age is taken as the numerator and the child's chronological age as the denominator, and the result is known as the Educational Quotient. For purposes of instruction and school organization, the Educational Quotient is becoming increasingly an instrument of value. It must be of particular use in such a case as that of transferring a child to a new school, where they want to know exactly where the child should be placed. The following example will illustrate the way in which the Educational Quotient of a boy, Richard, aged ten years and six months, would be calculated:

Richard's reading score	..	11 years, 3 months
,, arithmetic score	..	10 years, 2 months
,, composition score	..	12 years, 1 month
Total ..		33 years, 6 months

Educational age   = average or 11 years, 2 months

$$\text{Educational Quotient} = \frac{\text{Educational age} \times 100}{\text{Chronological age}}$$

$$= \frac{11 \text{ years, 2 months}}{10 \text{ years, 6 months}} \times 100 = \frac{134}{126} \times 100 = 106$$

In the old examination, the examiner's troubles begin after the students have written; in the new examination his arduous labours come before, and the valuation is largely automatic. There are three main types of questions which are now in use in the new examination. These are completion tests, true and false tests, and recognition tests.

In the Completion test a number of sentences or paragraphs are given from which a number of significant words are omitted, and blanks are inserted. The examiner's task is to complete the sense by supplying the missing words or phrases. Care has to be exercized in omitting words of such significance that only the person who knows the subject will be able to supply the omissions. I give a few examples from my psychology test, omissions occurring where the italicized words appear :

5. A reaction consists in the release by a *stimulus* of some stored up *energy* of an animal, and the direction of that *energy* into the form of some definite *response.*

18. If we mix *complementary* colours by rotation on a disc, the mixture takes place in the *retina*, and the result is neutral *grey.*

28. The puzzle-box experiment affords a typical example of *trial and error* learning with a gradual *elimination* of unsuccessful *responses.*

36. The difference between sensation and *perception* is that in the former we are *conscious* of *qualities*, and in the latter of objects.

The True and False test consists of presenting a large number of statements, approximately half of which are true and half false. The examinee is required to read through the statements and mark them, by some sign agreed upon, as to which are true and which false. This test has been criticized as one which gives too much encouragement to guessing. On the law of averages, guesses turn out to be half right and half wrong, so that if the scoring is done so as to reckon with that factor, there is no reason why it should prove an insuperable difficulty. At any rate, those who have experimented[1] most thoroughly with the true and false test claim that it is a most useful device. In scoring a performance, marks must be deducted for incorrect responses, so as to eliminate the guessing element. The usual method is to subtract the number of wrong responses from the number of right, since there are likely to be as many right guesses as wrong ones. This will yield a practically correct idea of the

---

[1] See Ballard, *The New Examiner*, pp. 87 ff. ; and McCall, *How to Measure in Education*, pp. 119 ff.

person's actual knowledge.   I shall give a few of the statements which I included in my psychology test, as examples :

3. Intelligence correlates very well with brain weight. . . . *False*.

23. An emotion is a conscious stirred-up state of the organism. . . . *True*.

32. Pain is an organic response to an objectively disagreeable stimulus. . . . *False*.

35. The olfactory nerve-cells are particularly irritable to musical notes. . . . *False*.

56. Meaningful sentences are usually easier to memorize than nonsense syllables. . . . *True*.

The Recognition test is in the form of certain statements with which the examinee is confronted.   The statements are incomplete, but a number of alternative words or phrases are presented, from which the examinee must select that which best completes the statement.   It involves a choice from several alternatives, and the alternatives require so to be formed that the candidate will have to know his subject and attend closely to select the best answer.   Neither the wrong alternatives of this test nor the false statements in the true and false test should be so obviously wrong that the examinee will be able to respond without serious attention.   Here again it is illustrated that the examiner's troubles come before rather than after the examination.   The following samples of the Recognition test are from my psychology test (the correct statements are marked 'x'):

6. The advantage of a stimulus-response psychology is—

    (*a*) It studies behaviour, and rules out introspection. . . .

    (*b*) It provides a good system before we begin to work.

    (*c*) It keeps close to the facts. . . x

    (*d*) It reduces the science to physiology. . .

14. After-images may be characterized as—

    (*a*) Phenomena characteristic of vision only. . .

    (*b*) Seeing the complement of a colour. . .

    (*c*) Intensified sensations. . .

    (*d*) After-sensations which occur in different senses. . . x

23. Forgetting is ordinarily due to—

    (*a*) Failure to make use of what is learnt. . . x

(b) Diseased nerve tissue. . . .

(c) Too rapid learning. . . .

(d) Misunderstanding the meaning. . . .

31. The characteristic feature of dreams is—

(a) They are 'wish-thoughts'. . . .

(b) They are illusions of perception. . . x

(c) They are so unreal. . . .

(d) Cognition is at rest. . . .

It is altogether likely that other types of questions will be devised as the new examination increases in popularity and use. As a means for disclosing and appraising mental products it is certainly far in advance of the older type. We may rest assured that the new examination has come to stay, for it not only affords a more precise criterion of individual differences of achievement, but also of educational progress and status. For that reason it is the most valuable instrument yet devised for the organization of a school, and it serves to emphasize the need already pointed out for more paedocentric instruction as differentiated from class teaching. It is much more scientific as a measurement of the progress of children, and consequently more valid as a measure of the results of teaching.

LITERATURE

W. A. McCall. *How to Measure in Education*. Macmillan, 1922.

Wilson and Hoke. *How to Measure*. Macmillan, 1921.

W. S. Monroe. *Measuring the Results of Teaching*. Houghton, Mifflin, 1918.

P. B. Ballard. *The New Examiner*. Hodder & Stoughton, 1923.

C. R. Stone. *Arithmetic Abilities and Some Factors Determining Them*. 1908.

Hollingworth and Winford. *The Psychology of Special Disability in Spelling*. Columbia University Press, 1919.

D. Starch. *Educational Measurements*. Macmillan, 1916.

Cyril Burt. *Mental and Scholastic Tests*. London County Council, P. S. King, 1921.

John Adams. *Modern Developments in Educational Practice*. University of London Press, 1922.

S. A. Courtis. *Teacher's Manual for Standard Practice Tests*. Harrap, 1916.

A. S. Woodburne. *Psychological Tests of Mental Abilities*. University of Madras, 1924.

CHAPTER XV

THE ACHIEVEMENT OF PERSONALITY

ELEMENTS IN THE MODERN CONCEPT OF PERSONALITY—THE SOCIAL
CHARACTER OF PERSONALITY—UNITY OF THOUGHT, FEELING AND
WILL—THE CONSCIOUSNESS OF PERSONAL IDENTITY—ABNORMAL
PERSONALITIES—COMPLEXES—THE GOAL OF EDUCATION.

IT is commonplace to speak of the goal of education as the
development of personality. Indeed, that aim is implicit even
when it is not explicit, for though we use such terms as 'culture'
or 'education' to express the goal of our endeavours, we imply
persons who are the subjects of culture or education. With
the development of new methods and new instruments, there is at
times a temptation to lose sight of the ultimate goal, so that we
need to remind ourselves frequently of our primary concern,
which is not with the text-books, curricula, time-tables, examinations, laboratories, libraries or institutions, but with persons.
The only excuse for attention to these other matters is that they
may be made the servants of personality.

Our concept 'person' is comparatively modern. There have
entered into it several elements from various sources, and we do
well to examine briefly these factors. The word itself owes its
origin to the Latin *persona*, a word whose meaning takes us back
to the old Roman and Greek dramas. In those dramas the same
actor often played several different rôles, and that necessitated
some sort of distinguishing tokens. These distinguishing tokens
were in the form of masks which were so designed that the
mouth acted as a megaphone, whereby the actor could make
himself heard, even by those in the distant parts of the amphi-
theatre. The Latin word for mask was *persona*, which is derived
from the verb *personare*, 'to sound through', or 'to fill with
sound'. From this original meaning, which had special reference
to the aspect of making themselves heard, the word came to be

combined with *dramatis*, 'of the drama', and thus the *dramatis persona* was an indication of the particular character being impersonated.

The Roman conception of personality added another factor, viz. the legal. According to Roman law, a person is an individual who possesses rights and obligations. The Romans had also the conception of 'natural rights' which they embodied in their legal conception. Roman jurists found in the concept of the law of nature a rational basis for political and moral relations. It is the rational nature of man which makes him social. From that arise the various principles of jurisprudence and morality. The social order affords man the opportunity for the realization of his own personality. This gave the State a strong argument for commanding the loyalty of individual citizens, for the political order was the sanctioned and appointed means for self-realization. Thus the Roman conception of personality was dominated by legal and political aspects. The Roman citizen had certain rights which were his by nature, but which the State protected for him; and in return he had certain obligations which he had to meet.

The science of grammar has added another aspect to the significance of personality. The three persons represent the speaker, the one spoken to, and the object spoken about. The word *I* suggests that there must be a *you* or a *thou* standing in distinction, and that in itself is an indication of the social aspect of personality. It has been repeatedly urged by moralists that egoism and altruism are mutually related. There can be neither an *ego* without an *alter*, nor an *alter* without an *ego*. Herbert Spencer expressed a truth in urging that either one pushed to extremes to the disregard of the other would be self-destructive. There is a constant inter-relationship between the self and the other, without which either word would be quite meaningless. Grammar thus offers to the school teacher a good instrument for bringing home to children one of the fundamental facts about themselves as moral persons.

Modern philosophical reflection has also contributed to our understanding of personality. By Immanuel Kant the absolute moral worth of the individual person was made central. Man is a rational being, a law unto himself. His criterion of conduct was so to live that if others followed the same rule of conduct perfect morality would abound. Such a life depended on the possession of a good will, and there is nothing on earth good except such a good will. So Kant realized the supreme dignity of the spirit and will of man, and made morality entirely personal. Personality has thus a distinctive character, and shines in its own light. It may be argued that Kant's conception over-emphasized both individualism and formalism. Be that as it may, we have to acknowledge the service which he rendered, in inspiring people to a high type of morality which views 'intelligence, wit, judgement, and the other talents of the mind, however they may be named, or courage, resolution, perseverance as qualities of temperament', as well as 'the gifts of fortune—power, riches, honour',[1] etc., as of subsidiary worth. Reverence for the worth of personality is thus primary in Kant. The motive for the performance of duty is not personal advantage, but reverence for one's self. Men must treat one another, not as means for furthering self-advantage, but with that honour which is becoming to the worth of personality.

Another factor which philosophy has contributed to the modern conception of personality is the conception of it as an ideal. It was developed by some of the Germans as a reaction to Hegelianism. Weisse emphasized the possible as ontologically superior to the actual, and Fichte developed the idea of the self-production of personality. Lotze, from the point of view of idealism, portrayed personality as gradually realizing itself. The coming to reality of the world of consciousness is the truest meaning of the world-process, so that personality is an indefinite ideal towards which man may progressively approach. Nietzsche has set up his ideal of a superman (Uebermensch) in contrast with the ordinary man of the common herd. It is an ideal which he leaves enveloped in a good deal of obscurity. Nevertheless, it is the conception of an ideal personality, possible of development beyond the most splendid achievements of the human race so far.

Still another influence has contributed to our idea of personality, viz. modern political thought. The old idea was that kings had divine rights, and were born to rule, whereas citizens were born to be ruled. But democratic thought is

---

[1] Kant, *Metaphysic of Morals*. English translation by Abbott, p. 9.

emphasizing the rights of the people. Nowhere is it expressed more finely than in the words of that superman, Abraham Lincoln: 'Government of the people, by the people, for the people.' The test of the worth of any government is not in its ability to argue for the divine right of its head, but in its value to the people. In a genuine democracy every personality will be given the opportunity to develop according to its maximum capacity. One of the educational products of democratic ideals is the special class or school for the feeble-minded. Put a feeble-minded child in a school along with forty others of normal intelligence, and he will never be able to keep pace with the progress of the class. Sub-normal children must be given opportunities to develop at the rate that their capacities admit, because, even though they be sub-normals, they are persons, and have a right to be allowed to do their best. It is one of the tasks of democratic education to see to it that none get unfair advantages and none unfair disadvantages. 'A democratic criterion', as Dewey says, 'requires us to develop capacity to the point of view of competency to choose and make its own career.'[1]

An analysis of personality from the psychological point of view is at once difficult and illuminating. Although it is admittedly very difficult, if not impossible, to define personality, yet we may be able, as the result of our investigations, to describe it in various particulars. Whatever we may gain towards the understanding of personality from any source is certain to be valuable to those who have to do with unfolding personalities. The subject is one of great complexity, for personality is the result of a peculiar combination of forces which have not, collectively at any rate, been scientifically analyzed.

1. There is one fact of fundamental importance which strikes us as soon as we begin to study personality, viz. that it is essentially social. We have already noted this in regard to the grammatical use of the word 'person'. Any individual's conception of himself is largely the outcome of his experience with other persons. And the way in which he is able to give

---

[1] Dewey, *Democracy and Education*, p. 139.

an account of himself is mainly with reference to others. I sometimes ask my students to write brief descriptions of themselves which would enable anyone who does not know them to identify them. Then we have these descriptions read and analyzed. It is amazing how largely the descriptions have to depend on social differentiations. The sorts of things which are included are names, family connections, caste, religion, town, college, academic standing, height, complexion, identification marks such as scars, and so on. The meanings of the various items are almost entirely social, they are designed to identify us and classify us in differentiation from other persons. Not only are our own conceptions of ourselves largely social products, but the social environment is of primary importance in determining our behaviour. The struggle to maintain existence is not carried on individually but in groups. Each of us is continually profiting by the experience of others, so that the social life affords a great conservation of human energy. Folkways are social forces furnishing us with interests, motives, habits, emotions, and mental concepts. In many cases the sense of social welfare dominates the idea of individual gain. The establishment of folkways is due to the gradual development of customs, and the individual's acquiescence goes on quite unconsciously. The authority of the group is exercised sometimes positively through traditions and rites, and sometimes negatively by restraints and taboos, and in more developed society by laws and public opinion.

A good deal of socially determined behaviour can be traced to suggestion. When people come together in social groups, especially where there is a community of interest or motive, they transmit impulses to one another, with the result that there is a re-enforcement, especially on the affective side. The behaviour of crowds is to a large extent explicable on this principle. A crowd may act either better or worse than the individuals composing it would have acted. Very frequently individuals who are ordinarily prudent, careful and tactful will throw their tact and prudence to the winds, and, under the suggestibility of the crowd, yield to intense passion, animal influence, and brute force. Thus by suggestibility we admit any notions whatsoever without definite motive, we assimilate them and act upon them.   The quality of suggestibility is one which varies greatly according to ethnological, geographical, environmental and other conditions.   It is ordinarily stronger in children that in adults, on which account it is of immense importance to teachers and parents.   Moreover, it is often a much more effective as well as facile instrument to use than coercion.   If the suggestion is tactfully thrown out, the child does the thing desired, and acts in the belief that it was his own initiative.   Thus this fundamentally social characteristic of personality may be turned to excellent account by the educationalist.

Folkways are not only responsible for many of the commonplace activities of life, but also for morality.   Does not our word 'morality' come from the Latin *mores*, folkways?   Morality takes its rise and continues to function in social relationships, man with man.   As Kant pointed out, the only object to which the word 'good' is applicable is personality.   Moral standards are socially originated.   They make vocal the group's conceptions of good and evil.   They are socially enforced also, for there is no other force by which they can be enforced than the social.   Conformity to the standard is socially motivated, for the love of approval, and the dislike of disapproval is a manipulation of the group consciousness.

The key to the understanding of the peculiar ways in which different people respond to a situation or to different situations is, in the majority of cases, to be found through an understanding of the social psychology of the group or groups to which they belong.   This is a fact of first-rate educational importance.   Too often teachers waste their energies in trying to fasten somebody else's response to a child's situation.   It is well to be abreast of all the known improvements in educational practice and method. But it is possible to make the mistake of trying to make wholesale transfers to new situations without much attention to adaptation.   My attention was drawn, e.g., to an adaptation, so-called, of an arithmetical test used in American schools to Indian conditions.   And in what did the adaptation consist?   It was confined to an alteration of the names to others familiar to Indian children, but it retained the dollar and cent as monetary units instead of trying to find problems of equivalent difficulty in rupees,

19

annas and pies. I am very much inclined to think that the social psychologist would have to criticize severely a good deal that has come into our Indian educational system by importation from the West with little of adaptation. Probably the most glaring mistake of all, from the viewpoint of group psychology, is the great stress that is laid upon a foreign language as the principal medium of instruction. A scientific study of social facts in India is sure to have a most salutary effect on the educational methods and practices which we use.

2. A second characteristic of personality is that it is an organic unity of cognitive, affective and conative elements. We are knowing, feeling and acting persons. By cognition we mean awareness of an object ; by affection the feeling-tone which accompanies experiences ; by conation the active side of consciousness which expresses itself in tendencies, impulses, desires and selected acts. In the old faculty psychology these three factors of the mental life were regarded as separate and distinct from one another, capable of analysis each in its own sphere. But the dominance of the functional point of view in the science has resulted in a complete reversal from that idea. First and foremost, the mental life is a unity, even as it is the mental life of a single unified psychophysical organism. We find it impossible to study the mental facts in separation from the physical, let alone to examine the various mental processes in isolation from one another. Every segment of behaviour has at once cognitive, affective and conative elements. What is it, we may ask, that constitutes the basic unity of these three factors ? For, though we deny to them any place as separate faculties in a compartmentalized mind, we recognize that the terms are still useful as indicating three important elements in the mental life. They function as an integral unity, yet for purposes of scientific analysis we may profit by studying the factors in separation. The chief thing to remember is that the unifying agency is the psycho-physical organism which in man we see developing into a personality. We have nothing to do with cognition, affection and conation, for these words are really abstractions used for descriptive purposes in respect to various elements of mental experience. It would be well in using them, as we observed in regard to reflexes and

instincts, were we to drop the substantives and use only the adjectival forms. It would be more correct to say that we have cognitive phases, affective tones, and conative tendencies of experience. There are no such things then as cognition, affection and conation, but there are persons who know, and feel, and act. Angell has put the matter in a striking way in regard to conation. He says: 'The term will is simply a convenient appellation for the whole range of mental life, viewed from the standpoint of activity and control over movement. The *whole mind active*, this is the will.'[1] He might have said with equal force that the terms cognition and affection are convenient appellations for the whole range of mental life, viewed from the points of view of awareness and feeling. The *whole mind aware*, this is cognitive consciousness. The *whole mind feeling*, this is affective experience. The important thing to remember is that personal experience is the fundamental basis for the unity in multiplicity of our experiences.

A study of the functions and inter-functions of these three elementary factors of mental life would take us through the whole gamut of individual psychology. The teacher who is concerned with the development of the personalities entrusted to his care would find that such a study would be very fruitful. This fact of a personal unity is exceedingly important. It would be a good preventive against some mistaken methods of instruction. He would realize that there is no mental receptacle to be filled with pre-digested knowledge. He would know that there are no feelings to be trained or subdued. He would not dream of wills to be broken or strengthened by pedagogical brute force. He would treat all of his children as persons, partly actual and partly potential, who are to be developed to think and feel and act in the most appropriate and most effective ways in all sorts of situations.

The integration and organization of life is through personality. This is applicable not alone to the traditional tripartite division of the elements of the mental life, but to the native and the acquired instincts and habits, motives and attitudes, physique and

---

[1] Angell, *Psychology*, p. 437.

temperament, judgement and reasoning, choice and effort. Personality implies the unified behaviour of a self that is self-determined, self-directing and self-conscious. And a developed personality is one that preserves the proper poise of all the elements, so that none shall be emphasized at the expense of others. A well-balanced personality is the goal of the educative process.

3. Personality involves a consciousness of personal identity. That does not mean, however, that the words 'person' and 'individual' are synonymous, for personality is something bigger, involving self-consciousness and social consciousness. An amoeba is an individual but cannot be a person. Though a person is an individual, an individual is not necessarily a person.

The consciousness of the self carries as its correlate the consciousness of a not-self. This is preceded in human experience by the ability to distinguish between persons and things. The mind of the infant, as James picturesquely remarked, is 'a big buzzing confusion'. It is a vague continuum, but before long he learns to distinguish *things* which behave with relative regularity and stability, from *persons* whose behaviour is more irregular. He finds that he can count on things behaving in certain ways under given conditions, but he can never be quite sure what persons are going to do. When he has once achieved the ability to classify the items of his environment into these two groups, it is not long until he classifies himself as a person, and attains a consciousness of selfhood. This distinction between the self and the not-self is important for the social consciousness, for one phase of it is a recognition of himself with relation to other selves.

Another phase of the consciousness of personal identity has been expressed by James as a distinction between 'I' and 'me', or the self as 'knower' and as 'known'. This consciousness is often accompanied by a budding self-assertiveness. The child objects to being ordered about, especially when the ordering is re-enforced by physical force. He expresses himself in various efforts to dominate situations, objects and other persons. This developing sense of personal identity needs skilful guidance, for there are grave dangers involved in undue emphasis on either assertiveness or submissiveness. The social life demands something of both, and in personality they must be preserved in proper balance. Every teacher with any considerable experience has had to do with children in whose personalities one or the other of these two elements was over-emphasized, and will realize how difficult it is to overcome these maladjustments. Much depends on the guidance which the child receives during the earlier, more plastic and formative years.

4. Much has been learned in regard to the nature of normal personality by the study of abnormal persons. We can do much to prevent children from developing in an unhealthy way, if we have observed the processes which in others have led to unhealthy results. Psychology has not yet accomplished nearly as much as it hopes from the study of multiple personality, mediumistic trance, hypnosis, dreams, insanity, and such phenomena. The very abnormality of the phenomena makes them all the more difficult of investigation. But what little knowledge has been acquired has resulted in increasing our understanding of the contrast between normal and abnormal processes in certain regards.

(a) Multiple personality may be two or more successive or simultaneous personalities. In that phenomenon the person suddenly loses the memory of his past life or normal life, and imagines himself to be quite a different individual. The character and temperament of the two personalities will, in many cases, be quite different, even opposite extremes. It is possible even to have an imagined alteration of sex. There is thus a splitting up of consciousness into sectors that appear to be quite unrelated to one another. The phenomenon is one of disintegration or dissociation, there usually being no remembering in the primary personality of what was done in the secondary, though there is often memory in the secondary personality of what was done in the primary, the subject frequently referring it to some other person. Dr. Morton Prince, who has made an extended investigation of this phenomenon, says: 'Intensive studies of multiple personality disclose the fact that the dissociation of one phase for another carries with it certain of the instincts innate in every organism. What I mean to say is, observation of psychopathological states has shown that instincts, such as play, hunger, anger, fear, love, disgust, the sexual instincts, etc., may be dissociated separately or in conjunction with complexes of ideas. In every case of multiple personality that I have had the opportunity to study, each phase has been shorn of one or more of the inborn psycho-physiological dispositions and I believe this obtains in every true case. As a result, certain sentiments and traits are lost, while those that are retained stamp an individuality upon the phase. And as the conative forces of the retained instincts are not balanced and checked by the dissociated opposing instincts, the sentiments which they form and the emotional reactions to which they give rise stand out as dominating traits. Thus one phase may be characterized by pugnacity, self-assertion, and elation—another by submission, fear and tender feeling; and so on.'[1]

The outstanding difference between multiple and normal personalities is that in the former there is disintegration, whereas in the latter there is integration, in the first dissociation where there would be association in the second. Observations of the facts of multiple personality serve to give an added emphasis to the facts of essential unity in normal experience. We have an opportunity of appreciating the significance of associative processes by seeing what takes place when they do not function normally. Multiple personality is a functional disorder which can frequently be successfully treated by hypnosis and suggestion. But if it is not treated in time, it may lead to a permanent disintegration and insanity.

(b) In hypnotism we encounter a number of facts and phenomena of a similar character to those which characterize multiple personality. By means of suggestion the hypnotist is able to induce an alteration of personality. It is quite feasible to bring changes in sensitivity, motor control, memory and temperament under the influence of hypnotic suggestion. Several theories have been proposed to account for it. Some of them are quite physiological, such as cerebral anæmia, cerebral congestion, temporary suppression of cerebral functions, abnormal cerebral

---

[1] Morton Prince, *The Unconscious*, pp. 299 ff.

excitability, or the independent functioning of a single cerebral hemisphere. Others say that in hypnosis normal consciousness is displaced by a dream consciousness. Still others propose the existence of two personalities in each organism, one functioning normally, and the other in hypnosis and sleep. But the theory which is today most attractive to students of the subject is that of mental dissociation; in the excessive suggestibility which is induced, there is dissociation of many normal processes, so that the subject may act at entire variance from his normal ways of behaviour. In this hypnotic state the subject may be able to solve problems which would ordinarily be too difficult for him. Or he may be cured of certain disorders. There are frequent cases on record in South India of cures of scorpion stings, hysteria and other disorders, which are without doubt due to the ultra-suggestibility of the subject with the exercise of hypnotic influence, which the person may not realize that he possesses.

One of the important uses which has been made latterly of hypnotic suggestion is for the treatment of multiple personality. By means of suggestion it has been found possible to induce the secondary personality. Then having brought it to consciousness, the suggestion is made that it is an undesirable personality, and ought not to be allowed to recur, or else that the secondary and primary are really one and must be so regarded. Dr. Mitchell, in his recent work on *Medical Psychology*,[1] has recorded several cures of this kind, and in some instances there had been no recurrence of the disorder after several years had elapsed.

The study of hypnosis may not be of direct value to the teacher, as no one would suggest turning a schoolroom into a laboratory for hypnotic treatment. But it throws much light on the questions of suggestibility and suggestion. Children will be found to vary greatly in suggestibility. Suppose you find Henry is not getting along well with his arithmetic lesson, and you say: 'What is the matter, Henry? Have you got a headache? I hope you are not getting fever.' Perhaps within an hour Henry will be feeling so badly, that he will have to be

---

[1] T. W. Mitchell, *Medical Psychology and Psychical Research*, 1922.

given leave to go home.   Whereas when you suggest the same explanation to Edward for his poor work, he at once resists, saying, ' No sir, there is nothing the matter with me.'   And he settles down to work to prove to you there is nothing the matter. The teacher must be a student of individual psychology to know what kind of suggestions to make in each case so as to induce the desired response.   Auto-suggestion or self-hypnotism is an instrument that a wise teacher may turn to good account for educational ends.

(c) Hysteria is a form of neural abnormality in which the higher nerve centres are disordered.   It manifests itself in a variety of symptoms, and may be due either to a predisposition or to a disturbance caused by exhaustion, fright or depression. It frequently appears during the adolescent period, when the life processes are undergoing important change.   Psychologically, hysteria is a milder form of the same type of abnormality which we observed to characterize multiple personality and hysteria, viz. dissociation.   In these cases the disintegrated portions may be only a group of sensory or motor discharges, the disappearance of which is less striking.   But if it be neglected, it may and often does lead to the more permanent disorder of insanity.   Parents and teachers, by judicious treatment of hysterical children may, in the majority of cases, lead them to a complete overcoming of the tendency, so that it ceases to recur.

(d) There are other abnormalities which might be discussed, as hallucinations, such as where the subject imagines himself made of some other material; emotional disturbances, as in melancholia; mediumistic trance, where the subject becomes relatively oblivious to sensory impressions and assumes a different personality, amnesia or loss of memory; and aphasia, where, due to cortical injury, the memory of sensory experiences is impossible.   In each of these cases that which impresses the observer most is the resultant disintegration or dissociation.   In some degree or other, all of these abnormalities act as disturbances to the otherwise integrative unity of the psycho-neural system. Temporarily or permanently, some portions of personality are split off from the normal whole.   So the comparative study of normals and abnormals helps us to a proper understanding and treatment of both.

5. Our understanding of personality is being considerably enhanced by the study of psycho-analysis. While psychology has devoted itself in the past largely to conscious mental processes, the psycho-analysts have directed considerable attention to the sphere of the unconscious. It is obvious that there are many mental forces and influences that are at work. 'Unconscious', as a technical term, has come into vogue quite recently, and some writers apparently regard it as a dumping ground for all the vagaries which they cannot understand. For some it is identical with the 'subconscious' or 'subliminal consciousness'. It would seem to be more scientific to restrict the term to describe those mental determinants of conscious processes or experiences which never become conscious. On that basis, we would then have two classes of mental phenomena, viz. conscious process and unconscious determinants of conscious processes. It has been suggested[1] on that basis that we would have two groups of unconscious determinants : the sentiments, and memories which are not recollections. Sentiments are our relatively permanent dispositions which predispose us to certain types of emotions and of actions. Though we may be conscious of possession of a particular sentiment, even as we are conscious of having a heart or a liver, yet the sentiment itself does not operate consciously. Then there is much of our past experience that is retained, and that exercises a powerful influence over us, though it never comes actually to the focus of consciousness. Attitudes, prejudices and customary modes of behaviour are examples in point. As we observed, retention is really a biological function, and a great mass of our possessions are retained quite unconsciously.

The psycho-analysts are responsible for another term which is intended to connote a characteristic feature of personal experience—the complex. Complexes have been defined as 'psychological constellations, formed by the attachment of the instinctive emotions to objects or experiences presented by the environment, but which, owing to their painful or repugnant character, are *unacceptable* to the "self".'[2] This meaning of the

[1] Drever, *An Introduction to the Psychology of Education*, pp. 22 ff.
[2] J. A. Hadfield, *Psychology and Morals*, p. 24.

term places the emphasis on the affective concomitant of a system of ideas, especially where it is personally distasteful, and hence repressed into the unconscious. But there is a wider use for the term to denote any system of ideas with its linkages of emotions, feelings and impulses, so that the recurrence of any element in the complex will tend to recall by association the experience in its entirety. There can be no doubt that those unconscious factors of experience, known as sentiments, prejudices, and habits, have much to do with determining the kinds of complexes which we form. Many of the abnormalities of dissociation, obsession, hallucination, hysteria and insanity are due to the operations of complexes. Perhaps all of them will eventually be so explained. These complexes find their nuclei around various centres, such as the ego, the herd, sex interests, war experiences, religious experiences, political obsessions, etc. Many of the psycho-analysts have done harm to their cherished cause by their reference of all complexes to a single nucleus, sex, fear, morals, or whatever it may be. But the very word 'complex' itself, so suggestive as to the character of the mental life, ought to be a sufficient guard against such one-track systems of explanation.

The method which is employed in psycho-analysis for the discovery of complexes is that of experiments in association. When a complex is repressed it frequently becomes the source of pathological nervous conditions, but if it be repressed thoroughly it may be difficult to get at the source of the trouble. Dream imagery is sometimes used as a starting place, and the subject is encouraged to let the mental processes proceed as in the case of uncontrolled association. In the schoolroom the teacher may, by such experimental methods, discover the mental background of pupils who are not doing as well as their intelligence would warrant, and thereby help children over their troubles, so that the best educational results may be possible. Teachers and parents have too often been responsible for the repression of certain complexes in children by an attitude of too great dominance. Injudicious punishments have frequently induced complexes, blunted personality, and thwarted the educative processes. The school is not a place where the teacher should seek to make his own personality dominate over the personalities of his pupils.

It should be a place where the interaction of personalities will bring about the harmonious and free development of both.

In conclusion, I may remind my readers of the goal of education, as it was so admirably stated by John Milton, three hundred years ago: 'I call, therefore, a complete and generous education that which fits a man to perform justly and magnanimously all the offices, both private and public, of Peace and War.' The very word[1] itself means getting something out of a person rather than putting something in. The child is a person, partially in actuality, partially in potentiality. It is the task of the educator to help the child to achieve actually what he is potentially. The mental processes which are to be developed are already in existence. The capacities of the child will not be added to or subtracted from, but they can be released for normal expression and progress. 'A good teacher', said President Hadley,[2] 'can show him (a boy) how to work to the best advantage and save waste effort; he can speed up the educational process by warning against false starts and unnecessary experiments; but in learning to do anything, whether to ride or to think, the boy is the active agent, the teacher is only the director, or at best the inspirer. Doing can be learned only by doing.'

[1] From the Latin *educare*, to educe, to lead out.
[2] Arthur Twining Hadley, 'What is Education?' in *Harper's Magazine*, Dec., 1922.

LITERATURE

John Dewey. *Human Nature and Conduct*. George Allen & Unwin, 1922.
John Dewey. *Democracy and Education*. Macmillan, 1915.
T. Mark. *The Unfolding of Personality*. University of Chicago Press, 1912.
Charles Baudouin. *Suggestion and Autosuggestion*. George Allen & Unwin, 1920.
J. A. Hadfield. *Psychology and Morals*. Methuen, 1923.
T. W. Mitchell. *Medical Psychology and Psychical Research*. Methuen, 1922.
Morton Prince. *The Unconscious*. Macmillan, 1914.
W. McDougall. *Outline of Psychology*. Methuen, 1924.
John Adams. *Modern Developments in Educational Practice*. University of London Press, 1922.

James Drever. *Introduction to the Psychology of Education*. Edward Arnold, 1923.

J. A. Thomson. *What is Man?* Methuen, 1923.

St. G. L. F. Pitt. *The Purpose of Education*. Cambridge University Press, 1924.

P. B. Ballard. *The Changing School*. Hodder & Stoughton, 1925.

J. J. Findlay. *The Foundations of Education*. University of London Press, 1925.

INDEX OF PERSONS

INDEX OF SUBJECTS